QuickBooks®
Simple Start™
FOR
DUMMIES®

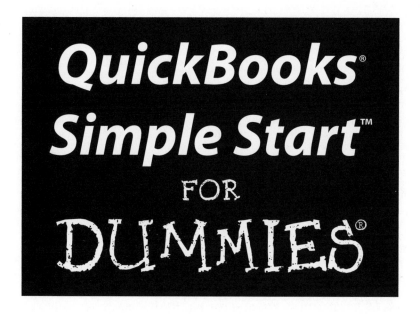

by Stephen L. Nelson, MBA, CPA, MS in Taxation

Wiley Publishing, Inc.

QuickBooks® Simple Start™ For Dummies®

Published by
Wiley Publishing, Inc.
111 River Street
Hoboken, NJ 07030-5774

Copyright © 2004 by Wiley Publishing, Inc., Indianapolis, Indiana

Published by Wiley Publishing, Inc., Indianapolis, Indiana

Published simultaneously in Canada

For general information on our other products and services or to obtain technical support, please contact our Customer Care Department within the U.S. at 800-762-2974, outside the U.S. at 317-572-3993, or fax 317-572-4002.

Wiley also publishes its books in a variety of electronic formats. Some content that appears in print may not be available in electronic books.

Library of Congress Control Number: 2004107899

ISBN: 978-0-7645-7462-7

Manufactured in the United States of America

10 9 8 7 6 5

1O/SS/QZ/QU/IN

WILEY

About the Author

Stephen L. Nelson, MBA, CPA, MS in Taxation has a simple purpose in life: He wants to help you (and people like you) manage your business finances by using computers. Oh, sure, this personal mandate won't win him a Nobel Prize or anything, but it's his own little contribution to the world.

Steve's education and experiences mesh nicely with his special purpose. He has a B.S. in accounting, an MBA in finance and a Master of Science in taxation. He's a CPA in Redmond, Washington. He used to work as a senior consultant and CPA with Arthur Andersen & Co. (er, yeah, that Arthur Andersen — but hey it was 20 years ago). Steve, whose books have sold more than 4 million copies in English and have been translated into 11 other languages, is also the bestselling author of *Quicken 2004 For Dummies* (from Wiley Publishing, Inc.).

Dedication

To the entrepreneurs and small-business people of the world. You folks create most of the new jobs.

Author's Acknowledgments

Hey, reader, lots of folks spent lots of time working on this book to make QuickBooks easier for you. You should know who these people are. You may just possibly meet one of them someday at a produce shop, squeezing cantaloupe, eating grapes, and looking for the perfect peach.

Those folks include my acquisitions editor, Bob Woerner, and my project editor, Beth Taylor, copy editor Christine Berman, and technical editor David Ringstrom.

Thanks to all for a job well-done!

Publisher's Acknowledgments

We're proud of this book; please send us your comments through our online registration form located at www.dummies.com/register/.

Some of the people who helped bring this book to market include the following:

Acquisitions, Editorial, and Media Development

Project Editor: Beth Taylor

Acquisitions Editor: Bob Woerner

Copy Editor: Christine Berman

Technical Editor: David Ringstrom

Editorial Manager: Leah Cameron

Media Development Manager: Laura VanWinkle

Media Development Supervisor: Richard Graves

Editorial Assistant: Amanda Foxworth

Cartoons: Rich Tennant (www.the5thwave.com)

Production

Project Coordinator: Adrienne Martinez and Maridee Ennis

Layout and Graphics: Lauren Goddard, Joyce Haughey, Stephanie Jumper, Barry Offringa, Jacque Roth, Heather Ryan

Proofreaders: John Greenough, Charles Spencer, Brian H. Walls, TECHBOOKS Production Services

Indexer: TECHBOOKS Production Services

Publishing and Editorial for Technology Dummies

    Richard Swadley, Vice President and Executive Group Publisher

    Andy Cummings, Vice President and Publisher

    Mary C. Corder, Editorial Director

Publishing for Consumer Dummies

    Diane Graves Steele, Vice President and Publisher

    Joyce Pepple, Acquisitions Director

Composition Services

    Gerry Fahey, Vice President of Production Services

    Debbie Stailey, Director of Composition Services

Contents at a Glance

Table of Contents

Introduction

1 think that running, or working in, a small business is one of the coolest things a person can do. Really. I mean it. Sure, sometimes the environment is dangerous. Kind of like the Old West. But it's also an environment in which you have the opportunity to make tons of money. And it's an environment in which you can build a company or a job that fits you. In comparison, many brothers and sisters working in big-company corporate America are furiously trying to fit their round pegs into painfully square holes. Yuck.

You're wondering, of course, what any of this has to do with this book or with QuickBooks Simple Start. Quite a lot, actually. The whole purpose of this book is to make it easier for you to run or work in a small business by using QuickBooks.

About QuickBooks Simple Start

Let me start off with a minor but useful point. QuickBooks comes in several different flavors: QuickBooks Simple Start, QuickBooks Pro, QuickBooks Premier, and QuickBooks Premier: Accountants Edition.

This book, however, talks about QuickBooks Simple Start. QuickBooks Simple Start is a skinny-ed down version of QuickBooks that's easier to use. The Simple Start version of QuickBooks isn't as powerful as, say, QuickBooks Premier. But that's okay. The big challenge with accounting software is figuring out how to get the program to work. And a simpler program — like QuickBooks Simple Start — will be much, much easier for you to figure out.

If you're using one of the other versions of QuickBooks, you use the regular *QuickBooks For Dummies* book. For example, if you're working with QuickBooks 2005 and you want a book, you should use the *QuickBooks 2005 For Dummies* book and not this one. Maybe you can return this book to the bookstore for an exchange.

About This Book

This book isn't meant to be read from cover to cover like some *Harry Potter* page-turner. Instead, it's organized into tiny, no-sweat descriptions of how you do the things you need to do. If you're the sort of person who just doesn't feel right not reading a book from cover to cover, you can, of course, go ahead and read this thing from front to back. You can start reading Chapter 1 and continue all the way to the end (which means through Chapter 20 and the Appendix).

I actually don't think this from-start-to-finish approach is bad, because I tell you a bunch of stuff. I tried to write the book in such a way that the experience isn't as bad as you might think, and I really do think you get good value from your reading.

But you also can use this book like an encyclopedia. If you want to know about a subject, you can look it up in the table of contents or the index. Then you can flip to the correct chapter or page and read as much as you need or enjoy. No muss, no fuss.

I should, however, mention one thing: Accounting software programs require you to do a certain amount of preparation before you can use them to get real work done. If you haven't started to use QuickBooks yet, I recommend that you read through the first few chapters of this book to find out what you need to do first.

Hey. There's something else I should tell you. I have fiddled a bit with the Windows display settings. For example, I've noodled around with the font settings and most of the colors. The benefit is that the pictures in this book are easy to read. And that's good. But the cost of all this is that my pictures look a little bit different from what you see on your screen. And that's not good. In the end, however, what the publisher has found is that people are really happier with increased readability. Anyway, I just thought I should mention this here, up front, in case you had any question about it.

What You Can Safely Ignore

Sometimes I provide step-by-step descriptions of tasks. I feel very bad about having to do this. So to make things easier for you, I describe the tasks by using bold text. That way, you know exactly what you're supposed to do. I also provide a more detailed explanation in the text that follows the step. You can skip the text that accompanies the step-by-step boldfaced directions if you already understand the process.

Here's an example that shows what I mean:

1. **Press Enter.**

   Find the key that's labeled Enter or Return. Extend your index finger so that it rests ever so gently on the Enter key. In one sure, fluid motion, press the Enter key by using your index finger. Then release your finger.

Okay, that example is kind of extreme. I never actually go into that much detail. But you get the idea. If you know how to press Enter, you can just do that and not read further. If you need help — maybe with the finger part or something — just read the nitty-gritty details.

Can you skip anything else? Let me see now. . . . I guess that you can safely ignore the stuff next to the Tip icons, too — even if the accumulated wisdom, gleaned from long hours slaving over a hot keyboard, could save you much weeping and gnashing of teeth. If you're someone who enjoys trying to do something another way, go ahead and read the tips.

What You Shouldn't Ignore (Unless You're a Masochist)

Don't skip the Warning icons. They're the ones flagged with the picture of the nineteenth-century bomb. They describe some things that you really shouldn't do.

Out of respect for you, I'm not going to put stuff such as "don't smoke" next to these icons. I figure that you're an adult. You can make your own lifestyle decisions. So I'm reserving the Warning icons for more urgent and immediate dangers — things akin to "Don't smoke while you're filling your car with gasoline."

Three Foolish Assumptions

I'm making three assumptions:

- ✔ You have a PC with Microsoft Windows 95 or later or Windows NT 4.0 or higher. (I took pictures of the QuickBooks windows and dialog boxes while using Windows XP, in case you're interested.)
- ✔ You know a little bit about how to work with your computer.
- ✔ You have or will buy a copy of QuickBooks Simple Start for each computer on which you want to run the program.

If you're just starting out with Microsoft Windows, peruse one of these books on your flavor of Windows, such as *Small Business Windows 98 For Dummies*, which I wrote; or *Windows 98 For Dummies*, *Windows 2000 Professional For Dummies*, *Microsoft Windows Me For Dummies*, or *Windows XP For Dummies* by Andy Rathbone (all published by Wiley).

How This Book Is Organized

This book is divided into five mostly coherent parts.

Part I: Getting Simple Started

Part I covers some upfront stuff that you need to take care of before you can start using QuickBooks Simple Start. For example, this part explains how to install and setup the program. I promise I won't waste your time here. I just want to make sure that you get off on the right foot.

Part II: Daily Chores

The second part of this book explains how you use QuickBooks Simple Start for your daily financial recordkeeping: preparing customer invoices, recording sales, and paying bills — that kind of stuff.

I guess you could say that these chores are just data entry stuff. And you'd be correct. But you'll be amazed at how much easier QuickBooks will make your life. QuickBooks is a really cool program.

Part III: Month-End and Year-End Routines

Part III talks about the kinds of things you should do at the end of the month or the end of the year. This part explains, for example, how you balance your bank account, create reports, and take care of some housekeeping tasks like backing up and restoring your QuickBooks data file.

While I'm on the subject, I also want to categorically deny that Part III contains any secret messages that you can decipher by reading backward. Yllaer.

Part IV: Real-Life Examples

Part IV provides detailed discussions of how you use QuickBooks Simple Start to accomplish specific accounting tasks (like fixed assets accounting or payroll) or how you use QuickBooks Simple Start in specific situations (like service businesses or retailing).

Part V: The Part of Tens

Gravity isn't just a good idea; it's a law.

By tradition, the same is true for this part of a *For Dummies* book. The Part of Tens provides a collection of lists: tips for business owners, tips for tricky bookkeeping situations, ideas for saving business taxes, ten things to do when you next visit Acapulco — oops, sorry about that last one. Wrong book.

Also by tradition, these ten-item lists don't need to have exactly ten items. You know the concept of a baker's dozen, right? You order a dozen dough-nuts but get 13 for the same price. Well, *For Dummies* ten-item lists have roughly ten items. (If the Dummies Man — the bug-eyed, paleface guy suffer-ing from triangle-shaped-head syndrome who appears on the cover of this book and on icons throughout these pages — were running the bakery, a ten-doughnut order might mean that you get anywhere from 8 to 13 doughnuts.) Do you believe that I'm an accountant? So exacting that it's scary.

Part VI: Appendix

An unwritten rule says that computer books have appendixes, so I include one. In Appendix A, I discuss how to calculate a business's profits in an accu-rate but still practical manner.

Conventions Used in This Book

To make the best use of your time and energy, you should know about the conventions I use in this book.

When I want you to type something such as **with a stupid grin, Martin watched the tall blonde strut into the bar and order grappa**, it's in bold let-ters. When I want you to type something that's short and uncomplicated, such as **Jennifer**, it still appears in boldface type.

Except for passwords, you don't have to worry about the case of the stuff you type in QuickBooks. If I tell you to type **Jennifer**, you can type **JENNIFER**. Or you can follow poet e. e. cummings' lead and type **jennifer**.

Whenever I tell you to choose a command from a menu, I say something like, "Choose File⇨Exit," which simply means to first choose the File menu and then choose the Exit command. The ⇨ separates one part of the command from the next part.

You can choose menus and commands and select dialog box elements with the mouse. Just click the thing you want to select.

While on the subject of conventions, let me also mention something about QuickBooks Simple Start conventions because it turns out that there's not really any good place to point this out. QuickBooks doesn't use document windows the same way that some other Windows programs do. Instead, it locks the active window into place.

Special Icons

Like many computer books, this book uses icons, or little pictures, to flag things that don't quite fit into the flow of things:

This icon is a friendly reminder to do something.

This icon points out nerdy technical material that you might want to skip (or read, if you're feeling particularly bright).

Whee! Here's a shortcut to make your life easier!

And this icon is a friendly reminder not to do something . . . or else.

Part I
Getting Simple Started

The 5th Wave   By Rich Tennant

With QuickBooks Simple Start, Tonto Was Finally Able To Calculate His Billable Hours As "Friend and Trusted Scout".

In this part . . .

All accounting programs — including QuickBooks — make you do a bunch of preliminary stuff. Sure, this is sort of a bummer. But getting depressed about it won't make things go any faster. So if you want to get up and go with QuickBooks Simple Start, peruse the chapters in this first part. I promise that I'll get you through this setup stuff as quickly as possible.

Chapter 1

Preparing to Use QuickBooks Simple Start

....

In This Chapter

▶ Choosing an appropriate entity form

▶ Installing the QuickBooks Simple Start software

▶ Running through the Setup Interview

....

1 know you're eager to get started. You've got a business to run. But before you can start using QuickBooks Simple Start, you need to perform some up-front work. You need to install the software and set up the containers you'll use for your accounting.

And here's something else. Even before you do that work — the installation and setup work — you really, really should think carefully about the entity form you've chosen to use for your business. (This thinking is important even if you're already been operating for a while because the entity form you use affects that way you and I, working together like a well-oiled machine, should set up QuickBooks Simple Start.)

So, this is what we'll do (you and I is what I mean by "we") in this chapter.

I assume that you know how Windows works. If you don't, take the time to read Chapter 1 of your Windows User's Guide. Or try the appropriate edition of *Windows For Dummies* by Andy Rathbone (Wiley).

Eenie, Meenie, Minie, Moe, Chose an Entity, and You're Ready to Go

You know what's weird? Most people seem to start businesses without spending any time thinking about what form the business entity should use. For example, people start businesses as simple sole proprietorships because they don't have the time to consider the other options. Or, just as bad, people start businesses as limited liability companies (also known as LLCs) or as corporations because that's the way Uncle Carl said you do it. (They may have run into Uncle Carl at the family reunion last year.)

You shouldn't take either of these approaches, however. You should carefully think about the appropriate business entity for two reasons, one pretty big and one sort of big.

- ✔ **The Pretty Big Reason.** Choosing the right entity saves you thousands in taxes and keeps your accounting simple and straightforward. Not surprisingly, choosing the wrong entity costs you thousands in taxes and turns your accounting into a nightmare from which you never really wake up.

- ✔ **The Sort of Big Reason.** During the QuickBooks setup process, artfully described in the later chapter section titled, "Running through the Setup Interview," you'll be asked to make accounting decisions that to a great extent depend on the entity form you've chosen.

So, you and I are going to have the talk. And by doing so, you're not going to fall into the traps that most people fall into, the "Gee I never thought of that" trap or the equally disastrous trap of getting half-baked tax and legal advice from some friend or relative.

For single-owner businesses

If you own a business in its entirety, you have four choices as to the entity you can use to operate your business.

In the following sections, I describe each of these entities and then identify the big benefits and drawbacks of each. Later in this chapter, I offer some general rules that you can use to make your decision.

Sole proprietorships: Fast, easy, and risky

Sole proprietorships don't require any special effort or paperwork or even a business license. If you start a business — even selling junk on eBay that you can't get anyone to haul away — you've got a sole proprietorship. If you start doing a little consulting on the side, you've got a sole proprietorship. If you do something else to make money on your own, well, you understand, right?

Just to clarify, I'm not saying that you don't need a business license from the local government authorities to operate your business. I'm quite sure that you do. I'm just telling you that, technically speaking, you don't create a sole proprietorship by getting a business license. You create one simply by starting some business activity.

Of course, sole proprietorships do have big benefits, but there is also a big drawback. The fact that you can create a sole proprietorship on the fly represents a benefit. A big one.

Another benefit is that with a sole proprietorship, you can keep your accounting simple. For example, you can report your business profits or losses to the federal and state government on a one-page tax form. And you can skip having to do any payroll tax accounting if you're the only person working in the business.

Hey, no kidding, simplicity is sweet when it comes to taxes and accounting, and it doesn't get any simpler than a sole proprietorship.

There's a big drawback with a sole proprietorship, however. And here it is: The debts of the business fall back onto the owner. In other words, if the business borrows $25,000 from the bank and then can't pay the money back, you, the owner have *unlimited liability* — you will have to pick up the tab. Ouch.

Single-member LLCs: Flexible safety

Single-member *limited liability companies,* or LLCs, get created when someone files articles of organization with the appropriate state government office. In Washington state where I live, for example, one files the form shown in Figure 1-1. Basically, you fill the blanks, write a check for $175 (state fees vary), and send the check and completed form to the Washington state Secretary of State. A few days (or a few weeks) later, you get an official looking document that tells you that your LLC exists.

Single-member LLCs deliver three big benefits to the small business owner. First, a single-member LLC (and other types of LLCs, too) limits your liability. In the previous section, I discuss how sole proprietorships work, that the owner of a sole proprietorship is ultimately responsible for business debt. LLCs don't work that way. If the owner can't pay a business debt, the LLC creditor can't look automatically to the LLC's owner or owners.

STATE OF WASHINGTON SECRETARY OF STATE

APPLICATION TO FORM A LIMITED LIABILITY COMPANY
(Per Chapter 25.15 RCW)
FEE: $175

- Please PRINT or TYPE in black ink
- Sign, date and return original AND ONE COPY to:

CORPORATIONS DIVISION
801 CAPITOL WAY SOUTH • PO BOX 40234
OLYMPIA, WA 98504-0234

- BE SURE TO INCLUDE FILING FEE. Checks should be made payable to "Secretary of State"

EXPEDITED (24-HOUR) SERVICE AVAILABLE – $20 PER ENTITY
INCLUDE FEE AND WRITE "EXPEDITE" IN BOLD LETTERS
ON OUTSIDE OF ENVELOPE

FOR OFFICE USE ONLY

FILED: /   /   UBI:

CORPORATION NUMBER:

Important! Person to contact about this filing | Daytime Phone Number (with area code)

CERTIFICATE OF FORMATION

NAME OF LIMITED LIABILITY COMPANY (LLC) *(Must contain the word "Limited Liability Company" "Limited Liability Co." "L.L.C." or "LLC")*

ADDRESS OF LLC'S PRINCIPAL PLACE OF BUSINESS

Street Address *(Required)* _____ City _____ State _____ ZIP _____

PO Box *(Optional – Must be in same city as street address)* _____ ZIP *(If different than street ZIP)* _____

EFFECTIVE DATE OF LLC *(Specified effective date may be up to 90 days AFTER receipt of the document by the Secretary of State)*

☐ Specific Date: _____ ☐ Upon filing by the Secretary of State

DATE OF DISSOLUTION *(If applicable)* | MANAGEMENT OF LLC IS VESTED IN ONE OR MORE MANAGERS
☐ Yes ☐ No

>>> PLEASE ATTACH ANY OTHER PROVISIONS THE LLC ELECTS TO INCLUDE <<<

NAME AND ADDRESS OF WASHINGTON STATE REGISTERED AGENT

Name _____

Street Address *(Required)* _____ City _____ State _____ ZIP _____

PO Box *(Optional – Must be in same city as street address)* _____ ZIP *(If different than street ZIP)* _____

I consent to serve as Registered Agent in the State of Washington for the above named LLC. I understand it will be my responsibility to accept Service of Process on behalf of the LLC; to forward mail to the LLC; and to immediately notify the Office of the Secretary of State if I resign or change the Registered Office Address.

Signature of Agent | Printed Name | Date

NAMES ADDRESSES OF EACH PERSON EXECUTING THIS CERTIFICATE *(If necessary, attach additional names and addresses)*

Printed Name _____ Signature _____

Address _____ City _____ State _____ ZIP _____

Printed Name _____ Signature _____

Address _____ City _____ State _____ ZIP _____

Printed Name _____ Signature _____

Address _____ City _____ State _____ ZIP _____

INFORMATION AND ASSISTANCE – 360/753-7115 (TDD – 360/753-1485)

025-001 (9/00)

FOR OFFICE USE ONLY

Figure 1-1:
The Washington State Articles of Organization form.

Because LLCs do by law limit the liability of an owner, business creditors (especially for new businesses) often won't loan the business money without first getting the owner to provide a personal guarantee. In effect, that personal guarantee trumps the liability protection offered by the LLC. Also, the

LLC liability protection (and corporate liability protection as well) often won't protect a business owner from what's called *tort liability.* For example, if you've got a roofing business and, by accident, you drop a hammer on someone's head, you're liable for that accident (in all probability). Even if your roofing company is an LLC. Furthermore, if some guy who works for you drops a hammer on someone's head, well, the LLC might not protect you from that liability.

Here's a second benefit that single-member LLCs deliver: It turns out that LLCs are chameleons for tax purposes. In other words, for purposes of reporting and paying your business income taxes, an LLC can be pretty much anything you want it to be. For example, even though your LLC is an LLC and gives you liability protection, the IRS happily treats it as a sole proprietorship (which will keep your accounting easy). Or if you want instead to have the LLC treated as a C corporation or an S corporation (two choices we'll talk about in the next sections), you can do that, too.

You tell the IRS how you want an LLC to be treated for tax purposes by using a special 8832 form (see Figure 1-2).

I need to also mention a quick third benefit, the less red tape and paperwork benefit. Let me back up a bit, though, by saying that corporations, an entity form that has been around for more than a century, also provide for limited liability. But, unfortunately, corporations also require a certain amount of legal fiddle-faddling. With a corporation, for example, you should have regular board of director meetings. And you should have annual stockholders meetings. An LLC doesn't require this extra work, however. In other words, with an LLC, you get the same liability limitation that a corporation provides. But you get to simplify your paperwork and red tape.

As far as I'm concerned, there are only two drawbacks — both minor. First, either you need to be able to fill out a simple form (see Figure 1-1 again) or you have to pay an attorney $1,000 to fill the form out. Second, you have to pay the state a one-time setup fee (of about $200, but the amount varies by state) and you have to pay (potentially) annual LLC fees. (These can actually be significant in some states like California.)

I think having an attorney do your LLC paperwork and setup is a good idea. I really do. If you have an attorney do it, the paperwork will get done right. You'll also get to ask all sorts of useful questions about how the liability protection really works and how one gets out of jury duty. However, if you're on such a limited budget that you can't afford an attorney — and so the choice is no LLC or a do-it-yourself LLC — hey, if it was me, I'd fill out the form myself. (I'd also get and read a book on how to set up your own LLC.)

Form **8832**
(Rev. September 2002)
Department of the Treasury
Internal Revenue Service

Entity Classification Election

OMB No. 1545-1516

Type or Print

Name of entity

EIN ▶

Number, street, and room or suite no. If a P.O. box, see instructions.

City or town, state, and ZIP code. If a foreign address, enter city, province or state, postal code and country.

1   **Type of election** (see instructions):

a ☐ Initial classification by a newly-formed entity.

b ☐ Change in current classification.

2   **Form of entity** (see instructions):

a ☐ A domestic eligible entity electing to be classified as an association taxable as a corporation.

b ☐ A domestic eligible entity electing to be classified as a partnership.

c ☐ A domestic eligible entity with a single owner electing to be disregarded as a separate entity.

d ☐ A foreign eligible entity electing to be classified as an association taxable as a corporation.

e ☐ A foreign eligible entity electing to be classified as a partnership.

f ☐ A foreign eligible entity with a single owner electing to be disregarded as a separate entity.

3   **Disregarded entity information** (see instructions):
a Name of owner ▶ ....
b Identifying number of owner ▶ ....
c Country of organization of entity electing to be disregarded (if foreign) ▶ ....

4   Election is to be effective beginning (month, day, year) (see instructions) . . . . ▶ ___ / ___ / ___

5   Name and title of person whom the IRS may call for more information | **6** That person's telephone number
( )

Consent Statement and Signature(s) (see instructions)

Under penalties of perjury, I (we) declare that I (we) consent to the election of the above-named entity to be classified as indicated above, and that I (we) have examined this consent statement, and to the best of my (our) knowledge and belief, it is true, correct, and complete. If I am an officer, manager, or member signing for all members of the entity, I further declare that I am authorized to execute this consent statement on their behalf.

Signature(s)	Date	Title

For Paperwork Reduction Act Notice, see page 4.   Cat. No. 22598R   Form **8832** (Rev. 9-2002)

Figure 1-2:
Form 8832 tells the IRS how your LLC should be treated for tax purposes.

C corporations: The traditional form

C corporations, which are just regular old corporations treated as corporations for tax purposes, sort of work like LLCs. You create a C corporation by filing articles of incorporation with the appropriate state government office.

In Washington state, for example, you file the articles with the Secretary of State. As with an LLC, you also send in a check. A few days (or weeks) later, you get an official looking document that tells you your corporation exists.

C corporations deliver three big benefits to small businesses. First, C corporations provide the same liability protection as LLCs. So that's cool. Second, C corporations can provide their employees with generous nontaxable fringe benefits (even employees who own the corporation) as long as the corporation isn't discriminating in favor of highly paid employees or owners. Third, C corporations separate the tax accounting of the business from the tax accounting of the owners. If a corporation makes money, that by itself doesn't affect the shareholders who own the corporation. Similarly, if a corporation loses money, that by itself, doesn't affect the shareholders. This Chinese wall element of the corporation often keeps the owners' (and the business's) finances simpler.

C corporations present some problems to small businesses, however. I've already mentioned that you encounter a certain amount of legal paperwork and red tape (that's a bummer). Any corporation complicates your tax accounting and payroll. Finally, you have to pay two taxes on the business profits if you operate as a C corporation.

This double-taxation thing can be confusing. Suppose that you've got a little corporation that makes, after paying all your expenses but before paying yourself a salary, $90,000. Further assume that you want that $90,000. Bad. So, here's the way that corporation tax accounting works. You can pay out as wages to yourself whatever portion of that $90,000 represents a fair salary to you. For example, if a guy who does your job makes $45,000 a year, you can pay $45,000 of the $90,000 as wages (to yourself). You'll personally get taxed on the wages. But the corporation will get to take a $45,000 deduction on its corporate tax return. If the corporation starts with $90,000 and then deducts $45,000 of shareholder salary, the corporation still has corporate profits of $45,000. And it's this remaining $45,000 that will get taxed twice. First, for example, the corporation will pay federal and state corporate income taxes on the $45,000. (You can figure these will run about $10,000.) This will leave $35,000. But if the corporation pays this $35,000 out to you (as a dividend, say), you'll have to pay personal income taxes on the $35,000. (You can figure these taxes will run another $10,000.) See the double taxation? It's the same $45,000 of profit, but the corporation pays taxes . . . and then the shareholder pays taxes.

S corporations: Complicated tax-saving machines

S corporations are regular old corporations that have made a special tax accounting election that lets them escape from the double-taxation I talk about in the previous paragraph. You make this election using a special form (see Figure 1-3).

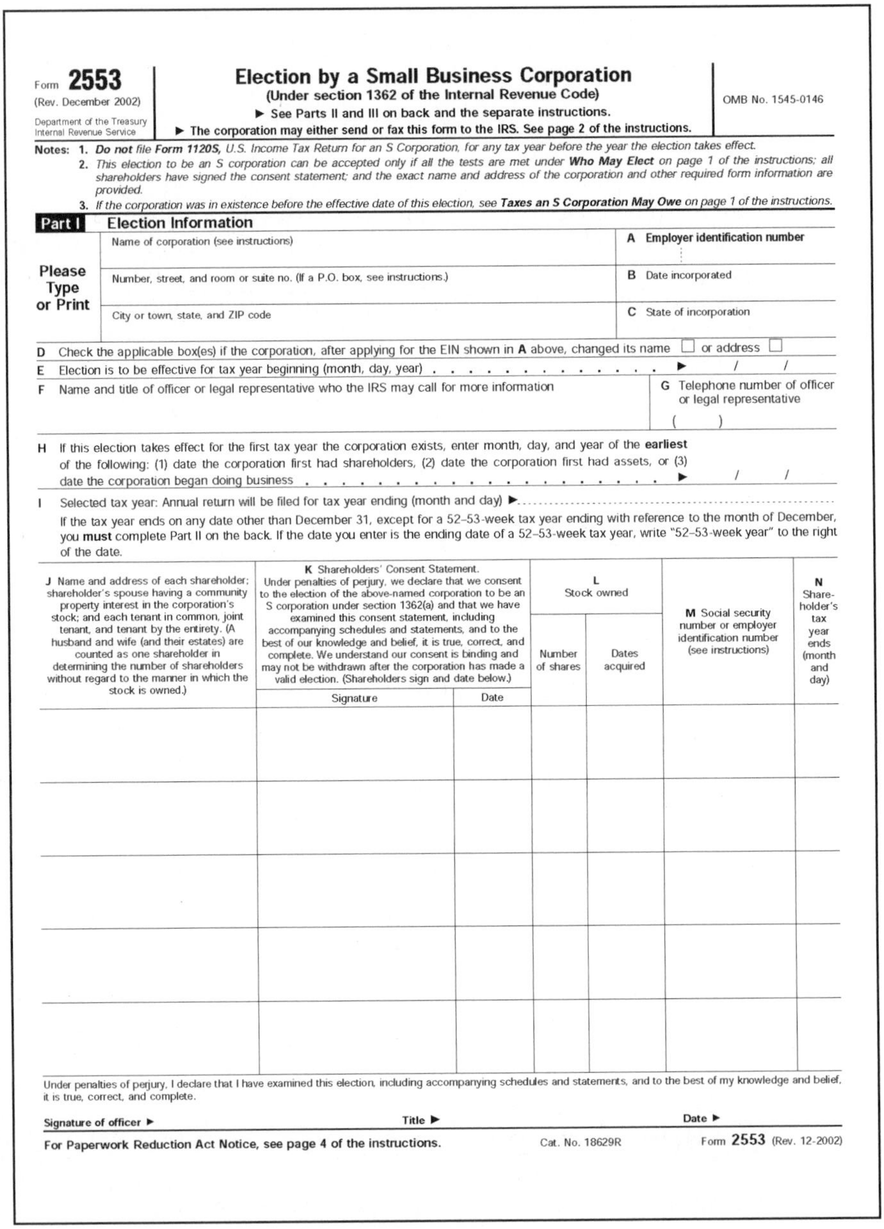

Form **2553** (Rev. December 2002) Department of the Treasury Internal Revenue Service

Election by a Small Business Corporation

(Under section 1362 of the Internal Revenue Code)

► See Parts II and III on back and the separate instructions.

► The corporation may either send or fax this form to the IRS. See page 2 of the instructions.

OMB No. 1545-0146

Notes: 1. *Do not file Form 1120S, U.S. Income Tax Return for an S Corporation, for any tax year before the year the election takes effect.*

2. *This election to be an S corporation can be accepted only if all the tests are met under **Who May Elect** on page 1 of the instructions; all shareholders have signed the consent statement; and the exact name and address of the corporation and other required form information are provided.*

3. *If the corporation was in existence before the effective date of this election, see **Taxes an S Corporation May Owe** on page 1 of the instructions.*

Part I Election Information

Please Type or Print		
	Name of corporation (see instructions)	A Employer identification number
	Number, street, and room or suite no. (If a P.O. box, see instructions.)	B Date incorporated
	City or town, state, and ZIP code	C State of incorporation

D Check the applicable box(es) if the corporation, after applying for the EIN shown in A above, changed its name ☐ or address ☐

E Election is to be effective for tax year beginning (month, day, year) . . . . ► / /

F Name and title of officer or legal representative who the IRS may call for more information

G Telephone number of officer or legal representative ( )

H If this election takes effect for the first tax year the corporation exists, enter month, day, and year of the **earliest** of the following: (1) date the corporation first had shareholders, (2) date the corporation first had assets, or (3) date the corporation began doing business . . . . ► / /

I Selected tax year: Annual return will be filed for tax year ending (month and day) ►

If the tax year ends on any date other than December 31, except for a 52–53-week tax year ending with reference to the month of December, you **must** complete Part II on the back. If the date you enter is the ending date of a 52–53-week tax year, write "52–53-week year" to the right of the date.

J Name and address of each shareholder; shareholder's spouse having a community property interest in the corporation's stock; and each tenant in common, joint tenant, and tenant by the entirety. (A husband and wife (and their estates) are counted as one shareholder in determining the number of shareholders without regard to the manner in which the stock is owned.)	K Shareholders' Consent Statement. Under penalties of perjury, we declare that we consent to the election of the above-named corporation to be an S corporation under section 1362(a) and that we have examined this consent statement, including accompanying schedules and statements, and to the best of our knowledge and belief, it is true, correct, and complete. We understand our consent is binding and may not be withdrawn after the corporation has made a valid election. (Shareholders sign and date below.)		L Stock owned		M Social security number or employer identification number (see instructions)	N Share-holder's tax year ends (month and day)
	Signature	Date	Number of shares	Dates acquired		

Under penalties of perjury, I declare that I have examined this election, including accompanying schedules and statements, and to the best of my knowledge and belief, it is true, correct, and complete.

Signature of officer ► Title ► Date ►

For Paperwork Reduction Act Notice, see page 4 of the instructions. Cat. No. 18629R Form **2553** (Rev. 12-2002)

Figure 1-3: Form 2553 tells the IRS you want to make the S corporation election.

Except for the actual S election, S corporations resemble C corporations. You set up an S corporation in the same way that you set up a C corporation. You have all the same paperwork and red tape headaches with an S corporation that you have with a C. You also have to file a corporate income tax return and put shareholder employees on the payroll. But S corporations deliver a couple of pretty sweet tax savings. First, S corporations aren't subject to corporate income tax (except in some special circumstances that don't apply if you immediately elect S status upon setting up the corporation). So there's no double-taxation worry with an S corporation. (We just talked about this in the section, "C corporations: The traditional form".)

But there's another benefit of operating as an S corporation. S corporations can often be used to save business owners from self-employment taxes. If you're a sole proprietor or a single-member LLC operating for tax purposes as a sole proprietor, you pay not only income taxes on your business profits but also self-employment taxes on your business profits. If you make $90,000, for example, you'll pay roughly $13,500 in self-employment taxes. (These taxes take the place of the Social Security and Medicare taxes that you would have paid had you kept that job you didn't like.)

Now, there's no way to get out from under these taxes if you're a sole proprietor. And, actually, partners in partnerships suffer from the same self-employment tax burden. But S corporations can sometimes be used to save self-employment taxes. What if, for example, you make $90,000 but incorporate and then immediately elect "S" status. In that case, the corporation will have to pay Social Security and Medicare taxes on the wages the corporation pays you. But not on the dividend the corporation pays you. If the corporation pays you $45,000 of wages and $45,000 of dividends, the corporation will pay roughly $6,750 in Social Security and Medicare taxes.

See the savings? One way you pay $13,500 in self-employment taxes. One way you (or actually, your corporation) pays $6,750 in Social Security and Medicare taxes.

The only trick with the self-employment tax savings gambit is that your salary must be reasonable. You can't pick a number out of thin air. And you can't simply set the salary to zero. (I recommend to my clients, for example, that they look up Bureau of Labor Statistics or Department of Commerce data on actual salaries paid to employees working a job like the one they do.)

So, S corporations are pretty cool for small businesses.

General rules for single-owner businesses

Based on the characteristics of sole proprietorship, single-member LLCs, and corporations, here are my traditional rules for small businesses:

1. If you've got a very small business — a few thousand in profits each year, for example — I think you go with a plain vanilla sole proprietorship. Sure, liability limitation would be nice. But the extra accounting and legal costs aren't, to my small, struggling mind, worth it.

2. If you've a small business that's making more than a few thousand in profits in year (or you plan for the business to make more than a few thousand in profits at some point), take the time and spend the money to set up a single-member LLC. But don't tell the IRS you want the LLC to be treated as a corporation. By telling the IRS nothing about the LLC — specifically by not filing the 8832 form shown in Figure 1-2), the LLC will be treated according to the default rules, which means for tax purposes, it'll be treated as a sole proprietorship. This keeps the accounting easy. But you get the limited liability protection you deserve.

3. If you've got a small business that's making in profits some multiple of what the business can fairly pay you as a salary, set up shop as a single-member LLC and then (with an attorney's or accountant's help) correctly file forms 8832 and 2553 (see Figure 1-2 and 1-3) so that your business is treated as an S corporation. You'll probably pay some extra taxes and more to get your tax return prepared. But you should end up with thousands of dollars in self-employment tax savings.

4. If you've got a good little business and, unfortunately, find yourself in a personal situation where you or a member of your family incurs frequent and large medical expenses, set up shop as a single-member LLC and then (with an attorney's or accountant's help) file a form 8832 to turn the business into a C corporation. When you do this, ask your attorney or accountant to help you set up a Sec. 105(b) medical reimbursement plan for employees. You'll pay slightly more in taxes and accountant's fees, but you'll be able to deduct all of your family's medical expenses.

Health insurance costs of self-employed people are 100 percent deductible no matter what entity form they choose for their businesses. So the preceding suggestion really concerns healthcare costs that aren't covered by a standard medical insurance policy. Unfortunately, uninsured healthcare costs might often be case where you or someone else in your family has a serious chronic illness.

For multiple-owner businesses

If you own a business with another person, you have four choices as to the entity you can use to operate your business. In the following sections, I describe each of these entities and then identify the big benefits and drawbacks of each. After that discussion, I offer some rules that you can use to nail down your choices.

Partnerships: The worst of all possible worlds

Partnerships, technically called general partnerships, form when two or more people team up in some profit-making venture or activity. In a sense, then, partnership creation occurs just as automatically as does sole proprietorship creation. And you might think that seems like a good idea.

I don't think, however, that the "fast and easy" or automatic creation feature can be called a benefit of partnerships. The reason is that in a partnership, each partner is personally liable for the business debts of the partnership. Partners may also have responsibilities to the partnership and their partners. What's more, partnership taxes and accounting are as complicated as corporate taxes and accounting.

Multiple-member LLCs: The new way to partner

Multiple-member LLCs are LLCs with multiple owners, or members. Sometimes, these multiple-member LLCs have one class or category of members, so they work like a regular partnership. Other times, these multiple-member LLCs have members who are managing members and members who are nonmanaging members.

Multiple-member LLCs get created when someone files an articles of organization form with the appropriate state government office. Earlier in the chapter in Figure 1-1, I showed a copy of the Washington state form that one files to set up an LLC. As I mention in that discussion, you fill the form's blanks, write a check, and then send the check and completed form to the appropriate state official. A few days or weeks later, you get an official looking document that tells you your LLC exists.

As with single-member LLCs, multiple-member LLCs deliver three big benefits to small business owners. First, the LLC limits your liability. If a sole proprietorship or general partnership can't pay some business debt, the owner or owners must pay. Or the owner who's got some money must pay. With a multiple-member LLC, however, if the LLC can't pay a business debt, the LLC creditor typically can't look to the LLC's owner or owners for payment.

As noted earlier, because LLCs do by law limit the liability of an owner, business creditors often won't loan the business money without first getting the owner to provide a personal guarantee — and that means the owners lose liability protection for that specific liability. What's more, LLC liability protection often won't protect a business owner from tort liability.

Here's a second benefit that multiple-member LLCs deliver: For purposes of reporting and paying your business income taxes, a multiple-member LLC can be a partnership, a corporation or even (in some cases) an S corporation. Even though your LLC is an LLC and gives you liability protection, the IRS is happy to treat it as a partnership. Or as a C corporation. Or as an S corporation. As I note earlier in the chapter, you tell the IRS how you want an LLC to be treated for tax purposes by using a special 8832 form (see Figure 1-2).

A third benefit of LLCs, at least as compared to corporations that also provide for limited liability, is that LLCs require less red tape and paperwork. With a corporation, for example, you should have regular board of directors meetings and annual stockholders meetings. An LLC doesn't require this extra work, however. So, with an LLC, you get the same liability limitation that a corporation provides but with simplified paperwork and red tape.

The two drawbacks of a multiple-member LLC are that you need to spend some money on legal fees by hiring a good attorney to help you through the process. Now, you may have read the earlier chapter discussion of single-member LLCs and may even recall my shoot-from-the-hip recommendation that you consider setting up a single-member LLC by yourself. I wouldn't do that if you've got multiple members. Call me a scaredy-cat. But with partners and almost certain future partner disagreements, you want a thoughtful veteran attorney to draft ancillary documents that'll let you efficiently manage the LLC (this is called the operating agreement document) and unwind the partnership when that time comes (usually done with a buy-sell agreement document). A second, usually minor, drawback to the multiple-member LLC form is that you have to pay the state a one-time setup fee (of about $200 but the amount varies by state) and you may have to pay annual LLC fees. (These can actually be significant in some states like California.)

C corporations: The same whether one shareholder or two

I discuss how C corporations work in an earlier chapter section titled, "C corporations: The traditional form." Pretty much everything I said there about how C corporations work for single-owner businesses also applies to C corporations owned by more than one owner. Go to that section to find out more.

S corporations: They work for multiple-owner firms, too

I also discuss how S corporations work in an earlier chapter section, "S corporations: Complicated tax saving machines." Again, almost everything I said there applies to businesses with more than a single owner. Go to that section to find out more.

Let me also point out that when you start talking about multiple-owner S corporations, things can become a little tricky. For example, the IRS has rules about who can and can't become an S corporation shareholder. (U.S. citizens and permanent residents are okay, but nonresidents and partnerships aren't, for example.) The IRS also has rules about the number of people who can become shareholders. (The rules limit sort of you to 75 shareholders.) What's more, the S corporation can have only one class of stock. (You can't, for example, have two classes of stock — such as common and preferred — that treat shareholders differently.)

With multiple owners, you're probably in a situation where you ought to sit down with a good attorney and accountant and get their help in selecting the appropriate entity form for your business.

General rules for multiple-owner businesses

Based on the characteristics of partnerships, multiple-member LLCs, and corporations, here are my traditional rules for small businesses with more than one owner:

1. Don't use a general partnership — even if you've got only a very small business generating a few thousand in profits each year. A partnership for a very small business presents too many liability, tax, and accounting problems.

2. If your business is at least modestly profitable (or you plan for the business to be modestly profitable), pay an attorney to set up a multiple-member LLC. As long as you don't do anything with that form I showed in Figure 1-2, the LLC will be treated according to the default rules, which means for tax purposes, it'll be treated as a partnership. And you'll get the limited liability protection you deserve.

3. If you've got a small business that's making in profits some multiple of what the business can fairly pay you and the other owner or owners as a salary, set up shop as a multiple-member LLC and then (with an attorney's or accountant's help) correctly file forms 8832 and 2553 (see Figure 1-2 and 1-3) so that your business is treated as an S corporation. You will pay some extra taxes and accountant's bills, but you and each of your partners should end up with thousands of dollars in self-employment tax savings.

Installing QuickBooks Simple Start

Hey, you thought I forgot this book is about QuickBooks Simple Start, didn't you? Don't worry. I didn't. In fact, here's where you install QuickBooks Simple Start right now. Just follow these steps:

1. **Get the QuickBooks Simple Start CD.**

   Rip open the QuickBooks package and get out the CD (which looks exactly like the ones that play music).

2. **Insert the CD in your CD-ROM drive.**

   If you have any amount of luck, Windows recognizes that you've inserted the QuickBooks Simple Start CD and displays a window that thanks you for purchasing QuickBooks Simple Start and asks if you want to "start." You do, so click the Start button and skip to Step 6.

3. **If nothing happened when you inserted the QuickBooks Simple Start CD, open the Control Panel window.**

In Windows XP, click the Start button and then choose Control Panel. In most versions of Windows, including Windows 2000, you click the Start button and then choose Settings⇨Control Panel from the Start menu. Figure 1-4 shows the Windows XP Control Panel window that appears.

4. **Start the Windows Install program.**

In most versions of Windows, you can do this by double-clicking the Add or Remove Programs icon. When the dialog box in Figure 1-5 appears, click Add New Programs, then click the CD or Floppy button, and then follow the on-screen instructions. You need to press the Enter key several times to move through some dialog boxes. Figure 1-5, I should mention, is the Windows XP Add or Remove Programs window. If you're using some other flavor of Windows, the window looks different. But it works in roughly the same way. After you see the first QuickBooks Simple Start window, click its Start button.

5. **Tell QuickBooks how you want to get started.**

After you click the Start button, QuickBooks Simple Start asks how you want to get started. But what it's really asking is whether you want to install the Simple Start software on your desktop computer — you would make this choice by clicking the Get Started with Desktop Edition button — or work with an online version over the Internet. You want to install the software on your desktop computer, so click the Get Started with Desktop Edition button.

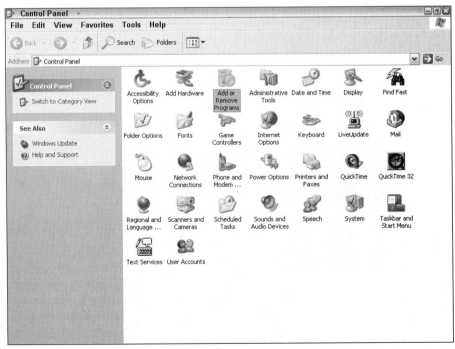

Figure 1-4:
The Control Panel window.

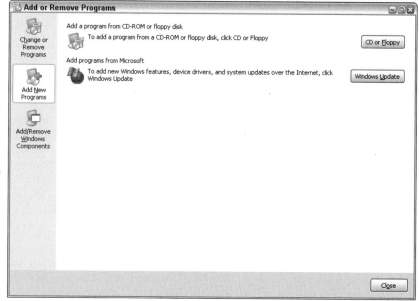

Figure 1-5:
The Add
or Remove
Programs
window in
Windows XP
Professional.

The QuickBooks setup process starts, and the InstallShield Wizard
window appears (Figure 1-6). Enter the CD key code (which is printed on
a yellow sticker on the back of the CD sleeve) and click Next to begin the
installation process. Then follow the on-screen instructions. If you have
a question about an installation option, just accept the QuickBooks suggestion by pressing Enter. (The suggested, or default, installation
options are fine for 999 out of 1,000 users.)

Figure 1-6:
The
InstallShield
Wizard.

6. **Click Next to begin copying the files.**

   QuickBooks gives you a summary of your installation choices and then tells you to click Next to begin copying the files. Do so. The QuickBooks installation program slowly begins extracting files from the CD. This process is slow. Think "glacier sliding down the side of a mountain." As the installation program runs, you should see a little bar that shows your progress.

   If you need to cancel the installation at any time, click Cancel. QuickBooks warns you that the setup is incomplete. That's okay — just start the setup from scratch next time around.

7. **After the Install program finishes, click Restart.**

   Congratulations. You're finished with the installation. You have a new item on the Programs menu and probably new shortcuts on your desktop.

   If you're installing QuickBooks Simple Start on a computer running Windows NT, Windows 2000, or Windows XP Professional, you need to log on as either the administrator or a user with administrator rights. With these operating systems, Windows security features require an administrator to install the QuickBooks Simple Start program.

Running through the Setup Interview

After you know what entity form your business will use and have the Quick-Books Simple Start software installed, you're ready to set up the QuickBooks data file. The data file is the container that QuickBooks Simple Start uses to hold your financial information.

Step-by-step help for the Setup Interview

To run through the Setup Interview, you start the QuickBooks Simple Start program and then, when prompted by QuickBooks, step through the Setup Interview.

Specifically, you take the following steps:

1. **Start QuickBooks Simple Start.**

   Before you begin the interview, you have to start QuickBooks Simple Start. To do so, double-click the QuickBooks Simple Start icon, which appears on the Windows desktop. Or, choose Start⇨Programs and then click the menu choices that lead to QuickBooks. (For example, I choose Start⇨QuickBooks Simple Start Edition.)

   The real fun begins at this point. The Setup Interview starts automatically, displaying the dialog box shown in Figure 1-7.

Welcome to the Setup Interview

Before you start billing your customers or tracking your expenses, you need to set up a company file to store the data you enter.

This Setup Interview will help you complete this task in just a few easy steps -- and it will guide you every step of the way.

If you make a mistake, you can click Prev to correct it. If you need to change the information at a later time, you can do so by choosing Company Information or Preferences from the File menu.

Click Next to begin.

Prev   Next   Cancel

Figure 1-7:
The Setup
Interview
dialog box.

If you're not starting QuickBooks for the first time but you want to step through the Setup Interview to set up a new company anyway, choose File➪New Company.

2. **Describe your business.**

   To begin the interview, click the Next button. The Setup Interview displays a window that asks you to enter your company's name and address. Fill in the blanks with the requested information.

3. **Identify your entity form choice.**

   To continue with the interview, click Next. The Setup Interview displays a window (not shown) that asks which entity form you've chosen for your business. Here's how you answer the question that this dialog box asks:

   • If you've chosen to operate as a sole proprietorship or as a single-member LLC that will be treated for tax purposes as a sole proprietorship, check the Sole Proprietorship button.

   • If you've chosen to operate as a partnership or as a multiple-member LLC that will be treated as a partnership for income tax purposes, check the Partnership or Limited Liability Company button.

   • If you've chosen to operate as an S corporation (this might be because you incorporated and then elected S status or because you set up an LLC and then double-elected S status), check the S corporation button.

   • If you've chosen to operate as a C corporation (this might be because you incorporate or setup an LLC and then elected to be treated as a corporation), check the Corporation button.

• If you're using QuickBooks Simple Start for a church or a nonprofit organization of some type, of course, check the Non-Profit Organization button.

One final point about this entity choice confusion: If you're currently operating as a sole proprietorship or a single-member LLC that's treated for income tax purposes as a sole proprietorship and you know that someday soon you'll make the elections necessary to turn the entity into a corporation, check the button that corresponds to the entity you'll become, not the entity form that you're currently using.

4. **Describe how you'll bill your customers.**

Click Next to move to the Setup Interview dialog box that asks how you'll bill your customers (see Figure 1-8). Mostly, you just answer the questions that the Setup Interview asks. But let me throw in my own two-cents' worth.

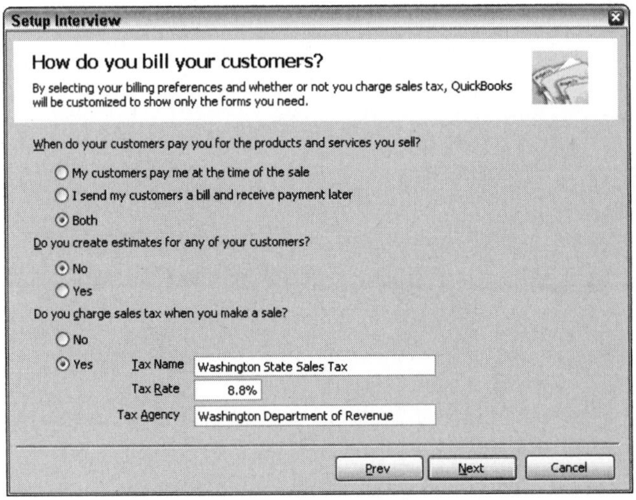

Figure 1-8:
The Setup
Interview
dialog box
that collects
billing
information.

• **Describe whether people pay in cash or on time.** See that first question about whether people pay you at the time of sale (presumably with cash or a check) or later after you invoice them? You need to answer this question by selecting the appropriate button. QuickBooks uses your question to this question to determine whether you need to print sales receipts (because yours is a point-of-sale business) or invoices (because you bill people and then they pay you later) or both.

• **Specify whether you create estimates for customers.** See that second question? The one that asks whether you create estimates — essentially "best guess" invoices — for your customers? You need to answer this question, too. If you do create (or you want to create) estimates, select Yes. If you don't, select No.

- **Indicate whether your customers are subject to sales tax.** If they are, click the Yes button. If you click the Yes button, you also need to label the sales tax you pay, specify the tax rate, and name the tax agency to which you remit the sales taxes. In Figure 1-9, for example, I provided the information necessary to put a line on receipts and invoices for Washington state sales tax. The sales tax equals 8.8 percent of the invoice or receipt total. And one remits the sales taxes (on a monthly or quarterly basis) to the Washington State Department of Revenue.

5. **Create the QuickBooks company file.**

   Click Next to move to the next Setup Interview dialog box. This dialog box informs you that QuickBooks is on the verge of creating the company file that'll store your accounting information. All you need to do is click Next. So click Next. When you do, QuickBooks displays the Save As dialog box (see Figure 1-9). Use this dialog box to name the QuickBooks company file. You simply enter the filename into the file name box and you click Save.

   You can also use the Save In box (shown at the top of the Save As dialog box) to specify the folder location that you want QuickBooks to use for the company file. But don't do it. I implore you. QuickBooks can lose track of where you store the company file if you put it someplace crazy and then create more than one company file. You don't want to lose your company file.

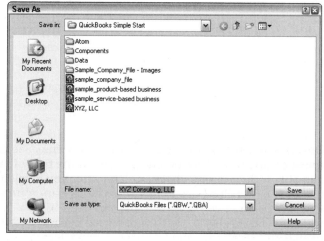

Figure 1-9:
Ah yes. The
Save As
dialog box.

After QuickBooks Simple Start creates the company file, it displays the usual QuickBooks Simple Start program window (see Figure 1-10). This is the same window you'll see from now on whenever you start QuickBooks.

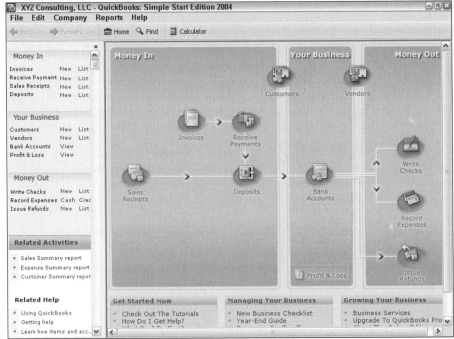

XYZ Consulting, LLC - QuickBooks: Simple Start Edition 2004

File   Edit   Company   Reports   Help

Figure 1-10:
The QuickBooks Simple Start program window.

After QuickBooks Simple Start starts, you may also see a message box that asks whether you want to register QuickBooks. You can use the product roughly a couple dozen times and then — whammo — either you register it or you can't use it. I don't like being forced to do something, but getting worked up about having to register QuickBooks is a waste of time. The simplest option is to just register. Here's how: When QuickBooks displays the message box that asks whether you want to register, click Online to register online or Phone to register over the phone. If you go with the phone option, QuickBooks displays another dialog box that gives you a telephone number to call and provides a space for you to enter your registration number. You can also register by choosing the File➪Register QuickBooks: Simple Start.

Should you get your accountant's help?

I think that most people should be able to set up QuickBooks Simple Start on their own. The trickiest part of this stuff isn't the software installation or setup — it's the entity choice stuff. And I tried to give you good detailed information on that at the very start of this chapter on that topic.

Having said that, however, if you've already been operating business for some time and have a current balance sheet and a year-to-date income statement, I suggest that you at least think about getting your accountant's help. Your accountant can do a much better job of giving you advice that may be specific to your situation. (Maybe you two can talk about the S election stuff.) And in many cases, your accountant can help you load into QuickBooks Simple Start the current balance sheet and year-to-date income statement information. What's more, your accountant probably knows your business and can keep you from making a terrible mess of things, just in case you don't follow my directions carefully.

If you do call upon your accountant to help you with the tasks in this chapter, I want to tell the accountant a couple of things. Tell your accountant that you're using QuickBooks Simple Start. And then when he says or she says, "Hmmmphf. I don't know the Simple Start program," tell them, "Ah, yeah you do. Simple Start is the same thing as regular QuickBooks . . . It's just that some of the features are hidden so it's easier for small business people."

Chapter 2

A Quick Tour of QuickBooks Simple Start

In This Chapter

▶ Using the Program window

▶ Using traditional menus

▶ Working with the Home page

▶ Using the navigation bar

▶ Getting help on Help

*A*fter you work with QuickBooks Simple Start awhile, you won't have any trouble finding your way around. But at the very start — those first few minutes and hours — you might find yourself slightly confused, sometimes befuddled, and often lost. The reason is that QuickBooks Simple Start uses an unusual interface.

Because the interface is a little funny, I want to take just a few pages to point out the components of the interface and tell you how to get around. I also want to go over the basics of using QuickBooks Simple Start menus and talk about the Help menu's commands. None of this stuff is difficult. You can finish in a few minutes.

Poking Around the Program Window

You see the Program window when you start the QuickBooks Simple Start program (see Figure 2-1). This is where it all happens — at least in an accounting sense.

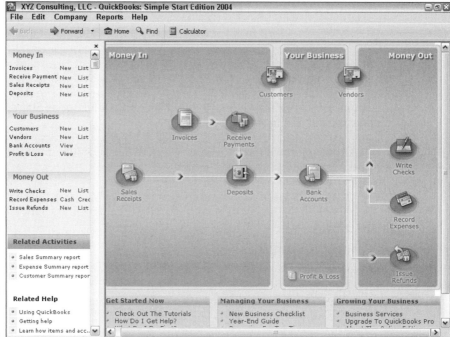

Figure 2-1:
The
QuickBooks
Simple Start
Program
window.

At the very top of the Program window, the Program window title bar appears. The Program Window title bar shows the name of the company. (In Figure 2-1, the title bar shows the name of the fictitious company I am using to illustrate QuickBooks Simple Start mechanics in this book: XYZ Consulting, LLC.) The Program window title bar also identifies the name of the program.

And, at the right end of the Program window title bar, Windows provides buttons you can click to minimize the Program window, restore the Program window, or you can close the Program window. The button that shows an X closes the QuickBooks Simple Start program window. The button that shows what looks like a little hyphen, or dash, minimizes the program window, so it appears only as a button on the Windows task bar. The other button — I don't even know how to describe it — alternately maximizes or unmaximizes (restores) the Program window.

Working with the Traditional Menus

Directly beneath the Program window title bar, QuickBooks Simple Start provides a menu bar and an icon bar. The menu bar is the horizontal list of names that, if clicked, displays menus of similar commands. In Figure 2-1, for example, the menu bar names the menus: File, Edit, Company, Reports, and Help. If you use the mouse to point to one of these menu names and click, QuickBooks Simple Start displays a list, or menu of roughly a dozen commands.

To display a menu, as you probably well know, you need to click the menu name with the mouse. Alternatively, you can press the Alt key and then the Letter key that corresponds to the underlined letter and the menu name. For example, if you press Alt and then the letter F, QuickBooks Simple Start displays the File menu (see Figure 2-2).

QuickBooks Simple Start doesn't underline letters in the menu name or command name until you press the Alt key.

Any valid command that you can choose in a particular setting appears in bold type. For example, in Figure 2-2, all of the menu commands appear in bold type. Therefore, any of the commands can be selected.

Figure 2-2:
The QuickBooks Simple Start File menu.

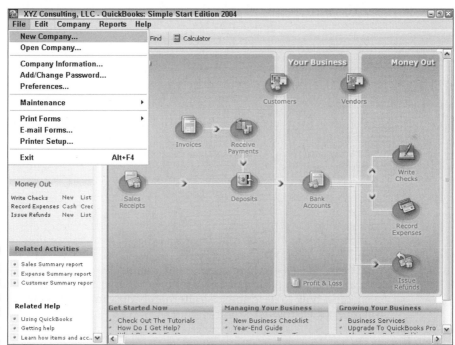

Figure 2-3 however shows the Edit menu. All of the Edit menu commands are grayed out. If a command is grayed out, QuickBooks Simple Starthas disabled the command. Disabled commands can't be chosen because they don't make sense to choose in the particular situation. Figure 2-3 shows something else interesting, too: For some menu commands, shortcut key combinations exist. For example, if you look closely at Figure 2-3, you'll see that the Undo command also can be chosen using the Ctrl+Z shortcut key combination. If you want to undo some editing, therefore, you can either choose the Edit➪Undo command or you can press Ctrl+Z.

Figure 2-4 shows the Company menu. Let me mention just a couple of things about this menu, too. First, note that some commands on a menu show a small arrowhead to the right of the command name. For example, in Figure 2-4, there is a small arrowhead that appears to the right of the Lists command, the Business Services command, and the For Your Accountant command. This arrowhead signals you that this menu command actually displays a submenu of additional commands. For example, if you choose the Company menu's Lists command, QuickBooks Simple Start displays the Lists submenu, as shown in Figure 2-5.

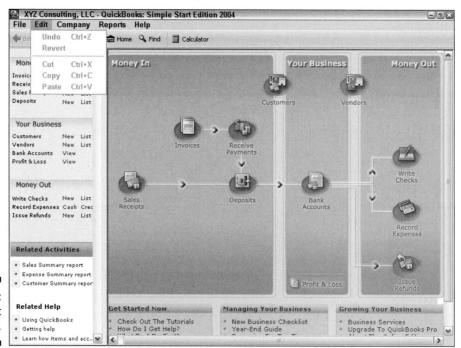

Figure 2-3:
The Edit
menu.

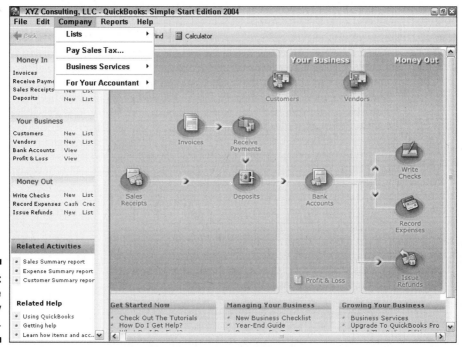

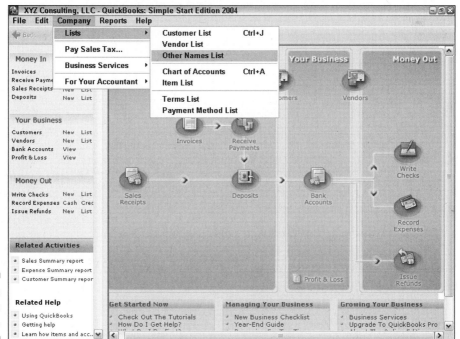

In Figure 2-4, there is one other little thing to notice. Some menu commands, if chosen, simply execute a command whenever you choose them. (The Undo command that I was just talking about works this way.) But other commands require more information from you before doing their thing. If a command requires more information, QuickBooks Simple Start displays a dialog box with which to collect that information. To show you that QuickBooks Simple Start will display a dialog box, it puts an ellipses, a series of dots or periods, after the command name. For example, in Figure 2-4, you can see that the Company⇨Pay Sales Tax command name is followed with dot dot dot. This alerts you to the fact that if you do choose the Company menu's Pay Sales Tax command, QuickBooks Simple Start will display a dialog box that it uses to collect information about how it should execute the command.

Using the icon bar

Beneath the menu bar, QuickBooks Simple Start displays an icon bar. The icon bar provides Back and Forward buttons to move to the previously displayed window or the recently displayed window, a Home button that redisplays the QuickBooks Simple Start Home Page (which shows in Figure 2-1), a Find button that displays a Find window that you can use to search for transactions, and a Calculator button that you can click to start the Windows Calculator accessory (see Figure 2-6). The Calculator accessory — a separate small program that comes with Windows — lets you add, subtract, multiply, and divide numbers. This baby is a handy tool to keep just a click away.

Figure 2-6:
The
Windows
Calculator.

A Few Words about Document Windows

QuickBooks Simple Start stacks document windows on top of the Home page flow chart shown in Figure 2-1.

For fun, and also to see how all this works, click the Icon bar's Find button. Don't worry. I don't expect you to know how to operate this window on your own. (Although you could figure it out pretty quickly . . .) But notice that when you do click the Find button, QuickBooks Simple Start displays the Find window (see Figure 2-7). And notice that the Find window sits on top of the QuickBooks Simple StartHome window.

To move back to the previously displayed window — in the example here that means the QuickBooks Simple StartHome window — you click the Back button on the icon bar. If you click the Back button to move back a window, you can then click the Forward button to move forward a window. If you happen to be following along in front of your computer, go ahead and noodle around with the Back and Forward buttons to make sure you know how they work. To click a window, you can click its Close box. The Close box is the little red box marked with an X that sits in the upper-right corner of the document window area.

One other little thing to note about the Back and Forward buttons is this: See the small arrowhead to the right of the Back and Forward buttons? If you click that Arrow button, QuickBooks Simple Start displays a list of the previously displayed document windows or the subsequently displayed document windows. You can select one of the windows listed to jump right to that window.

At any time, you can jump directly to the Home window by clicking the Home button on the icon bar.

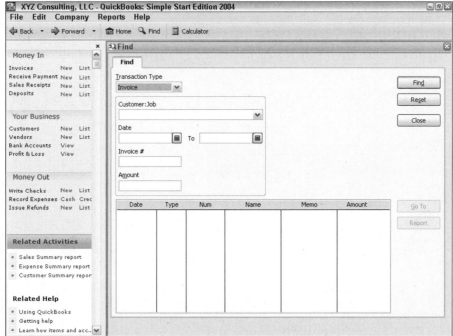

Figure 2-7:
The
QuickBooks
Simple Start
Program
window
showing
the Find
window.

Understanding the Home Window

The Home window (see Figure 2-1 near the beginning of the chapter) presents a flow chart of the QuickBooks Simple Start accounting process. The Home window also provides icons you click to access menu-like thingies.

Touring the Money In, Your Business, and Money Out areas

The Home window breaks the small business accounting process into three areas: the Money In area, the Your Business area, and the Money Out area. Take a look at Figure 2-1 to see what I mean. Each of these three areas — Money In, Your Business, and Money Out — is clearly labeled.

Within a particular area, such as the Money In area, QuickBooks Simple Start displays little icons, or pictures, for each step of the process. For example, in the Money In area you can see an icon for Sales Receipts. If you point to an icon, QuickBooks Simple Start displays a pop-up window that explains what that step in the accounting process entails. Figure 2-8, for example, shows the sales receipts menu-like feature.

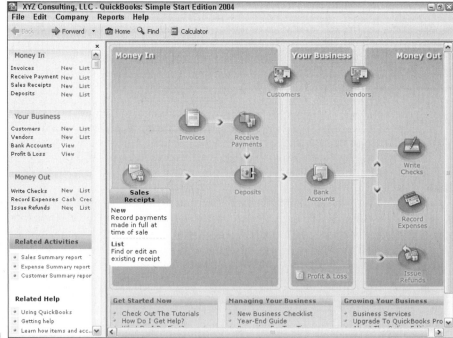

Figure 2-8:
The QuickBooks Simple Start Home window with the Sales Receipts icon selected.

I suggest taking a look at the Home page's flow chart. Go ahead — spend some time examining it. (Perhaps for a few minutes right now?)

By looking at the flow chart you can see that money comes into the business in two basic ways. You can invoice a customer and then later receive payment on the invoice, or you can to receive cash for some item you sell. No matter which way you get this money, QuickBooks Simple Start also shows what happens next: You deposit the money into your bank account.

Similarly, the Money Out area explains how your cash outflows work. Look closely at the Money Out area, and you'll see that cash flows out of the business because you write checks (obviously), record expenses, and (occasionally) because you issue refunds to customers.

In the Your Business area of the QuickBooks Simple Start Home window, you can see clickable icons for Customers, Vendors, Bank Accounts, and Profit & Loss. If you click either the Customers or Vendors buttons, you see the pop-up menu-like things that let you display customer or vendor lists — or add names to the customer or vendor lists. If you click the Bank Accounts button, you display the register for a bank account. If you click the Profit & Loss icon, QuickBooks Simple Start produces a profit and loss statement so you can see how your business is doing.

The Home page basement

Beneath the flow chart that represents the lion's share of the Home window, QuickBooks Simple Start displays three mini-lists of features related to starting the new business or getting started with QuickBooks: the Get Started Now list, the Managing Your Business list, and the Growing Your Business list.

The Get Started Now list provides three useful hyperlinks: Check Out The Tutorials, How Do I Get Help, and What Do I Do First. To use one of these Help tools, simply click the hyperlink and then follow the on-screen instructions. For example, if you click the Check Out The Tutorials hyperlink, QuickBooks Simple Start displays the QuickBooks Simple Start tutorial window, as shown in Figure 2-9.

This window lists seven different multimedia lessons that you can step through to find out about how to navigate within QuickBooks, set up a checking account, bill a customer, receive payment from a customer, record a deposit, write a check, and even check how the business is doing. If you click on a particular video tutorial, it starts. Figure 2-10 shows the video tutorial window. Note that the video tutorial window includes Pause, Rewind, and Back buttons (see lower-right corner), which you use to control the video.

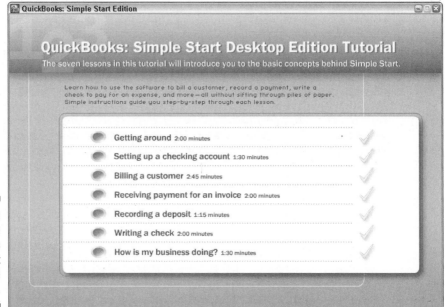

Figure 2-9:
The
QuickBooks
Simple Start
tutorial
window.

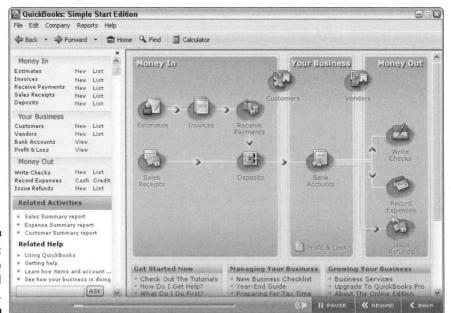

Figure 2-10:
The video
tutorial
window.

If you've got decent multimedia capabilities on your computer, do take the QuickBooks Simple Start tutorials. Each tutorial takes only a minute or two, and is a great way to get comfortable with QuickBooks Simple Start.

The Managing Your Business list includes three hyperlinks, too: New Business Checklist, Year-End Guide, and Preparing For Tax Time. Again, you can access one of these features by clicking the appropriate hyperlink. QuickBooks Simple Start then displays another window that provides information on the selected topic or access to information on the selected topic. Figure 2-11 for example, shows the QuickBooks Simple Start New Business Checklist. You can use this checklist as a way to strategize about your business, think about choice-of-entity decisions, and prepare important or necessary forms, permits, and license applications.

The Growing Your Business list supplies three hyperlinks: Business Services, Upgrade to QuickBooks Pro, and About the Online Edition. These links lead to sales literature about other accounting products and services that Intuit would like to sell you.

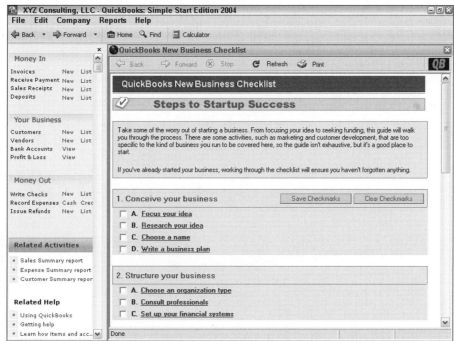

Figure 2-11: The New Business Checklist.

Using the Navigation Bar

Along the left edge of the QuickBooks Simple Start Program window, the navigation bar appears (you can peek at Figure 2-11 to see this). The navigation bar provides clickable hyperlinks you use to display windows that you use to collect accounting information. But here's the weird thing: These clickable hyperlinks, for the most part, are the same as the commands that get displayed when you click a Home page icon.

Let me show you what I mean. If you take a peek at the Money In area of the navigation bar, for example, you see four items listed: Invoices, Receive Payment, Sales Receipts, and Deposits. These four items correspond to the four icons in the Money In area. (You'll need to look at Figure 2-8 to see this.)

Next to most navigation bar list items is the word New, List, or both the words New and List. These New and List buttons are clickable links you use to either create a new thing like the item listed or to create a list of things like the item listed. For example, if you click the word New that is next to the Invoices item on the navigation bar — I'm going to call this the Invoices New hyperlink — QuickBooks Simple Start displays a window you can use to create a new invoice (see Figure 2-12). If you click the list item that is next to the sales receipts item, QuickBooks displays a list of the sales receipts you recorded.

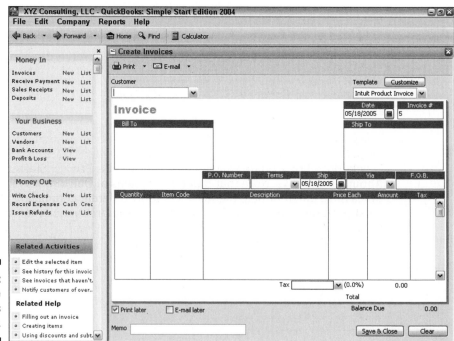

Figure 2-12: The Create Invoices window.

Not all of the navigation bar items include both a New and List hyperlink. Note, for example, that the Bank Accounts navigation bar item includes only a View hyperlink. And the same is true for the Profit and Loss navigation bar item. Just so you know, when you click one of these View hyperlinks, QuickBooks Simple Start displays bank account information or profit and loss statement information. The Record Expenses item in the navigation bar also provides two unique hyperlinks: Cash and Credit. If you click the Cash item, QuickBooks Simple Start displays a window you can use to record cash expense. And if you click the Credit hyperlink, QuickBooks Simple Start displays a window you can use to record a credit card charge.

If you scroll down the navigation bar, QuickBooks Simple Start displays two other sets of tools: the Related Activities set of hyperlinks and the Related Help set of hyperlinks. You use the Related Activities hyperlinks to produce reports that summarize sales revenue, tally business expenses, and report customer information.

The Related Help hyperlinks let you access the QuickBooks Simple Start Help file and Help tool merely by clicking the appropriate hyperlink: Using QuickBooks, Getting Help, Learn How Items and Accounts Work Together, and To See How Your Business is Doing. You can also search for help information on a specific topic by entering a word or phrase into the Ask box and then clicking the Ask command button.

Help on Help

The QuickBooks Simple Start Help feature provides a number of powerful tools to help you find out about using QuickBooks Simple Start. To access Help, select the Help menu. When you do, QuickBooks Simple Start displays the Help menu.

The QuickBooks Simple Start 2004 Help menu lists nine commands: Search Help, Help Index, Support Center, Tutorials, Internet Connection Setup, Buy QuickBooks Pro, Update QuickBooks, QuickBooks Privacy Statement, and About QuickBooks. Note that different versions of QuickBooks might sometimes have different help menus and supply different commands. But for the most part, the QuickBooks Help menu works in pretty much the same way. In the following paragraphs, I briefly describe how each of the commands shown in Figure 2-13 works.

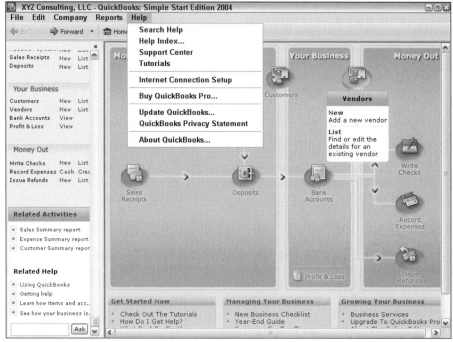

Figure 2-13:
QuickBooks
Help pane
shows
up on the
left side of
the window.

The Search Help command

If you choose the Help menu's Search Help command, QuickBooks Simple
Start displays the Help pane on the left side of the window (see Figure 2-13).
To use the QuickBooks Help pane, type your question into the Ask box. When
you finish, click the Ask button. QuickBooks Simple Start then displays the
list of help topics that might or might not answer your question. To see a particular help topic, click the topic. QuickBooks Simple Start then displays the
actual selected topic in the right pane of the window.

The Help Index command

If you choose the Help menu's Help Index command, QuickBooks Simple Start
also displays the Help window (see Figure 2-14). However, this version of the
Help window shows you a complete index of the Help topics available for
QuickBooks Simple Start. You can scroll down the list of Help Index topics, find
the topic you want, select it, and then click the Display button. Alternatively,

you can type in a word or short phrase into the text box and then click the Display button. No matter which method you use to identify the Help topic you want to display information for, QuickBooks Simple Start uses the right half of the QuickBooks Help window to display the actual Help topic information.

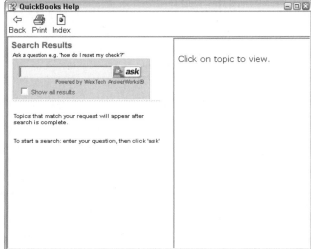

Figure 2-14:
The
QuickBooks
Help
window
showing the
Help Topic
Index.

The Support Center command

The Help menu's Support Center command displays the document window that explains how to get help for QuickBooks Simple Start. The Support Center window, for example, tells you about the QuickBooks extensive online knowledge base, it tells you about telephone technical support, and it can even help you locate a certified QuickBooks Pro Advisor. (A Pro Advisor, by the way, is simply someone who's agreed to pay Intuit $500 to $600 a year for a copy of the QuickBooks Simple Start program and a listing of the QuickBooks Web site. And, oh yes, there is a simple test you need to take.)

The Tutorials command

The Help menu's Tutorials command displays the Tutorials window. You can get to any of QuickBooks Simple Start seven multimedia tutorials from the Tutorials window. Earlier in the chapter, I make a plug for these tutorials. I think they're a great way to spend a few minutes of your time.

The Internet Connection Setup command

If you choose the Help menu's Internet Connection Setup command, Quick-Books Simple Start displays an Internet Connection setup dialog box. This dialog box lets you tell QuickBooks Simple Start how your computer connects to the Internet. You probably don't need to use this command. Windows takes care of your Internet connection for you.

The Buy QuickBooks Pro command

The Help menu's Buy QuickBooks Pro command lets you upgrade from QuickBooks Simple Start to QuickBooks Pro. All you do is choose the command and then follow the online instructions. Perhaps this paragraph is a reasonable place to mention that QuickBooks Simple Start is actually a fully powered version of QuickBooks with some pretty front-end ornaments that hide most of the complexity in the regular QuickBooks program. You can get rid of these pretty front-end ornaments by choosing the Buy QuickBooks Pro command and paying a bit of money.

The Update QuickBooks command

Recent versions of QuickBooks contain an automatic update feature. If you tell QuickBooks to do so, it uses your Internet connection to download product updates from the Intuit site. In this manner, QuickBooks can automatically grab fixes from the Intuit Web site.

If you choose the Help menu's Update QuickBooks command, QuickBooks Simple Start displays the Update QuickBooks window, as shown in Figure 2-15. You can force an update of the QuickBooks program by clicking the Update Now button.

Alternatively, you can use the Options tab (shown in Figure 2-16) to turn off or turn on the automatic update feature. To turn on or turn off the automatic update feature, predictably, you click the Automatic Update Yes or the Automatic Update No button. The list box at the bottom of the Options tab identifies which kind of updates you want QuickBooks to download automatically: Service Messages, Payroll Tax Table Information, Employee Organizer Data, and E File and E Pay data. You simply select the update you want. But note that the payroll stuff isn't available within QuickBooks Simple Start, so you wouldn't "update" for that.

If you click the Update Now tab, QuickBooks Simple Start displays some information about when it last updated or attempted to update the QuickBooks files. You can also click this tab's Get Updates button to get updated stuff. And you can click this tab's Stop Updates button to terminate an update session.

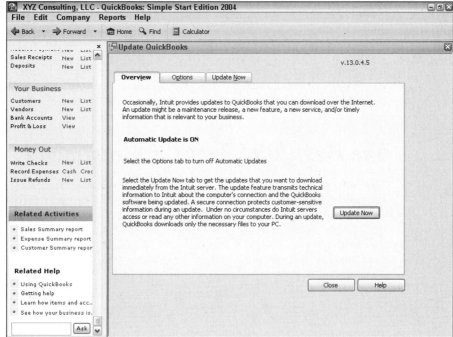

Figure 2-15:
The Overview tab of the Update QuickBooks window.

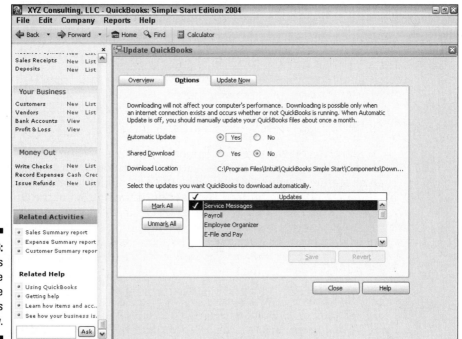

Figure 2-16:
The Options tab of the Update QuickBooks window.

The QuickBooks Privacy Statement command

The Help menu's QuickBooks Privacy Statement command gives you the privacy statement that QuickBooks is required to share because it's a financial services company. Enough said.

The About QuickBooks command

The Help menu's About QuickBooks command displays the About QuickBooks window, which gives you the install key code, the registration number, and the serial number for your copy of QuickBooks Simple Start.

Chapter 3

Creating Lots of Lists

*O*kay, even after you've installed, set up and poked around the QuickBooks Simple Start program, you still have some work to do before you begin your bookkeeping. Specifically, you need to make some lists for QuickBooks. For example, you need to make a list of your customers (or at least most of them). And a list of your vendors (the people you buy stuff from). And a list of the products or services you sell. And a few other things as well.

In this chapter, I walk you through the steps for setting up these lists. Let me make a couple of comments, though, just in case you're now moaning and groaning about the project that setting up QuickBooks Simple Start has become. First, these lists will, in the end, save you enormous amounts of time — potentially hours and hours each month.

Second, making these lists won't actually take that long. Even if you have several dozen customers, and several dozen vendors, and a bunch of things you sell, you'll still be looking at not much more than a couple of hours work. And after that? After that, it'll all be smooth sailing.

The Magic and Mystery of Items

Items are things you sell. And you need to make a list of these items in order to easily and quickly prepare invoices and sales receipts.

Before you start adding to your Item List, I need to tell you that QuickBooks Simple Start isn't very smart about its view of what you sell. It thinks that anything you stick on an invoice or sales receipt is something you're selling.

If you sell blue, yellow, and red coffee mugs, for example, you probably figure (and correctly so) that you need to add descriptions of each of these items to the Item list: blue mug, yellow mug, and red mug. But if you add sales tax to an invoice, well, guess what? QuickBooks Simple Start again thinks that you're adding another item. And if you put a discount item on your invoice — perhaps a discount for wholesalers — QuickBooks Simple Start thinks that discount is an item, too.

Although QuickBooks Simple Start is a wonderful accounting program, it is still only a computer program. It's not an artificial intelligence program. It doesn't pick up on the little subtleties of business — such as the fact that, even though you charge customers for freight, you're not really in the shipping business.

Each entry on the invoice or sales receipts — the mugs you sell, the subtotal, the discount, and the sales tax — is an *item*. Yes, I know. This setup is weird. But getting used to the wackiness now makes the discussions that follow much easier to understand.

If you want to see a sample invoice, take a peek at Figure 3-1. See those first three items: blue mugs, red mugs and yellow mugs? You can see the sense of calling them *items*, right? These mugs are things you sell. But then suppose that you give frequent buyers of your merchandise a 25-percent discount. In order to include this discount in your accounting, you need to add a Subtotal item to tally the sale and then a Discount item to calculate the discount (see Figure 3-1). See it? Kind of weird, eh?

Everything that appears on an invoice or a purchase is an item that needs to be described in your Item List. QuickBooks Simple Start supplies a discount, subtotal, and sales tax item for you, automatically. But you need to add every other item to the list.

I describe creating invoices and sales receipts in Chapter 4.

Adding items you might include on invoices

To add invoice or purchase order items to the Item List, follow these steps:

1. **Choose Company➪Lists➪Item List.**

   QuickBooks Simple Start displays the Item List window, shown in Figure 3-2. The Item List window displays any items you've already added as well as the sales tax, discount, and subtotal items that QuickBooks Simple Start automatically adds (usually) during the setup.

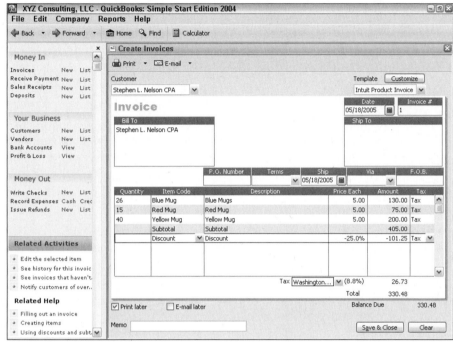

Figure 3-1:
A sample
QuickBooks
Simple Start
invoice.

2. **Right-click the window and choose New from the shortcut menu.**

   QuickBooks Simple Start displays the New Item window, shown in Figure 3-3.

3. **Type an item number or name.**

   Then type a short description of the item

4. **Describe the item in more detail.**

   Move the cursor to the Description text box and type a full description. This description then appears on the invoice. You can type quite a bit of text — and it's not a bad idea to do so because lots of text means you can describe the item in lots of detail.

5. **Tell QuickBooks Simple Start how much to charge for the item.**

   Move the cursor to the Price box. Then type the price per unit. If you're selling products, like tacky coffee mugs, this then is the price you'll charge per mug. If you're selling services, the price is the price per hour of labor or perhaps per task.

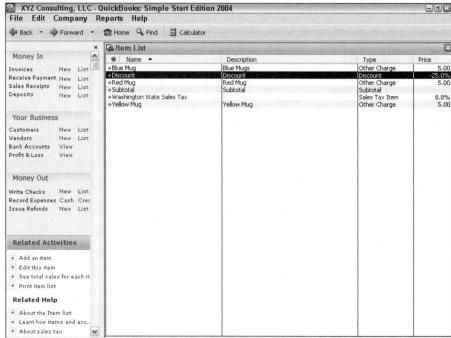

Figure 3-2:
The
QuickBooks
Simple Start
Item List
window.

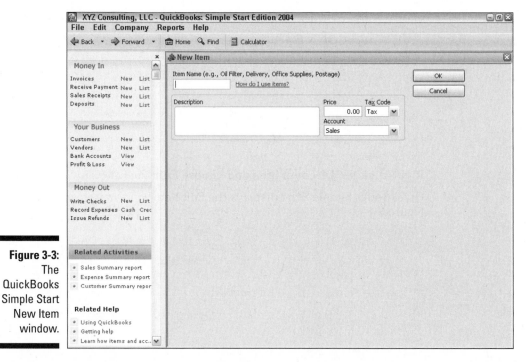

Figure 3-3:
The
QuickBooks
Simple Start
New Item
window.

6. **Indicate whether the item is subject to sales tax.**

   Use the Tax Code drop-down list box to indicate whether the item is subject to sales tax. In general, services are not subject to sales tax, wholesale products are not subject to sales tax, and retail sales are subject to sales tax. By the way, if sometimes an item is subject to sales tax and sometimes it's not, don't worry. Just use the Tax Code box to indicate whether the item is usually taxable or nontaxable.

   The Taxable check box appears only if you told QuickBooks Simple Start in the Setup Interview that you charge customers sales tax.

7. **Identify income account to use for tracking the income that you receive from selling the item.**

   Probably you'll just use the account that QuickBooks Simple Start suggests, which is Sales. But if you use more than one income account to track your sales, you would specify which income account is appropriate for this particular item.

8. **Click OK when you're finished.**

   Click OK to add the item to the list and return to the Item List window.

Editing the discount item

QuickBooks Simple Start supplies a discount item that you can use to calculate a discount amount based on the previous invoice item. But, initially, the discount item doesn't have any discount percentage or discount amount set.

To edit the discount item so you can actually use it on an invoice, follow these steps:

1. **Choose Company⇨Lists⇨Item List.**

   QuickBooks Simple Start displays the Item List window, shown in Figure 3-2.

2. **Right-click the Discount item and choose Edit from the shortcut menu.**

   QuickBooks Simple Start displays the Edit Item window, shown in Figure 3-4.

3. **(Optional) Edit the discount item name.**

   You can change the name of the discount. Just edit the contents of the Item Name/Number box.

4. **(Optional) Add a discount description.**

   For example, you can add the discount description "preferred customer discount" or "wholesalers discount."

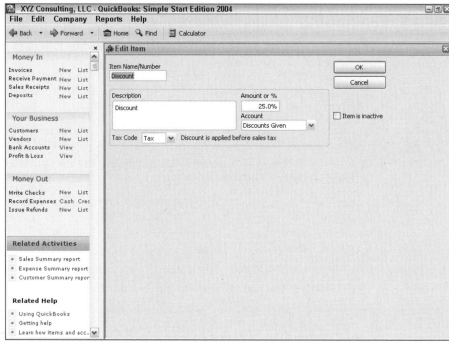

Figure 3-4:
The
QuickBooks
Simple Start
Edit Item
window.

5. **Describe the discount.**

   You use the Amount or % box to describe the discount. If the discount is a set dollar amount, enter that amount into the Amount or % box. For example, if the discount is a $75 discount, enter **75** into the box. If the discount is a percentage amount, enter the percentage amount and the % symbol into the Amount or % box. For example, if the discount is 25 percent, enter **25%** into the box.

6. **(Optional) Change the account you'll use to track discounts.**

   Initially, QuickBooks Simple Start uses the Discounts Given account to track discounts. If you want to use some other account, however, select that account from the Account drop-down list box.

7. **Click OK to save your changes.**

Editing other items

You can edit any other item in the manner I just described for the discount item. Simply display the Item List window, right-click the item, choose Edit from the shortcut menu, and then make your changes.

In Figure 3-1, I show an invoice that uses both a Subtotal item and a Discount item. If you're interested in how discount and subtotal items work, look back there.

Customers Are Your Business

This is sort of off the subject of lists, but I read about a survey that some business school had conducted. In the survey, people who wanted to start a business were asked what is the most important thing that a person needs to start a business. Almost all of them answered, "Cash." The same survey also asked a large number of people who had already started businesses — many of whom had been running their businesses successfully for years — what's the most important thing that a person needs to start a business. They all answered, "Customers."

Weird, huh? I do think that those survey results are true, though. You need customers to get into business. Everything else — including cash — is secondary. But I've sort of gotten off track. I'm supposed to be describing how you add to your Customer List. Here's the blow-by-blow:

1. **Choose Company⇨Lists⇨Customer List.**

    The Customer List window appears (see Figure 3-5).

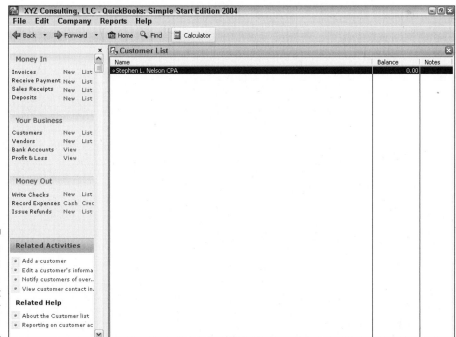

Figure 3-5:
The QuickBooks Simple Start Customer List window.

2. **Right-click the list and choose New from the shortcut menu.**

   QuickBooks Simple Start displays the Address Info tab of the New Customer window, as shown in Figure 3-6. Use this window to describe the customer in as much detail as possible.

3. **Type the customer's name.**

   Enter the name of the customer as you want it to appear in the Customer List into the Customer Name box. This isn't the name that goes on invoices, by the way. So you don't need to be all official and formal. This is the name that you use within QuickBooks Simple Start to identify the company.

4. **Give the company a name.**

   That's right, type the customer's company name into the Company Name box. This name does appear on invoices and sales receipts. Here's where you want to be official and formal.

5. **(Optional) Give the name of your contact, along with other pertinent information.**

   Move the cursor to the Mr./Ms. text box and type the appropriate title. Same with the First Name, M.I., and Last Name text boxes. (QuickBooks Simple Start automatically types the names into the Contact text box as you type them. Nice touch, eh?)

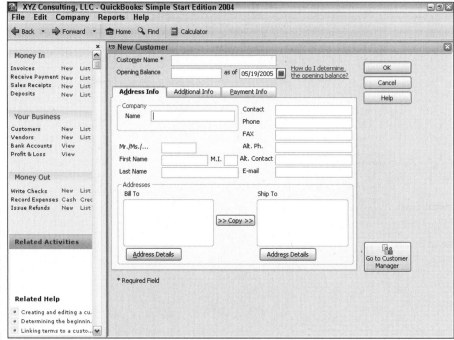

Figure 3-6: The Address Info tab of the New Customer window.

Go ahead and fill in the Phone, FAX, Alt. Ph. (alternate phone), and E-mail text boxes while you're at it.

6. (Really optional) Give the name of your alternate contact.

Move the cursor to the Alt. Contact text box and type the name of the alternate contact.

7. Give the billing address.

You can use the Bill To text box to provide the customer's billing address. QuickBooks Simple Start copies the Company and Contact names to the first lines of the billing address, so you need to enter only the address. To move from the end of one line to the start of the next, press Enter.

8. Give the shipping address.

You can use the Ship To text box to provide the customer's shipping address if this address differs from the Bill To address. (If it's the same, just click Copy.) You enter this information in the same way that you enter the Bill To address. A few deft mouse clicks. Some typing. You're done.

9. (Optional) Click the Additional Info tab and record some more data.

If you want, click the Additional Info tab. When you do, QuickBooks Simple Start displays the tab shown in Figure 3-7. You can use this tab to describe the default payment terms for the customer.

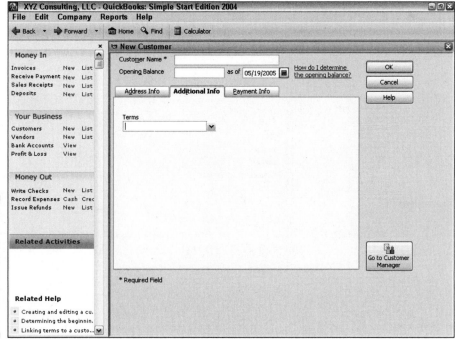

Figure 3-7:
Set the default payment terms using the Additional Info tab.

The little things do matter

If you're not familiar with how payment terms work, you can get a bird's-eye view here. For the most part, payment terms just tell the customer how quickly you expect to be paid. For example, Net Due Upon Receipt means that you expect to be paid as soon as possible. If Net is followed by some number, as in Net 15 or Net 30, the number indicates the number of days after the invoice date within which the customer is supposed to pay. So Net 15 means that the customer is supposed to pay within 15 days of the invoice date.

Some payment terms, such as 2 percent 10 Net 30, include early payment discounts. In other words, the customer can deduct 2 percent from the bill if it's paid within 10 days. Either way, the customer must pay the bill within 30 days. I also talk briefly at the very end of this chapter about creating payment method descriptions in QuickBooks. (See the "Working with the Payment Methods List" section.)

10. **(Optional) Click the Payment Info tab and record some more data.**

You can click the Payment Info tab and then use its boxes to record bits of customer information: preferred payment method, credit card number, and the credit card name, address, and expiration date (see Figure 3-8).

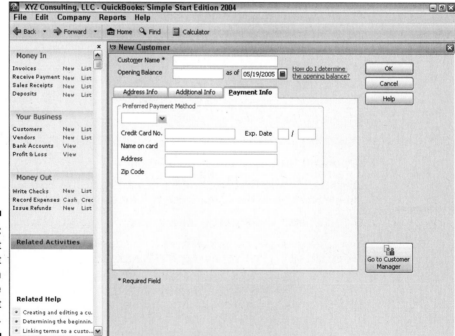

Figure 3-8:
Collect
payment
information
with the
Payment
Info tab.

11. **Save the customer information.**

    Click OK to add the customer to the list and return to the Customer List window.

 If you want to change some bit of customer information, display the Customer List window, double-click the customer account you want to change, and then make changes by using the Edit Customer window.

Adding Vendors to Your Vendor List

Adding vendors to your Vendor List works the same basic way as adding customers to your Customer List does. Here's how to get the job done:

1. **Choose the Company⇨Lists⇨Vendor List command.**

    QuickBooks Simple Start displays the Vendor List window. Along with listing your vendors, it lists any sales tax agencies that you identified as part of setting up QuickBooks Simple Start to handle sales tax.

2. **Click the Vendor button and choose New from the drop-down menu.**

    QuickBooks Simple Start displays the New Vendor window, as shown in Figure 3-9. You use this window to describe the vendors and all their little idiosyncrasies.

3. **Give the vendor's name.**

    The cursor is already in the Vendor Name text box. All you have to do is type the vendor's name as you want it to appear on the Vendor List. If you want to list your vendors by company name, enter the company name. To list them by the first or last name of the sales representative, enter one of these names.

4. **Give the official company name.**

    This is usually the name that'll get printed on checks. But see Step 8, too.

5. **(Optional) Give the name of your contact.**

    Fill in the Mr./Ms., First Name, M.I., and Last Name text boxes. QuickBooks Simple Start fills in the Contact text box for you automatically.

6. **Give the address to which you're supposed to mail checks.**

    You can use the Address text box to provide the vendor's address. QuickBooks Simple Start copies the Company and Contact names to the first line of the address, so you need to enter only the street address, city, state, and zip code. To move from the end of one line to the start of the next, press Enter.

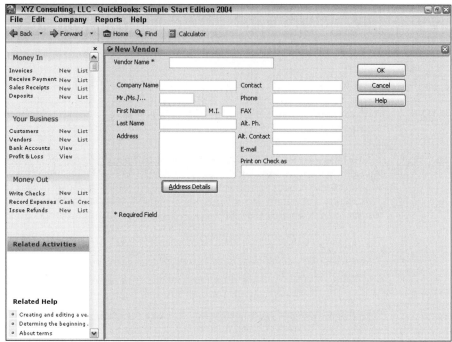

7. **(Optional) Give the vendor's telephone and fax numbers and, if available, the e-mail address.**

   The window also has an Alt. Ph. text box for a second telephone number. They thought of everything, didn't they?

8. **Verify the Print on Check As text box.**

   QuickBooks Simple Start assumes that you want the company name to appear on any checks you write for this vendor. If not, change the text box to whatever you feel is more appropriate.

9. **Save the vendor information.**

   Click OK to add the vendor to the list and return to the Vendor List window.

If you want to change some bit of vendor information, display the Vendor List window, double-click the vendor that you want to change, and then make changes by using the Edit Vendor window.

Working with the Other Names List

Okay, you've got customers (or you will have shortly). And you've got vendors (probably). But what about people who don't neatly fit into either the customer or vendor category? For example, what if you write checks to shareholders or partners owning the corporation. Or what if you're going to pay some employees. Hmmm. I know, you can add these people to the Other Names List.

To add a name to the Other Names List, choose the Company➪Lists➪Other Names List command. QuickBooks Simple Start then displays the Other Names List window. To add someone to the Other Names List, right-click the window and choose the New command. Then, when QuickBooks Simple Start displays the New Name window (see Figure 3-10), describe the person and click OK.

To change some bit of other names list information, display the Other Names List window, double-click the person that you want to change, and then make changes by using the Edit Name window

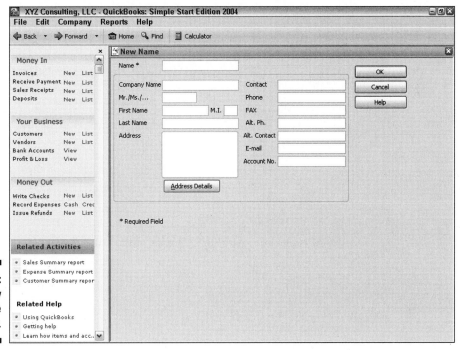

Figure 3-10:
The New
Name
window.

Noodling with the Chart of Accounts List

When you set up QuickBooks Simple Start, it builds a list of accounts that it will use to track your income and expenses as well as your assets, liabilities, and owner's equity. (QuickBooks Simple Start largely bases this chart of accounts on the type of entity you choose, and I discuss entities in some detail in Chapter 1.)

I explain how to work with the Chart of Accounts List, but you should know that unless you're a pretty good accountant and already know QuickBooks Simple Start well, you should probably leave the Chart of Accounts List alone.

Adding accounts

To add accounts to the chart of accounts, follow these steps:

1. **Choose Company➪Lists➪Chart of Accounts to display that window.**

   QuickBooks Simple Start displays the Chart of Accounts window, shown in Figure 3-11.

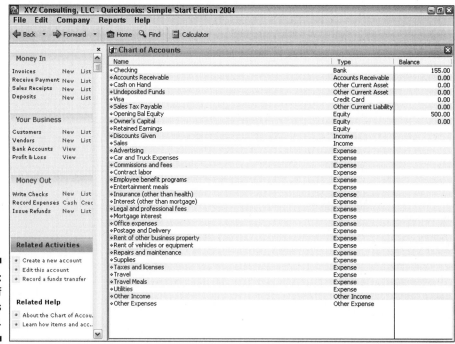

Figure 3-11: The Chart of Accounts window.

2. Right-click the list and choose New from the shortcut menu.

QuickBooks Simple Start displays the New Account window, as shown in Figure 3-12. Use this window to describe the account in as much detail as possible.

3. Identify the type of account you're adding.

QuickBooks Simple Start accounts fall into one of 15 different categories. Accounts that appear on the balance sheet fall into one of these categories: bank, accounts receivable, other current asset, fixed asset, other asset, accounts payable, credit card, other current liability, long term liability, equity. Accounts that appear on the profit and loss statement fall into one of these categories: income, cost of goods sold, expense, other income, and other expense. As a practical matter, you pick an account type that corresponds to the specific area on the balance sheet or profit and loss statement where an account should appear.

4. Name the account.

Provide a name for the account. This name appears on your financial statements, so you want to be descriptive but also concise.

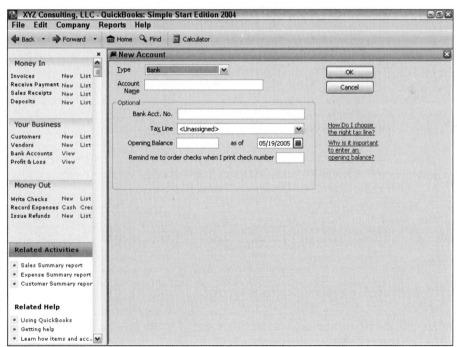

Figure 3-12:
The New Account window.

5. **Provide any other account information.**

   QuickBooks Simple Start collects different types of accounts for different types of businesses. Figure 3-12 shows the text boxes that QuickBooks Simple Start uses to collect bank account information. For other types of accounts, QuickBooks Simple Start collects different information.

   You don't want to enter a starting balance as part of setting up a new account. The right approach is to use a journal entry to record starting account balances.

6. **Click OK to save the new account.**

Editing accounts

To edit an account, display the Chart of Accounts window, right-click the account that you want to change, choose Edit from the shortcut menu, and then make changes by using the Edit Account window.

Deleting accounts

You can delete an account that you haven't used by right-clicking the account and then choosing Delete from the shortcut menu. Note, however, that you can't delete an account if the account has been used.

If you want to remove an account that you once used but no longer use, right-click the account and then choose Make Inactive from the shortcut menu. Note that you shouldn't do this unless the account shows a zero balance.

To later "re-activate" an account, choose Show All from the shortcut menu, select the account, and then choose Make Active from the shortcut menu.

Working with the Terms List

QuickBooks Simple Start maintains a Terms list, which you use to specify what payment terms are available. To add terms, choose Company➪Lists➪ Terms List. When you choose this command, QuickBooks Simple Start displays the Terms List window. To add more terms, right-click the window, choose New from the shortcut menu, and then fill in the window that QuickBooks Simple Start displays (see Figure 3-13).

You name the payment terms using the Terms text box. To create the typical pay within a certain number of days of the invoice date, mark the Standard button and then specify the number of days after the invoice date that payment is due.

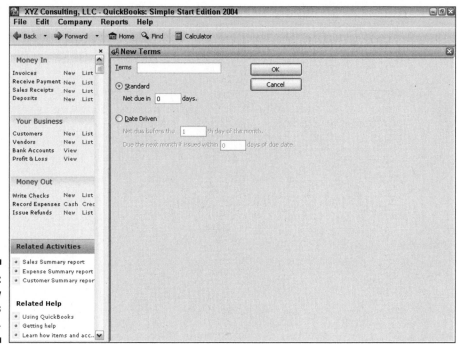

Figure 3-13:
The New
Terms
window.

You can also create a date-driven due date by marking the Date Driven button. In this case, you need to specify which day of the month that payment is due — and when the due date should just skip ahead to the next month because the invoice date is already so close to the due date. (In other words, if invoices are due on the 1st, should an invoice that you bill on the 31st really be due on the 1st, one day later?)

Working with the Payment Method List

QuickBooks Simple Start provides descriptions for the usual payment methods. But you can add to these by choosing Company⇨Lists⇨Payment Method. QuickBooks Simple Start actually displays the Payment Method window. To add more methods, right-click the window, choose New from the shortcut menu, and then fill in the window that QuickBooks Simple Start displays (see Figure 3-14). Simply name the payment method (using the Payment Method box) and then identify the type of payment (using the Payment Type) drop-down list box.

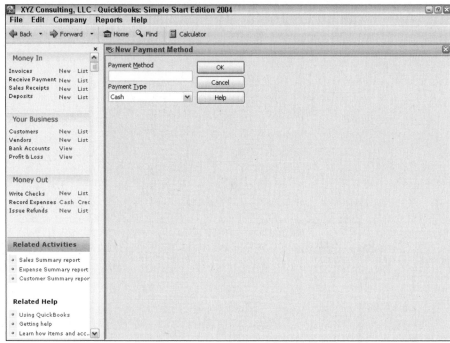

Figure 3-14:
The New
Payment
Method
window.

Part II
Daily Chores

In this part . . .

Okay. You've got QuickBooks Simple Start set up. Or maybe you were lucky enough to have someone else do all the dirty work. But all that doesn't matter now. It's in this part where the rubber really hits the road. You need to start using QuickBooks to do a bunch of stuff on a regular, and maybe daily, basis. Invoice customers. Record customer payments. Pay bills. This part describes how you do all these things.

Chapter 4

Invoicing Your Customers

. . . .

. . . .

*I*n this chapter, I describe how to create and print invoices in QuickBooks Simple Start, as well as how to record credit memos and issue refunds.

You find out how to use the QuickBooks invoice form to bill customers for the goods you sell. I also describe how to use the credit memos form to handle returns and canceled orders for which you've received payments and how to issue refunds.

Making Sure That You're Ready to Invoice Customers

You already should have installed QuickBooks, of course. (I describe how in Chapter 1.) You should also be comfortable navigating within QuickBooks. (I describe this in Chapter 2.) You also want to have your Customer and Items Lists set up. (I describe how you work with the Customer and Items Lists in Chapter 3.)

As long as you've done all this prerequisite stuff, you're ready to start. If you don't have one of the prerequisites done, you need to complete them before going any further.

Preparing an Invoice

After you complete all the preliminary work, preparing an invoice with QuickBooks Simple Start is a snap. If clicking buttons and filling in text boxes are becoming old hat to you, skip the following play-by-play commentary and simply click the Invoices New hyperlink and then fill in the Create Invoices window and click the Print button. If you want more help than a single sentence provides, keep reading for step-by-step instructions.

In the following steps, I describe how to create the most complicated and involved invoice around: a *product invoice.* Some fields on the product invoice don't appear on the *service* or *professional invoice,* but don't worry if your business is a service or professional one. Creating a service or professional invoice works basically the same way as creating a product invoice — you just fill in fewer fields. And keep in mind that you start with Steps 1 and 2 no matter what type of invoice you create. Without further ado, here's how to create an invoice:

1. **Click the Invoices New hyperlink.**

   As an alternative to the Invoices New hyperlink, you can also click the Invoice icon on the Home window and then click New.

   The Create Invoices window appears, shown in Figure 4-1.

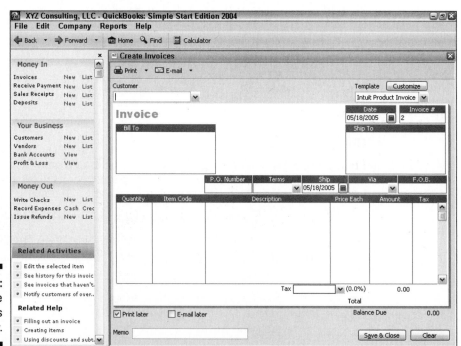

Figure 4-1:
The Create
Invoices
window.

2. **Select the template, or invoice form, that you want to use from the Template drop-down list box.**

   QuickBooks Simple Start comes with three predefined invoice forms: Product, Professional, and Service. Which one appears by default depends on which one you told QuickBooks Simple Start you wanted to use in the Setup Interview. You can also slightly customize an invoice template by clicking the Customize button. I describe customizing invoice forms in the "Customizing Your Invoices and Credit Memos" section, later in this chapter.

3. **Identify the customer.**

   Activate the Customer drop-down list by clicking the down arrow at the right end of the box. Scroll through the Customer list until you see the customer name that you need, and then click it.

   If you don't see the customer name — perhaps because this is the first time you're invoicing this person or business — enter the customer's name into the Customer box. For example, if you were invoicing me, you might enter "Stephen L. Nelson" into the box. Then press the Tab key. QuickBooks Simple Start displays a Customer Not Found message (see Figure 4-2). The message box asks what you want to do and provides three command buttons: QuickAdd, Setup, and Cancel. You, my friend, want to click QuickAdd.

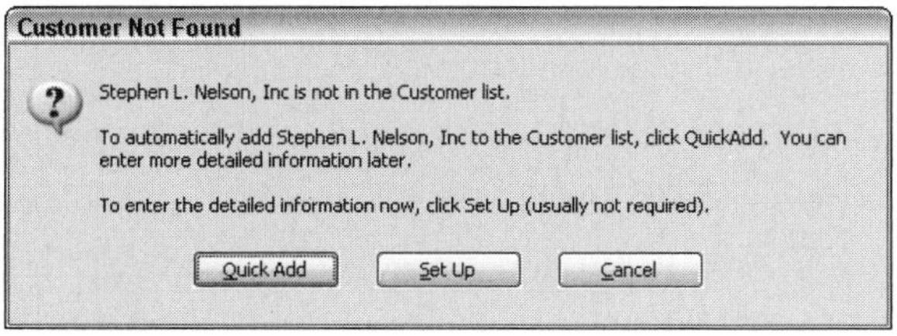

Figure 4-2:
The
Customer
Not Found
message
box.

Customer Not Found

Stephen L. Nelson, Inc is not in the Customer list.

To automatically add Stephen L. Nelson, Inc to the Customer list, click QuickAdd. You can enter more detailed information later.

To enter the detailed information now, click Set Up (usually not required).

[Quick Add]   [Set Up]   [Cancel]

4. **Give the invoice date.**

   Press Tab several times to move the cursor to the Date text box. Then enter the correct date in MM/DD/YYYY format. You also can use the following secret codes to change the date:

   • **Press** + (the plus symbol) to move the date ahead one day.

   • **Press** – (the minus symbol) to move the date back one day.

   • **Press T** to change the date to today's date (as specified by the system time that your computer's internal clock provides).

   • **Press M** to change the date to the first day of the month (because *M* is the first letter in the word *month*).

- **Press H** to change the date to the last day of the month (because *H* is the last letter in the word *month*).

- **Press Y** to change the date to the first day of the year (because, as you no doubt can guess, *Y* is the first letter in the word *year*).

- **Press R** to change the date to the last day of the year (because *R* is the last letter in the word *year*).

You can also click the button on the right side of the Date field to display a small calendar. To select a date from the calendar, just click the date you want. Or click the arrows on the top-left and top-right sides of the calendar to display the previous or next month.

5. (Optional) Enter an invoice number.

QuickBooks Simple Start suggests an invoice number by adding 1 to the last invoice number that you used. You can accept this addition, or, if you need to have it your way, you can tab to the Invoice # text box and change the number to whatever you want.

6. Fix the Bill To address, if necessary.

If the information is available, QuickBooks Simple Start grabs the billing address from the Customer list. You can change the address for the invoice by replacing some portion of the usual billing address. You can, for example, insert another line that says, "Attention: William Bobbins," if that's the name of the person to whom the invoice should go.

Obviously, if this is the first time you've entered an invoice for the customer and you just "quick added" the customer following my earlier instructions, you should fill in the complete address information.

7. Fix the Ship To address, if necessary.

I feel like a broken record, but here's the deal: If it's available, QuickBooks Simple Start also grabs the shipping address from the Customer list. So, if the shipping address has something unusual about it for just this one invoice, you can change the address by replacing or adding information to the Ship To address block.

You can also add the shipping address information to the invoice by typing it into the box.

8. (Optional . . . sort of) Provide the purchase order number.

If the customer issues purchase orders, enter the number of the purchase order that authorizes this purchase in the P.O. Number text box.

9. Specify the payment terms.

To specify the payment terms, click the arrow at the end of the Terms drop-down list box and select something from it.

10. **Specify the shipping date if it's something other than the invoice date.**

    To specify the date, simply move the cursor to the Ship text box and then type the date in MM/DD/YYYY fashion. You can move the cursor by pressing Tab or by clicking the text box.

    One other quick point: all those secret codes I talk about in Step 4 for changing the invoice date? They also work for changing the shipping date.

11. **Specify the shipping method.**

    You can probably guess how you specify the shipping method, but parallel structure and a compulsive personality force me to continue. So, to specify the shipping method, move the cursor to the Via drop-down list, activate the list, and then select a shipping method.

    By the way, you can add new shipping methods to the list by choosing Add New and then filling out the cute little dialog box that QuickBooks Simple Start displays. Setting up new shipping methods is really easy. Really easy.

12. **Specify the FOB point by using the F.O.B. text box.**

    FOB stands for *free-on-board*. The FOB point is more important than it first seems — at least in a business sense — because the FOB point determines when the transfer of ownership occurs, who pays freight, and who bears the risks of damage to the goods during shipping.

    If a shipment is free-on-board at the *shipping* point, the ownership of the goods being sold transfers to the purchaser as soon as the goods leave the seller's shipping dock. (Remember that you're the seller.) In this case, the purchaser pays the freight and bears the risk of shipping damage. You can specify the FOB shipping point either as FOB Shipping Point or by using the name of the city. If the shipping point is Seattle, for example, FOB Seattle is the same thing as FOB Shipping Point. Most goods are shipped as FOB Shipping Point, by the way.

    If a shipment is free-on-board at the *destination* point, the ownership of the goods that are being sold transfers to the purchaser as soon as the goods arrive on the purchaser's shipping dock. The seller pays the freight and bears the risk of shipping damage. You can specify the FOB destination point either as FOB Destination Point or by using the name of the city. If the destination point is Omaha, for example, FOB Omaha is the same thing as FOB Destination Point.

13. **Enter each item that you're selling.**

    Move the cursor to the first row of the Quantity/Item Code/Description/Price Each/Amount/Tax list box. Okay, I know that isn't a very good name for it, but you know what I mean, right? You need to start filling in the line items that go on the invoice. After you move the cursor to a row in the list box, QuickBooks Simple Start turns the Item Code field into a drop-down list box. Activate the Item Code drop-down list box of the first empty row in the list box and then select the item.

When you select the item, QuickBooks Simple Start fills in the Description and Price Each text boxes with whatever description and price you've entered in the Item list. (You can edit the information for this particular invoice if you need to.) Enter the number of items sold in the Quantity text box. (After you enter this number, QuickBooks Simple Start calculates the amount by multiplying Quantity by Price Each.) If you need other items on the invoice, use the remaining empty rows of the list box to enter each one. If you selected the Taxable check box when you added the item to the Item list, the word *Tax* appears in the Tax column to indicate that the item will be taxed. (If the item is nontaxable [or you feel like being a tax evader for no good reason], click the Tax column and select *Non.*)

You can put as many items on an invoice as you want. If you don't have enough room on a single page, QuickBooks Simple Start adds as many pages as necessary to the invoice. Information about the invoice total, of course, goes only on the last page.

14. Enter any special items that the invoice should include.

If you haven't worked much with the QuickBooks Simple Start item file, then you have no idea what I'm talking about. (For more information about adding to and working with lists in QuickBooks, cruise through Chapter 3.)

To describe any of the special items — such as subtotals or discounts — activate the Item Code drop-down list box of the next empty row and then select the special item. After QuickBooks Simple Start fills in the Description and Price Each text boxes, edit this information (if necessary). Describe each of the other special items — subtotals or discounts — that you're itemizing on the invoice by filling in the empty rows in the list box.

If you want to include a Discount item and have it apply to multiple items, you need to stick a Subtotal item on the invoice after the inventory or other items you want to discount. Then stick a Discount item directly after the Subtotal item. QuickBooks Simple Start calculates the discount as a percentage of the subtotal.

15. Specify the sales tax.

If you specified a tax rate in the Customer list, QuickBooks Simple Start uses it as a default. If it isn't correct, move the cursor to the Tax list box, activate the drop-down list, and select the correct sales tax.

16. (Truly optional) Add a memo.

You can add a memo description to the invoice if you want to. This memo doesn't print on invoices. Memo descriptions give you a way of storing information related to an invoice with that invoice. Figure 4-3 shows a completed Create Invoices window.

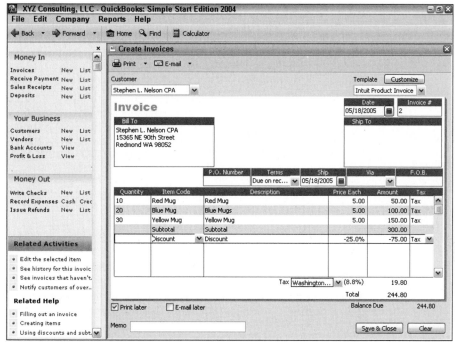

Figure 4-3:
A
completed
Create
Invoices
window.

17. **If you want to delay printing this invoice, deselect the Print Later check box that's in the lower-left area of the Create Invoices window.**

    I want to postpone talking about what selecting the Print Later check box does until I finish the discussion of invoice creation.

18. **Click Save & Close to save the invoice.**

    QuickBooks Simple Start saves the invoice that's on-screen.

Fixing Invoice Mistakes

Everyone makes mistakes. You don't need to get worked up over mistakes that you make while entering information in invoices, though, because in the following sections, I show you how to fix the most common mistakes you might make on your invoices.

If the invoice is still displayed on-screen

If the invoice is still displayed on-screen, you can just move the cursor to the box or button that's wrong and then fix the mistake. Because most of the bits of information that you enter in the Create Invoices window are short and sweet, you can easily replace the contents of some fields by typing over whatever's already there. To start the invoice over again, just click the Clear button. To save the invoice after you've made your changes, click Save & Close.

If you need to insert a line in the middle of the invoice, right-click the invoice and then choose Insert Line or Delete Line from the shortcut menu that appears.

If the invoice isn't displayed on-screen

If the invoice isn't displayed on-screen, you can use the Invoices list to get back to the Create Invoices window. Choose the Invoices List hyperlink from the navigation bar or click the Invoices icon in the Home window and choose List. QuickBooks Simple Start displays the Invoices You've Created window (see Figure 4-4).

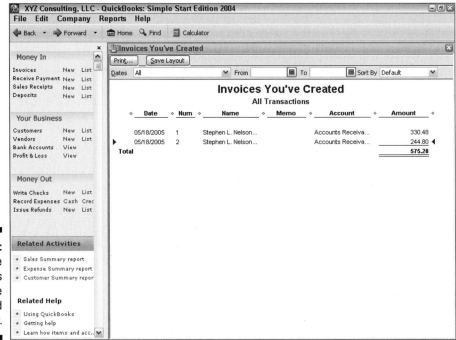

Figure 4-4: The Invoices You've Created window.

Double-click the invoice you want to edit. QuickBooks Simple Start displays the Create Invoices window with the selected invoice. You can make your changes in the usual way. Just remember to click Save & Close when you're done. (If you don't remember to click Save & Close when you're done, QuickBooks Simple Start reminds you.)

If you've printed the invoice, you also can make the sort of change I describe in the preceding paragraphs. For example, you can use the Invoices You've Created window to locate the invoice that has the error. And you can change the error and print the invoice again. I'm not so sure that you want to go this route, however, if you've already sent the invoice. You might want to consider fixing the invoice by issuing either a credit memo (if the original invoice over-charged) or another invoice (if the original invoice undercharged). I suggest issuing a credit memo (which I show you how to do in the appropriately titled section "Issuing a Refund," later in this chapter) or another invoice because life can get awfully messy if you or your customer has multiple copies of the same invoice floating around and causing confusion.

Deleting an invoice

I hesitate to mention this, but you also can delete invoices. Procedurally, deleting an invoice is easy. You just display the invoice in the Create Invoices window and choose Edit⇨Delete Invoice. When QuickBooks Simple Start asks you to confirm your deletion, click Yes. But read the following paragraph first. You might not want to delete the invoice.

Even though deleting invoices is easy, it isn't something that you should do casually or for fun. Deleting an invoice is okay if you've just created it; only you have seen it, and you haven't yet printed it. In this case, no one needs to know that you've made a mistake. It's your private secret. But the rest of the time — even if you've created an invoice that you don't want later — you should keep a copy of the invoice in the QuickBooks Simple Start system. By doing so, you have a record that the invoice existed, which usually makes it easier to answer questions later.

"But how do I correct my books if I leave the bogus invoice?" you ask.

Good question. To correct your financial records for the invoice that you don't want to count anymore, simply void the invoice. The invoice remains in the QuickBooks Simple Start system, but it doesn't count it (it loses its quantity and amount information). Good news — voiding an invoice is just as simple as deleting one. Just display the invoice in the Create Invoices window and then choose Edit⇨Void Invoice.

Issuing a Refund

Credit memos can be a handy way to fix data-entry mistakes that you didn't find or correct earlier. Credit memos are also handy ways to handle things such as customer returns and refunds. If you've prepared an invoice or two in your time, you'll find that preparing a QuickBooks Simple Start credit memo is a lot easier than using old-fashioned methods. Follow these steps:

1. **Click the Issue Refund New hyperlink.**

   The Issue Refund New hyperlinks about two thirds of the way down the navigation bar with the Money Out actions. QuickBooks Simple Start displays the Create Credit Memos/Refunds window, shown in Figure 4-5.

2. **Identify the customer.**

   Activate the Customer drop-down list. Then select the customer by clicking it.

3. **Date the credit memo (going steady is optional).**

   Press Tab to move the cursor to the Date text box. Then enter the correct date in MM/DD/YYYY format. You also can use the secret date-editing codes that I describe in the section "Preparing an Invoice" earlier in the chapter. Oh, boy.

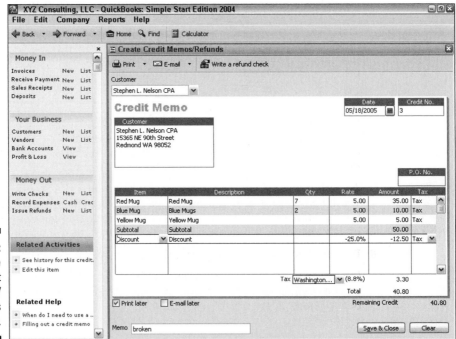

Figure 4-5:
The Create Credit Memos/Refunds window.

4. (Optional) Enter a credit memo number.

QuickBooks Simple Start suggests a credit memo number by adding 1 to the last credit memo number you used. You can accept the number or tab to the Credit No. text box to change the number to whatever you want.

5. Fix the Customer address, if necessary.

QuickBooks Simple Start grabs the billing address from the Customer List. You can change the address for the credit memo by replacing some portion of the usual billing address. Typically, you should use the same address for the credit memo that you used for the original invoice or invoices.

6. (Optional . . . sort of) Provide the purchase order number.

If the credit memo adjusts the total remaining balance on a customer purchase order, you should probably enter the number of the purchase order into the P.O. No. text box.

Here's my logic on this suggestion for those readers who care: If you billed your customer $1,000 on P.O. No. 1984, which authorizes a $1,000 purchase, you've "used up" the entire purchase order — at least according to the customer's accounts payable clerk who processes your invoices. If you make sure that a credit memo for $1,000 is identified as being related to P.O. No. 1984, however, you essentially free up the $1,000 purchase balance, which might mean that you can use, or bill on, the purchase order again.

7. If the customer is returning items, describe each item.

Move the cursor to the first row of the Item/Description/Qty/Rate/ Amount/Tax text box. In the first empty row of the box, activate the Item drop-down list and then select the item. After you select it, QuickBooks Simple Start fills in the Description and Rate text boxes with whatever sales description and sales price you entered in the Item list. (You can edit this information if you want, but it's not necessary.) Enter the number of items that the customer is returning (or not paying for) in the Qty text box. (After you enter this number, QuickBooks Simple Start calculates the amount by multiplying Qty by Rate.) Enter each item that the customer is returning by filling in the empty rows of the list box.

As with invoices, you can put as many items on a credit memo as you want. If you don't have enough room on a single page, QuickBooks Simple Start keeps adding pages to the credit memo until you're finished. The total information, of course, goes on the last page.

8. Describe any special items that the credit memo should include.

If you want to issue a credit memo that shows other items that appear on the original invoice — subtotals and discounts, for example — add descriptions of each item to the Item list.

To add descriptions of these items, activate the Item drop-down list of the next empty row and then select the special item. (You activate the list by clicking the field once to turn it into a drop-down list box and then by clicking the field's down arrow to access the list box.) After QuickBooks Simple Start fills in the Description and Rate text boxes, edit this information (if necessary). Enter each special item — subtotal, discount, freight, and so on — that you're itemizing on the credit memo.

If you want to include a Discount item, you need to stick a Subtotal item on the credit memo after the inventory or other items that you've discounted. Then stick a Discount item directly after the Subtotal item. In this way, QuickBooks Simple Start calculates the discount as a percentage of the subtotal.

9. **Specify the sales tax.**

Move the cursor to the Tax list box, activate the list box, and select the correct sales tax.

10. **(Optional, but a really good idea. . . .) Add a memo.**

You can use the Memo text box to add a memo description to the credit memo. I suggest that you use this description to explain your reasons for issuing the credit memo and to cross-reference the original invoice or invoices. Note that the Memo field prints on the Customer Statement. Figure 4-6 shows a completed Create Credit Memos/Refunds window.

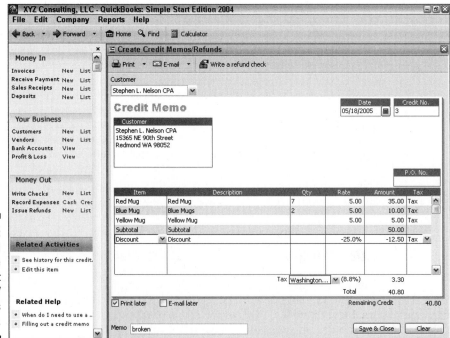

Figure 4-6:
A completed
Create
Credit
Memos/
Refunds
window.

11. **If you want to delay printing this credit memo, clear the Print Later check box.**

    I want to postpone talking about what selecting the Print Later check box does until I finish the discussion of credit memo creation. Coverage on printing invoices and credit memos comes up in the following section.

12. **Click Save & Close to save the credit memo.**

    QuickBooks Simple Start saves the credit memo that's on-screen.

 To print a refund check, click the Write a Refund Check button after you've filled out the Create Credit Memos/Refunds window. QuickBooks Simple Start displays the Write Checks window and automatically fills out the check, linking it to the memo. Chapter 5 describes how to use the Write Checks window to make payments.

Fixing Credit Memo Mistakes

Sure, I can repeat the same information that I gave you in the section, "Fixing Invoice Mistakes," and leave you with a strange feeling of déjà vu. But I won't.

 Here's everything you need to know about fixing credit memo mistakes: You can fix credit memo mistakes the same way that you fix invoice mistakes. If you need more help, refer to the earlier section "Fixing Invoice Mistakes."

Printing Invoices and Credit Memos

As part of setting up QuickBooks, you selected an invoice type. I assume that you have the raw paper stock for whatever invoice type you chose. If you're going to print on blank letterhead, for example, I assume that you have letterhead lying around. If you decide to use preprinted forms, I assume that you've ordered those forms and have received them.

I also assume that you've already set up your printer. If you've ever printed anything, your printer is already set up. Really.

Loading the forms into the printer

This part is easy. Simply load the invoice forms into the printer the same way you always load paper. Because you have one of about a jillion different printers, I can't give you the precise steps that you need to take, but if you've used a printer a bit, you should have no problem.

Wait a minute. What's that? Your printer is brand-new, and you've never used it before? Okay, here's one of my weird ideas: Use a pencil or something else that's heat-resistant (so that it won't melt and gum up the insides of the printer) to draw an arrow on a piece of paper. (Do not, repeat, do *not* use a crayon. And don't let your children watch you do this.) Draw the arrow so that it points toward the top edge of the paper. Load the paper in the printer, with the arrow face up, and note which direction the arrow is pointing. Print something. Anything. When the paper comes out, notice whether the image faces the same direction as the arrow and whether it's on the same side of the paper as the arrow. With this information and a little logic, you should be able to figure out how to load forms correctly.

Setting up the invoice printer

You need to set up the invoice printer only once, but you need to specify a handful of general invoice-printing rules. These rules also apply to credit memos and purchase orders, by the way.

To set up your printer for invoice printing, follow these steps:

1. **Choose File⇨Printer Setup and, in the Form Name drop-down list box, select Invoice.**

   QuickBooks Simple Start displays the Printer Setup dialog box, shown in Figure 4-7.

2. **Select the printer that you want to use to print invoices.**

   Activate the Printer Name drop-down list to see the installed printers. Select the one that you want to use for printing invoices and purchase orders.

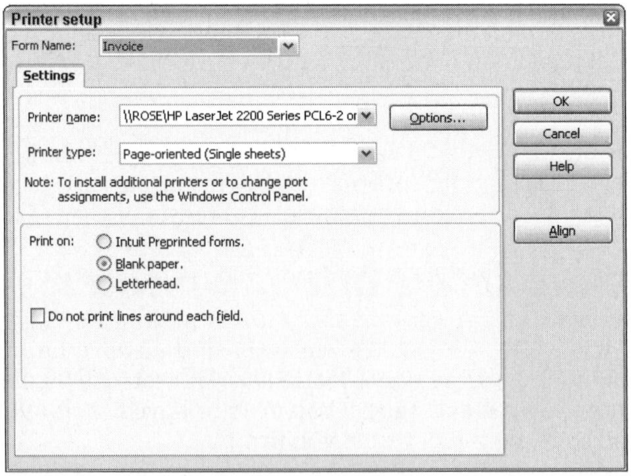

Figure 4-7:
The Printer Setup dialog box.

3. (Optional) Select the printer type.

The Printer Type drop-down list describes the kind of paper your printer uses. You have two choices: *Continuous* and *Page-Oriented.* Continuous means that your paper comes as one connected ream with perforated edges. Page-Oriented means that your paper is in single sheets.

4. Select the type of invoice form.

Select the option button that describes the type of form that you want to print on: Intuit Preprinted Form, Blank Paper, or Letterhead. Then select the Do Not Print Lines Around Each Field check box if you don't like the nice little boxes QuickBooks Simple Start creates to separate each field.

5. (Optional, but a really good idea. . . .) Print a test invoice on real invoice paper.

Click the Align button. When QuickBooks Simple Start displays the Align Printer dialog box, choose the type of invoice you want to print from the list and then click OK. When QuickBooks Simple Start displays the Fine Alignment dialog box, shown in Figure 4-8, click Print Sample to tell QuickBooks Simple Start to print a test invoice on whatever paper you've loaded in the invoice printer.

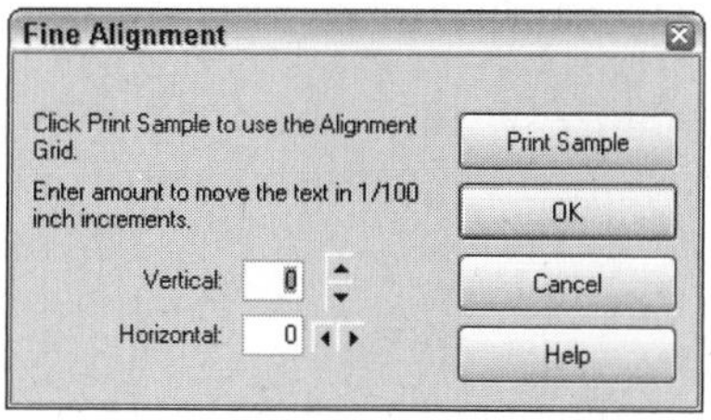

Figure 4-8: The Fine Alignment dialog box.

The test invoice that QuickBooks Simple Start prints gives you a chance to see what your invoices will look like. The invoice also has a set of alignment gridlines that prints over the Bill To text box. You can use these gridlines if you need to fine-align your printer.

6. Fix any form-alignment problems.

If you see any alignment problems after you complete Step 5, you need to fix them. (Alignment problems usually occur only with impact printers. With laser printers or inkjet printers, sheets of paper feed into the printer the same way every time, so you almost never need to fiddle with the form alignment.)

To fix any big alignment problems — like stuff printing in the wrong place — you need to adjust the way the paper feeds into the printer. When you finally get the paper loaded as best you can, be sure to note exactly how you have it loaded. You need to have the printer and paper set up the same way every time you print.

For minor, but nonetheless annoying, alignment problems, use the Fine Alignment dialog box's Vertical and Horizontal boxes to adjust the form's alignment. Then print another sample invoice. Go ahead and experiment a bit. You need to fine-tune the printing of the invoice form only once. Click OK in the Fine Alignment dialog box when you finish to have QuickBooks Simple Start redisplay the Printer Setup dialog box.

Clicking the Options button in the Printer Setup dialog box (refer to Figure 4-7) opens the selected printer's Windows printer setup information, where you can do such things as specify quality settings or print order. Because this information relates to Windows and not to QuickBooks, I'm not going to explain it. If you're the curious type or accidentally click it and then have questions about what you see, refer either to your Windows User's Guide or the printer's user guide.

7. **Save your printer settings stuff.**

   After you finish fiddling with all of the Printer Setup dialog box's boxes and buttons, click OK to save your changes.

   If you want to always print a particular form using some particular settings (maybe you always print two copies of an invoice, for example), see the "Customizing Your Invoices and Credit Memos" section, later in this chapter.

You can print invoices and credit memos either one at a time or in a batch. How you print them makes no difference to QuickBooks Simple Start or to me, your humble author. Pick whatever way seems to fit your style the best. The following sections show you how.

Printing invoices and credit memos as you create them

If you want to print invoices and credit memos as you create them, follow these steps:

1. **Click the Print button after you create the invoice or credit memo.**

   After you fill in the boxes in the Create Invoices window or the Create Credit Memos/Refunds window, click the Print button. QuickBooks, ever the faithful servant, displays either the Print One Invoice dialog box (shown in Figure 4-9) or the Print One Credit Memo dialog box (which looks almost like the Print One Invoice dialog box).

2. **(Optional) Select the type of invoice or credit memo form.**

   If you're using a different type of invoice or credit memo form than you've described for the invoice printer setup, select the type of form that you want to print on in the Print On box. You can choose Intuit Preprinted Forms, Blank Paper, or Letterhead.

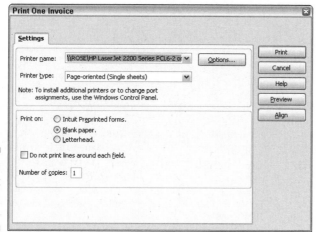

Figure 4-9:
The Print
One Invoice
dialog box.

You shouldn't have to worry about printing test-invoice or credit-memo forms or fiddling with form-alignment problems if you addressed these issues when you set up the invoice printer. So I'm not going to talk about the Align button here. If you want to do this kind of stuff and you need help, refer to the preceding section, "Setting up the invoice printer," in which I describe how to print test forms and fix form-alignment problems.

3. Print the form.

Click the Print button to send the form to the printer. QuickBooks Simple Start prints the form.

4. Review the invoice or credit memo and reprint the form, if necessary.

Review the invoice or credit memo to see whether QuickBooks Simple Start printed it correctly. If the form looks wrong, fix whatever caused the problem (perhaps you printed it on the wrong paper, for example) and reprint the form by clicking the Print button again.

Printing invoices in a batch

If you want to print invoices in a batch, you need to select the Print Later check box that appears in the lower-left corner of the Create Invoices window. This check mark tells QuickBooks Simple Start to put a copy of the invoice on a special invoices-to-be-printed list.

When you later want to print the invoices-to-be-printed list, follow these steps:

1. Display the Create Invoices window (click the Invoices New hyperlink, for example), click the arrow next to the Print button, and choose Print Batch from the drop-down menu.

What am I printing on?

Sometimes people get confused about the difference between preprinted forms, letterhead, and plain paper. Here's the scoop: Preprinted forms have your company name, perhaps your logo, and a bunch of other boxes and lines (often in another color of ink) already printed on them. Preprinted forms are often multipart forms. (Examples of preprinted forms come in the QuickBooks box.)

Letterhead is what you usually use for letters that you write. It has your company name and address on it, for example, but nothing else. To save you from having to purchase preprinted forms, QuickBooks enables you to use letterhead

to create invoices and forms. (To make the letterhead look a little more bookkeeperish, QuickBooks draws lines and boxes on the letterhead so that it looks sort of like a preprinted invoice.)

Plain paper is, well, plain paper. Nothing is printed on it. So QuickBooks needs to print everything — your company name, all the invoice stuff, and optionally, lines and boxes. For what it's worth, I use plain paper invoices for my CPA business. Plain paper invoices work fine. (I do use nice heavy paper — you know, to maintain a bit of class.)

QuickBooks Simple Start displays the Select Invoices to Print dialog box, shown in Figure 4-10. This box lists all the invoices you marked as Print Later that you haven't yet printed.

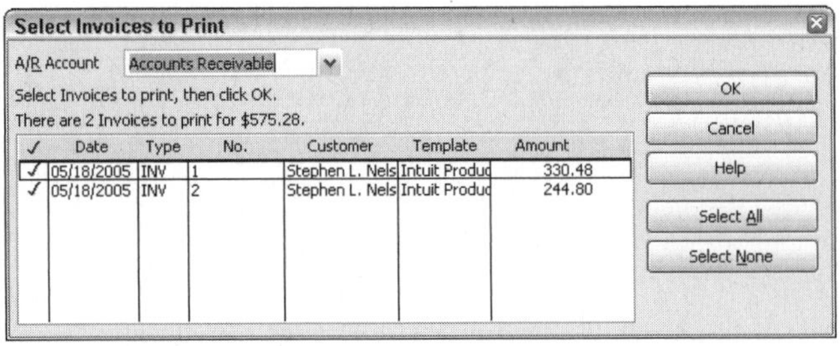

Figure 4-10: The Select Invoices to Print dialog box.

2. **Select the invoices that you want to print.**

   Initially, QuickBooks Simple Start marks all the invoices with a check mark, indicating that they will be printed. You can select and deselect individual invoices on the list by clicking them. You also can use the Select All and the Select None buttons. Click Select All to select all the invoices. Click Select None to deselect all the invoices.

3. **Click OK.**

   After you correctly mark all the invoices you want to print — and none of the ones you don't want to print — click OK. QuickBooks Simple Start displays the Print Invoices dialog box, shown in Figure 4-11.

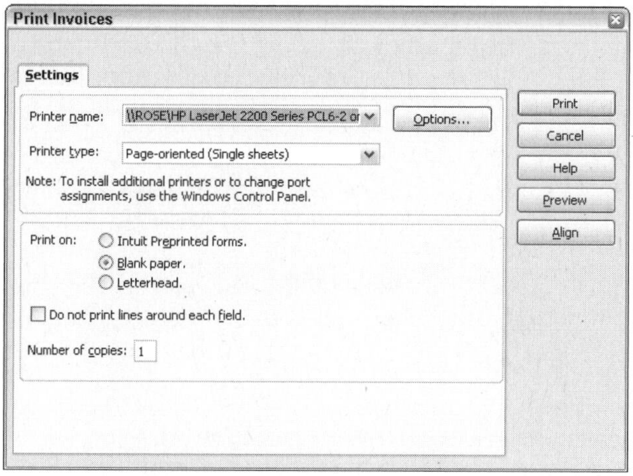

Figure 4-11:
The Print
Invoices
dialog box.

4. **(Optional) Select the type of invoice form.**

   If you use a different type of invoice form than you described during the invoice setup, select the type of form that you want to print on by using the Print On options. You can choose Intuit Preprinted Forms, Blank Paper, or Letterhead.

5. **Print the forms.**

   Click the Print button to send the selected invoice forms to the printer. QuickBooks Simple Start prints the forms and then displays a message box that asks whether the forms printed correctly.

6. **Review the invoice forms and reprint them if necessary.**

   Review the invoices to see whether QuickBooks Simple Start printed all of them correctly. If all the forms look okay, click OK in the message box. If one or more forms don't look okay, enter the invoice number of the first bad form in the message box. Then fix whatever problem fouled up the form (perhaps you printed it on the wrong paper, for example) and reprint the bad form(s) by clicking the Print button again. (The Print button is in the Print Invoices dialog box.)

Printing credit memos in a batch

If you want to print credit memos in a batch, you need to select the Print Later check box that appears in the lower-left corner of the Create Credit Memos/Refunds window. Selecting this check box tells QuickBooks Simple Start to put a copy of the credit memo on a special credit-memos-to-be-printed list.

Printing credit memos in a batch works similarly to printing invoices in a batch. Because I describe how to print invoices in a batch in the preceding section, I'm going to speed through the following description of printing credit memos in a batch. If you get lost or have questions, refer to the preceding section.

When you're ready to print the credit memos that are on the to-be-printed list, follow these steps:

1. **Display the Create Credit Memos/Refunds window, click the arrow next to the Print button, and choose Print Batch from the drop-down menu.**

   QuickBooks Simple Start displays the Select Credit Memos to Print dialog box.

2. **Select the credit memos that you want to print.**

3. **Click OK to display the Print Credit Memos dialog box.**

4. **Use the Print Credit Memos dialog box to describe how you want your credit memos to be printed.**

5. **Click the Print button to send the selected credit memos to the printer.**

   QuickBooks Simple Start prints the credit memos.

Sending Invoices and Credit Memos via E-Mail

If you have e-mail already set up on your computer, you can e-mail invoices and credit memos rather than print them. To e-mail an invoice or credit memo, click the E-mail button, which appears at the top of the Create Invoices window. (The button shows a picture of a little envelope with a green arrow.) QuickBooks Simple Start displays the Send Invoice window, shown in Figure 4-12.

To send your invoice via e-mail, enter the e-mail address of the business you want to bill or refund money to, edit the message as appropriate, and then click the Send Now button. The first time you try to e-mail invoices, QuickBooks Simple Start collects a bit of information from you so you can sign up for the invoice e-mailing service. QuickBooks Simple Start also tries to sell you additional services — for which there are modest charges.

If you want to wait to send your invoice, click the Send Later button while in the Send Invoice window, or select the E-Mail Later check box in the lower-left corner of the invoice window; QuickBooks Simple Start batches your e-mail invoices together. You can send the entire batch later by clicking the arrow next to the Send button and choosing the Send Batch command.

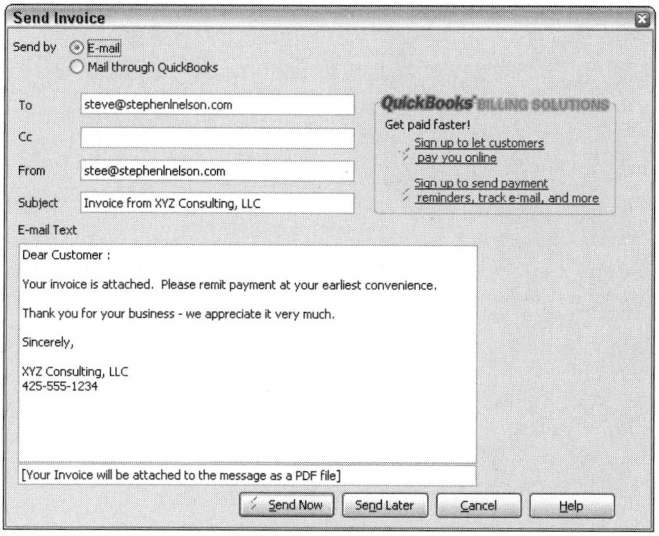

Figure 4-12:
The Send
Invoice
window.

Customizing Your Invoices and Credit Memos

QuickBooks Simple Start doesn't let you customize your invoices or credit memos much. (In comparison, the full-blown versions of QuickBooks let you do just about anything — which can be pretty useful.) You can, however, customize your invoices by putting a logo on the invoice or credit memo form. To make this change, follow these steps:

1. **Display the Invoice window or the Create Credit Memos/Refunds window.**

2. **Click the Customize button.**

   QuickBooks Simple Start displays the Customize Invoice or Customize Credit Memo/Refunds window. Figure 4-13 shows the Customize Invoice dialog box. Note that you can use the Customize window to add and remove company information to the invoice or credit memo. You do this by marking and unmarking the Print Company Name and Print Company Address boxes.

3. **Select the Use Logo check box.**

   QuickBooks Simple Start displays the Select Image dialog box (see Figure 4-14). Use the Look In drop-down list box to identify the folder holding the logo graphic image file. Then select the graphic image from the list shown in the middle of the dialog box. Click OK, and QuickBooks Simple Start returns to the Customize Invoice dialog box.

4. **Click OK to save your invoice customization changes.**

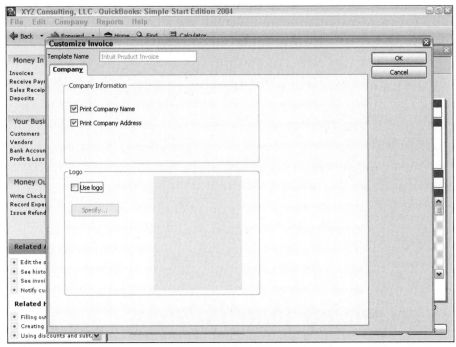

Figure 4-13:
The
Customize
Invoice
dialog box.

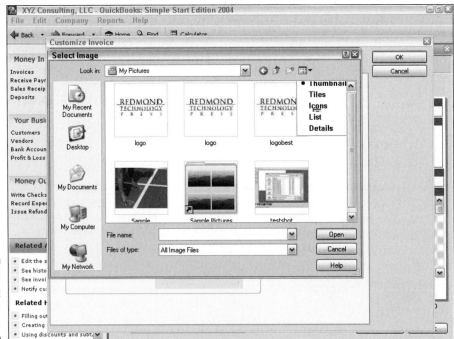

Figure 4-14:
The Select
Image
dialog box.

Chapter 5

Paying Bills

· ·

· ·

QuickBooks Simple Start gives you two ways to pay and record your bills. You record bills when you write a check. And you can record bills when you charge an amount on your credit card. Both payment methods are commonly used by small businesses, so you'll want to find out how to deal with both transactions.

Recording Your Bills by Writing Checks

When you write a check to pay some vendor or supplier directly, you record the bill, or expense, as you write the check. (This sounds obvious, I know, but the process actually works a little differently when you pay some vendor or supplier by charging your credit card.)

Now, although recording your bills by writing checks isn't tricky, you do have a couple of options for how you go about doing this. There's a slow way (which is neat because you get to collect quite a bit of information about the check and can even print the check). And there's a fast way (which is what you'll probably usually use).

Writing checks the slow way

Using the Write Checks window is the slow way, but it enables you to print a check.

To use the Write Checks window to write checks, follow these steps:

1. **Click the Write Checks icon and then New.**

   Alternatively, select Write Checks New from the Navigators list.

2. **(If prompted) Create a bank account.**

   If this is the first time you've used QuickBooks Simple Start to pay a bill, it asks if you want to create a bank account. In this case, click Yes. When QuickBooks Simple Start displays the New Account dialog box (see Figure 5-1), use the Account Name box to name the bank account and the Opening Balance box to specify the current bank account balance. It's not essential, but you can also use the As Of box to specify the date that the opening balance is correct using the MM/DD/YYYY format. After you click OK, the Write Checks window appears, as shown in Figure 5-2.

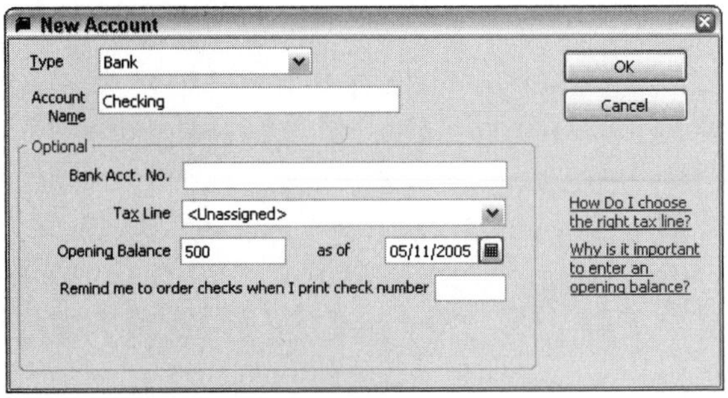

Figure 5-1: The New Account dialog box.

Notice that Write Checks window has three parts:

- The check part on the top, which you no doubt recognize from having written thousands of checks in the past.
- The buttons — Print, Update Amount, Save & Close and Clear — on the top and bottom.
- The Expense Category, Amount and Memo columns near the bottom of the window. This part is for recording what the check is for, as I explain in Steps 9, 10, and 11.

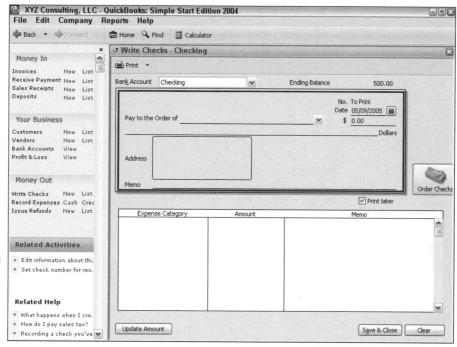

Figure 5-2:
The Write
Checks
window.

3. **Click the Bank Account drop-down list and choose the account from which you want to write this check.**

   This step is very important if you have more than one account. Make sure that you choose the correct account; otherwise, your account balances in QuickBooks Simple Start will be incorrect. Of course, if you've only got one bank account, perhaps the bank account you just set up in Step 2, this third step is necessary.

4. **Specify the check date.**

   Click in the Date box and type the check date. You enter the date using the MM/DD/YYYY format. For example, you enter November 26, 2005 as 11/26/2005. You can enter today's date by pressing the *T* key, the first and last date of the year by pressing the *Y* or *R* keys, and the first and last date of the month by pressing the *M* or *H* keys. You can adjust the date one day at a time by pressing the + and – keys. You can also click the button to the right of the Date box to get a pop-up calendar. To select a date from the pop-up calendar, click the calendar day that you want to use.

5. **Fill in the Pay to the Order Of line.**

To specify who the check pays, type the payee name into the Pay to the Order Of box.

Note that you only need to type a payee name once. If you've written a check to this person or party before, you can open the Pay to the Order Of drop-down list box (by clicking the little arrowhead that appears at the right end of the box). When QuickBooks Simple Start displays a list of previous payees, you can select one by clicking its name.

Alternatively, if you've written a check to this person or party before, QuickBooks Simple Start AutoFill feature fills in the name of the payee in the Pay to the Order Of line for you after you start typing the name. (AutoFill does so by comparing what you type with names shown in the Customer, Vendor, and Other Names Lists that QuickBooks Simple Start maintains.) AutoFill also puts the payee's address in the Address box — if you've previously collected that information. The AutoRecall feature will even fill out the entire check for you, based on the last check that you wrote to this vendor.

If you've never paid anything to this person before, the program displays a Name Not Found message box after you enter the name on the Pay to the Order Of line. You can either click Quick Add or Set Up to add the payee name to one of your lists. (To find out how to do so, check out the "To Quick Add or to Set Up?" sidebar, elsewhere in this chapter.) But for now, know that you can probably just click Quick Add — that's simplest — and then, when asked to which list the payee name should be "quickadded," select vendor, customer or "other" as appropriate.

6. **Type the amount of the check.**

   Now comes my favorite part. I've always found it a big bother to write out the amount of checks. I mean, if you write a check for $21,457.00, how do you fit twenty-one thousand, four hundred fifty-seven dollars, and no cents on the line? Where do you put those hyphens, anyway?

   All you have to do with QuickBooks Simple Start is enter the amount next to the dollar sign and press Tab. When you press Tab, QuickBooks Simple Start writes out the amount for you on the Dollars line. At moments like this, I'm grateful to be alive in the twenty-first century when computer technology can do these marvelous things for me.

7. **(Optional) Fill in the Address text box.**

   You need to fill in this box only if the address isn't there already and you intend to send the check by mail in a window envelope.

8. **(Optional) Fill in the Memo line.**

   You can put a message to the payee on the Memo line — a message such as "Quit bleeding me dry." But you usually put an account number on the Memo line so that the payee can apply your payment properly your account number.

If you try to click Save & Close and close the dialog box after completing Steps 1 through 8, QuickBooks Simple Start tells you that you can't and tries to bite your leg off. Why? Because you can't write a check unless you fill out the Expense information. You use the Expense Category, Amount and Memo columns to describe what the check pays.

9. **Move the cursor down to the Expense Category column and enter an expense account name.**

   Chances are that you want to enter the name of an account that's already on the list of accounts that QuickBooks Simple Start set up for your business. (QuickBooks Simple Start sets up a list of accounts, also known as a chart of accounts, based on the type of entity you operate.) If that's the case, move the cursor to a field in the Expense Category column, and QuickBooks Simple Start turns the field into a drop-down list box. Click the down arrow to see a list of all your accounts. You'll probably have to scroll down the list to get to the expense accounts. Click the one that this check applies to. For example, a check to pay your landlord is probably rent. A check to pay some big box store for pencils and paper is probably office supplies.

   If you need to create a new expense account category for this check, choose Add New from the top of the list to see the New Account dialog box. Fill in the information and click OK.

   What if the money that you're paying out with this check can be distributed across two, three, or four expense accounts? Simply click the row below the expense category and amount that you just entered. The down arrow appears next to the cursor. Click the down arrow and enter another expense account, and another, and another, if you want to.

To Quick Add or to Set Up?

If you click Quick Add in the Name Not Found message box, you see a Select Name Type message box, asking whether the payee is a Vendor, Customer, or Other. Most likely, the payee is a vendor, in which case you click Vendor (but you can, of course, click one of the other options). The address information that you write on the check goes in the Vendor List — or Customer List, or Other Names List, depending on what you clicked. (See Chapter 3 if you're in the dark about adding to your lists.)

Choosing Set Up in the Name Not Found message box is a little more interesting. When you choose this option, you also see the Select Name Type box. Click Vendor, Customer, or Other. Click OK, and then you see the New *Whatever* List window.

By the way, my long-suffering technical editor David wants me to point out that using the Quick Add method is sort of lazy. With Quick Add, QuickBooks Simple Start only requires you to collect a minimal amount of information.

10. Tab over to the Amount column, if necessary, and change the numbers around.

If you're distributing this check across more than one account, make sure that the numbers in the Amount column correctly distribute the check to the appropriate accounts. See Figure 5-3.

11. If you want to, enter words of explanation or encouragement in the Memo column.

Someday, you might have to go back to this check and try to figure out what these expenses mean. The Memo column might be your only clue. Enter some wise words here: "May rent," "copier repair," or "company party."

When you finish adding items, you might want to use one of the following options that appear in the Write Checks window:

- Click the Print button to print the check in the Write Checks window. This option doesn't print all the checks that you have written and marked to be printed, however. (I explain in detail how to print checks in the later chapter section, "Printing Checks.")

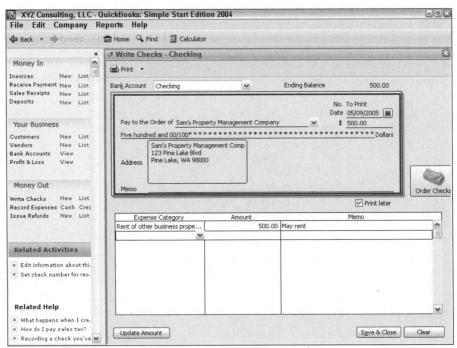

Figure 5-3:
A completed
check.

- The Clear button deletes any information that you've entered into the Write Checks window.

- The Update Amount button totals the individual expenses summarized in the Expense Category and Amount columns. It then puts the total onto the face of the check in the check amount box.

- The Print Later check box designates the check for printing. Select this check box if you want to later print the check. Deselect this check box if you're recording a handwritten check.

12. **Click Save & Close to finish writing the check.**

    Click Save & Close to tell QuickBooks Simple Start that you want to save the check and close the Write Checks window.

Writing checks the fast way

If you want to record a bill that you won't pay with a QuickBooks-printed check, you can record your check directly into the bank account register. This method is the fast and easy way to go; follow these steps:

1. **Click the Bank Accounts icon and then Register.**

   Alternatively, select Bank Accounts View from the Navigators list.

2. **(If prompted) Create a bank account.**

   If this is the first time you've used QuickBooks Simple Start to pay a bill, it asks if you want to create a bank account. In this case, click Yes. When QuickBooks Simple Start displays the New Account dialog box (see Figure 5-1), use the Account Name box to name the bank account and the Opening Balance box to specify the current bank account balance. It's not essential, but you can also use the As Of box to specify the date that the opening balance is correct using the MM/DD/YYYY format.

   The Bank Account register appears, as shown in Figure 5-4. (If you have more than one bank account, you have to select the proper account from the drop-down list and click OK.) The cursor is at the end of the register, ready and waiting for you to enter check information.

3. **Fill in the information for the check.**

   Notice that the entries you make are the same ones that you would make on a check. You should enter the date, the check number, the payee, the payment amount, the expense category (this goes into the Account box), and, optionally, a memo description.

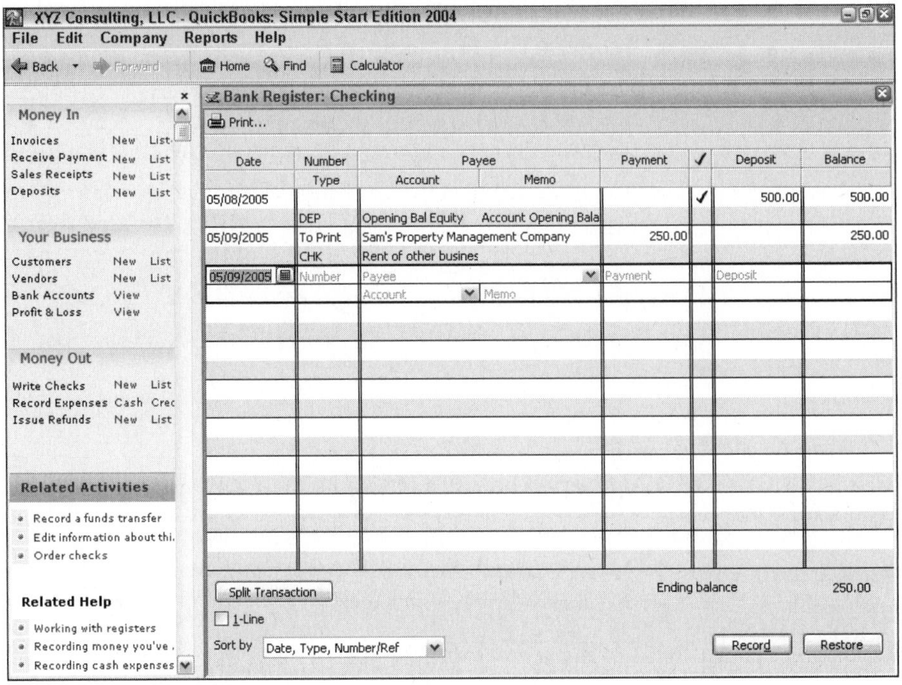

Figure 5-4:
The bank
account
register.

You want to note three important things about the register:

- If you enter a Payee name that QuickBooks Simple Start doesn't recognize, you see the Name Not Found message box, and you're asked to give information about this new, mysterious vendor. To see what to do next, go back to the preceding set of instructions on writing a check the slow way.

- You have to choose an expense category name from the account box. Chances are, you can find the right one in the Account drop-down list, but if you can't, enter one of your own. QuickBooks Simple Start displays the Account Not Found message box and asks you to fill in the information about this new account.

- To record a check that pays more than a single expense, click the Split Transaction button (shown in the bottom-left corner of the window) to display a little box (see Figure 5-5) that you can use to input multiple expense accounts and amounts.

4. **When you finish filling in the check information, click Record.**

   You click Record, of course, to record the check.

   By the way, if you realize that you've made a mistake and haven't yet clicked Record to record the check, you can click the Restore button to go back to square one. Clicking Restore blanks out what you just entered so that you can start over again.

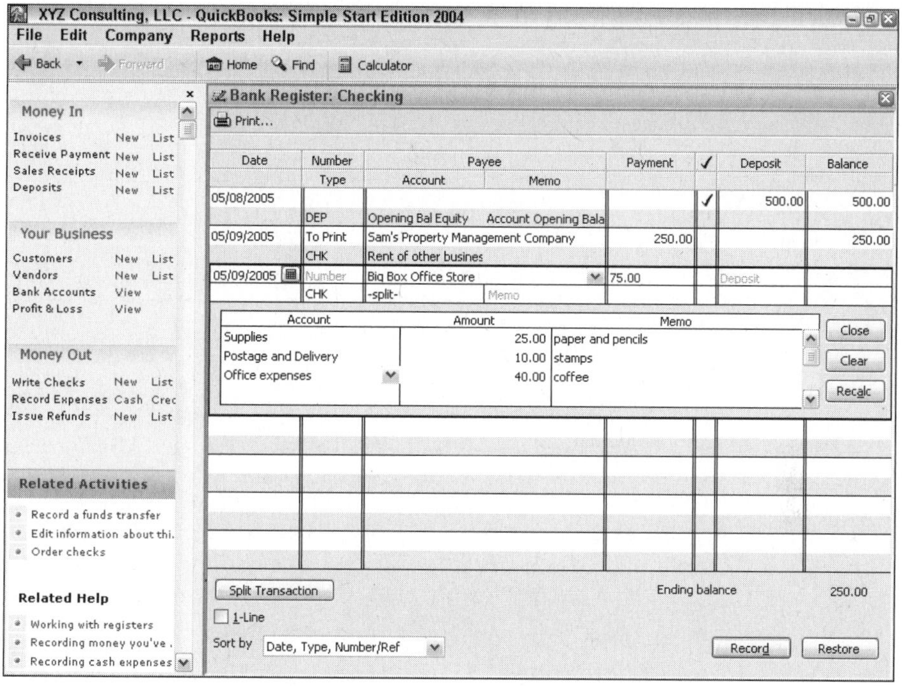

Figure 5-5:
The bank
account
register with
the split
transaction
area
showing.

Recording Your Bills by Charging a Credit Card

Commonly, you'll pay business expenses by charging an amount on your credit card. To record the bill or expense you pay through a credit card charge, you follow these steps:

1. **Select Record Expenses Credit from the Navigators list.**

2. **(If prompted) Create a credit card account.**

   If this is the first time you've used QuickBooks Simple Start to record a credit card charge, QuickBooks Simple Start asks if you want to create a bank account. In this case, click Yes. When QuickBooks Simple Start displays the New Account dialog box (see Figure 5-6), use the Account Name box to name the credit card account and the Opening Balance box to specify the current credit card balance. It's not essential, but you can also use the As Of box to specify the date that the balance is correct using the MM/DD/YYYY format. After you click OK, the Credit Card Register window appears, as shown in Figure 5-7.

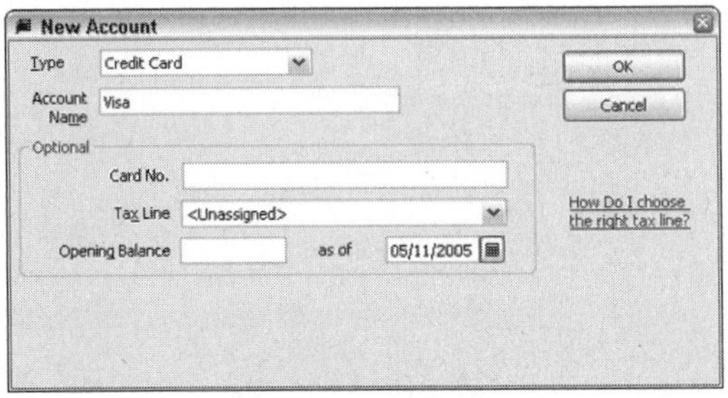

Figure 5-6:
The New
Account
dialog box.

3. **Specify the charge date.**

Click in the Date box and type the check date. You enter the date using the MM/DD/YYYY format. For example, you enter November 26, 2005 as 11/26/2005. You can enter today's date by pressing the *T* key, the first and last date of the year by pressing the *Y* or *R* keys, and the first and last date of the month by pressing the *M* or *H* keys. You can adjust the date one day at a time by pressing the + and – keys. You can also click the button to the right of the Date box to get a pop-up calendar. To select a date from the pop-up calendar, click the calendar day that you want to use.

4. **(Optional) Enter a reference number for the charge.**

I really don't know what you'd enter into the Ref field. A secret number? That monstrously long number off the credit card statement? Who knows.

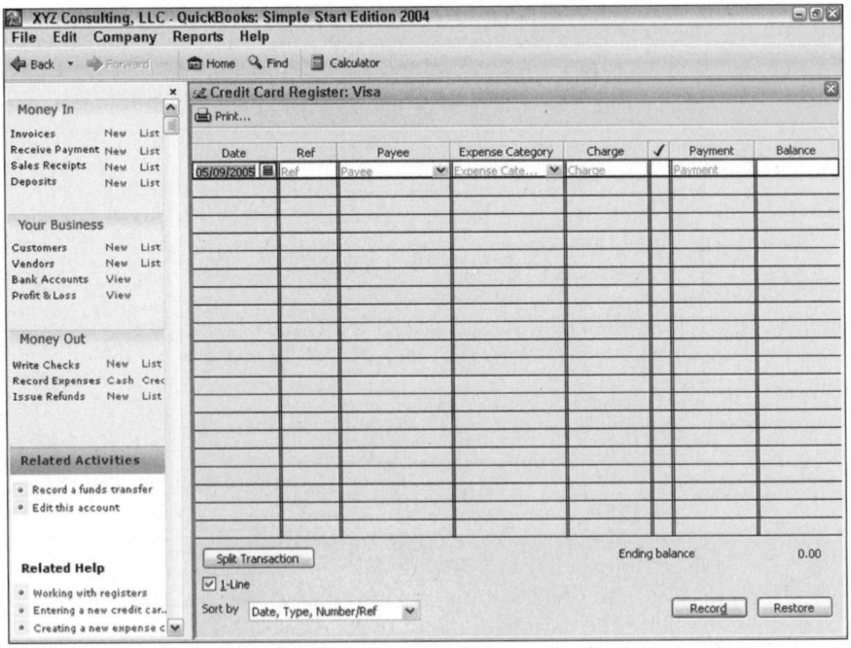

Figure 5-7:
The Credit
Card
Register
window.

5. **Fill in the Payee.**

   To specify who the charge paid, type the vendor or merchant name into the Payee box.

   Note that you only need to type a payee name once. If you've written a check to this person before or charged an amount with this person before, you can open the Payee drop-down list box (by clicking the little arrowhead that appears at the right end of the box). When QuickBooks Simple Start displays a list of previous payees, you can select one by clicking its name.

   Alternatively, if you've written a check to or made a credit card charge with this person before, QuickBooks Simple Start AutoFill feature will fill in the name of the payee in the Pay to the Order Of line for you after you start typing the name. (AutoFill does so by comparing what you type with names shown in the Customer, Vendor, and Other Names Lists that QuickBooks Simple Start maintains.)

   If you've never paid anything to or charged an amount with this person before, the program displays a Name Not Found message box after you enter the name into the Payee box. You can either click Quick Add or Set Up to add the payee name to one of your lists. (To find out how to do so, check out the "To Quick Add or to Set Up?" sidebar, earlier in this chapter.)

6. **Type the amount of the charge.**

   Use the Tab key or the mouse to select the Charge box. Then, type in the charge amount. Can I be a little compulsive here? You want to stick the amount in the Charge column. You don't want to stick the amount into the Payment column. You'll use the Payment column when you pay off the credit card balance (or some portion of the credit card balance) as described in the later chapter section, "Paying Your Credit Card Bill."

7. **(Optional) Fill in the Memo line.**

   If you want to record additional information about the charge, unmark the 1-Line box at the bottom of the Credit Card Register window. Quick-Books Simple Start expands the register from a one-line format to a two-line format (see Figure 5-8). Now use the Memo line to record some extra bit of credit card charge information that you want to record but haven't been able to store elsewhere. Perhaps a brief notation as to the business purpose of the charge?

8. **(Optional) Split the charge.**

   What if the money that you're charging can be distributed across two, three, or four expense accounts? Click the Split Transaction button. QuickBooks Simple Start opens a little, cute, pop-up split transaction area that lets you split a charge amount into several different expense categories and amounts (see Figure 5-9). Use the Expense Category column to describe the expense accounts. Use the Amount column to specify the expense amounts.

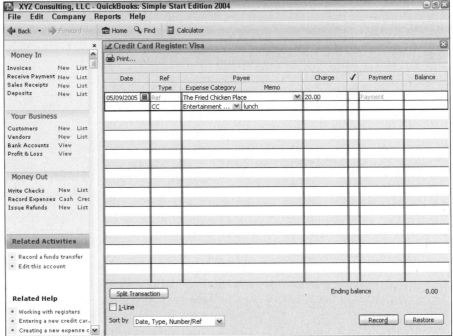

Figure 5-8:
The two-line
Credit Card
Register
window.

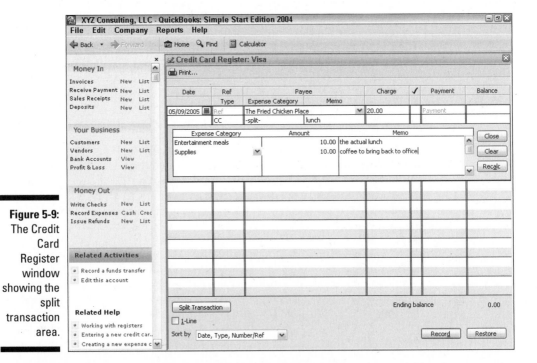

Figure 5-9:
The Credit
Card
Register
window
showing the
split
transaction
area.

The individual split transaction details must match (in amount) the total amount you enter into the Charge box on the Credit Card Register window. You can, however, tell QuickBooks Simple Start to enter the total of the individual split transaction details into the Charge box. Simply click the Recalc button. Or, if you want to start over, click the Clear button to erase the split transaction details.

9. **Click the Record button to finish recording the credit card charge.**

Paying Your Credit Card Bill

So here's a question: The preceding section, "Recording Your Bills by Charging a Credit Card," describes how you record credit card charges you've made. But how do you record that check you write to pay the credit card bill?

If you've read this chapter from the start, you already know the answer to this question. You record a check that pays a credit card bill in the same way that you record any other check. The only difference — the only difference — is that rather than specify an expense category for the check, you specify the credit card account. Figure 5-10 shows how a $500 check that pays a credit card bill looks, for example.

Let me make a couple quick observations about what happens, accounting-wise, when you charge money on a credit card and when you later pay off the credit card.

First, when you charge some amount on a credit card, the charge counts as an expense at the moment you charge. That's why, to be accurate in your accounting, you want to record credit card charges in the manner described in the preceding section. By recording a credit card charge in the QuickBooks Simple Start in this manner, you also keep track of your increasing credit card balance.

Second, when you pay the credit card bill, you don't need to record any expense (you've already done that). What you need to do is show that the credit card balance and the bank account balance decrease by the amount of the payment. Which is why you record the payment using not an expense category but the actual credit card account. If this seems weird, think about it this way: In effect, when you pay a credit card balance, you're transferring money from one account (your bank account) to another account (your credit card account).

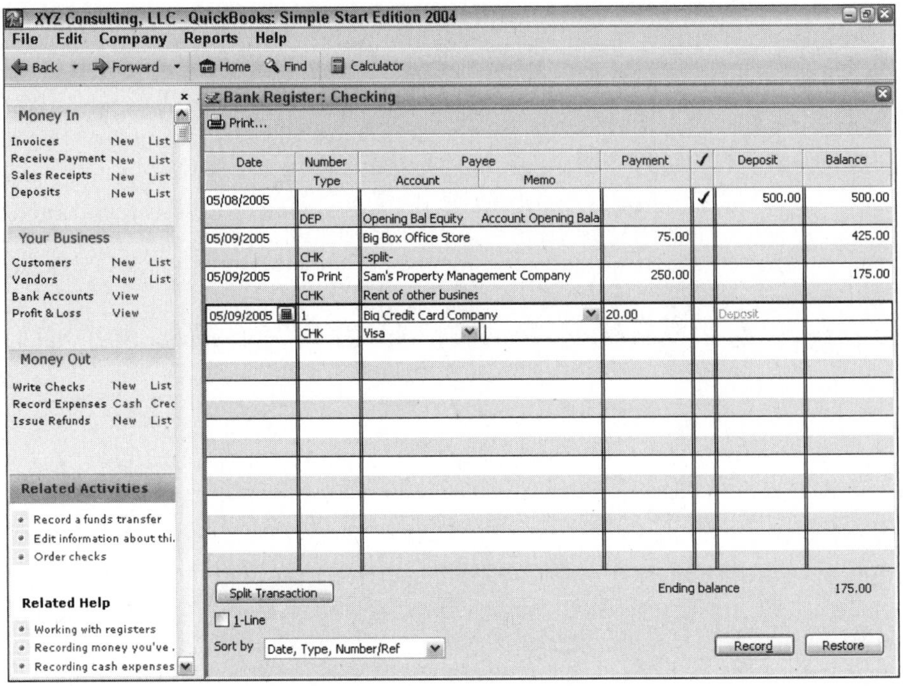

Figure 5-10: How a check transaction looks when it pays the credit card bill.

Editing Checks and Charges

Suppose that you accidentally enter the same check twice or enter a credit card charge that was from your personal credit card and not your business credit card. (Just because you're tracking bills by computer doesn't mean that you don't have to look over the things carefully anymore.) Here's how to edit and delete checks and charge transactions that you incorrectly entered into the bank account or credit card register:

1. **Locate the transaction in the bank account or credit card register by using one of the following methods:**

   • If you know roughly what day you entered the bill, you can scroll through the list to find it. The entries are listed in date order. (Select the 1-Line check box to display each bill on one line rather than on two lines to make the scrolling go faster.)

- If you don't remember the date, use the Find command (which I describe in a nearby sidebar).

2. **Select the check or charge transaction that you want to edit or delete by putting the cursor anywhere in the bill.**

3. **Edit or delete the transaction.**

   To edit the selected transaction, simply edit the contents of the field that need to change. If the payee name is wrong, for example, correct the text shown in the payee field. If the amount is incorrect, adjust the value shown in the amount field.

   If you want to delete the selected transaction, choose the Edit⇨Delete Check or Edit⇨Delete Charge command.

   QuickBooks Simple Start confirms that you really, truly want to delete the transaction, and if you click OK, it dutifully deletes the check or charge from the register.

   You can also void a check or charge transaction. To void the selected check or charge, choose the Edit⇨Void Check or Edit⇨Void Charge transaction. Voiding a transaction (rather than deleting) makes sense when you want to keep a record of the transaction's deletion. The voided transaction is marked "void" in the register and its amount set to zero. The voided transaction, therefore, doesn't affect your books. But you have a record that the transaction was entered and then cancelled.

Using the Find command

When you can't remember the information you need to find a particular entry or transaction, you can search for the information by using the Find command and window. For example, if you can't recall when you entered the bill, click the Find command button, which appears at the top of most register windows. QuickBooks Simple Start opens the Find window. Use the Transaction Type drop-down list box to select the type of transaction you want to locate. You can also use the Customer, Job, Date From and To, Invoice #, and Amount boxes to further describe the transaction or transactions that you're looking for.

After you finish specifying what the transactions you want to find look like, click the Find button, and the transactions that match all your search criteria appear in the list at the bottom of the window. Click the transaction that you want to examine more closely and then click Go To. QuickBooks Simple Start opens the appropriate window and takes you right to the transaction. Very snazzy, I do believe.

Printing Checks

Printing checks in QuickBooks Simple Start is quick and easy. You just need to make sure your printer is set up correctly. And you will need to order some preprinted checks from Intuit.

QuickBooks Simple Start has check forms that you can buy, and I recommend using them if you print checks. After all, the QuickBooks Simple Start checks were made to work with this program. And all banks accept these checks.

Getting the Printer Ready

Before you can start printing checks, you have to make sure that your printer is set up to print them. You also have to tell QuickBooks Simple Start what to put on the checks — your company name, address, logo, and so on. And you might try running a few sample checks through the printer to see whether they come out all right.

Follow these steps to set up the printer:

1. **Choose File⇨Printer Setup.**

   The Printer Setup dialog box appears, as shown in Figure 5-11.

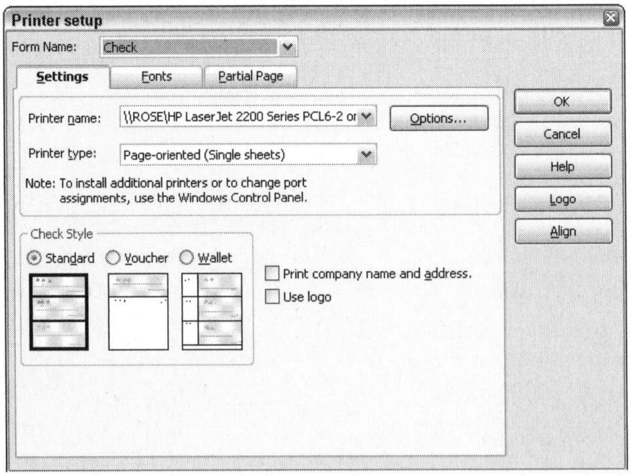

Figure 5-11: The Printer Setup dialog box.

2. Select Check from the Form Name drop-down list box.

QuickBooks Simple Start sets your printing options differently depending on which form you want to print. For printing checks, you want to choose the Check from the Form Name drop-down list box at the top of the dialog box.

3. In the Printer Name drop-down list box, click the down arrow and select the printer that you have.

When you installed QuickBooks, it had a frank, software-to-software talk with Windows to find out what kind of printer you have, among other things. Your printer is probably already selected, but if it's not, select the correct printer.

4. Set the correct Printer Type option, if necessary.

This box is probably already filled in, too, thanks to that frank discussion I mention in Step 3. But if it isn't, click the down arrow and choose Continuous or Page-Oriented. (The former is generally for dot matrix printers and the latter for laser and inkjet printers, but it really just depends on what kind of paper you use for your printer.)

5. Select the appropriate Check Style.

Now you're cooking. This step is where you get to make a real choice. Standard checks are sized to fit in legal envelopes. Voucher checks are the same width as standard checks, but they're much longer. When you choose the Voucher option, QuickBooks Simple Start prints voucher information as well — the items and expense tabulations from the bottom of the Write Checks window. QuickBooks Simple Start also provides information about the checking account that you're writing this check on. The Wallet option is for printing checks that are small enough to fit in — you guessed it — a wallet.

6. (Optional) Click the Options button and then adjust your printer options.

QuickBooks Simple Start displays your printer's Properties dialog box. Use this dialog box to specify print quality, number of copies, and other options specific to your printer. When you're finished, click OK to return to the Printer Setup dialog box.

7. Click the Fonts tab of the Printer Setup dialog box and then the Fonts button on that tab to customize the fonts on your checks.

When you click either the Font button or the Address Font button on this tab, you see the Select Font dialog box (shown in Figure 5-12) or the Select Address Font dialog box. You use the Address Font button to designate how your company's name and address look and the Font button to designate what all other print on your checks looks like. Here's your chance to spruce up your checks and make your company's name stand out.

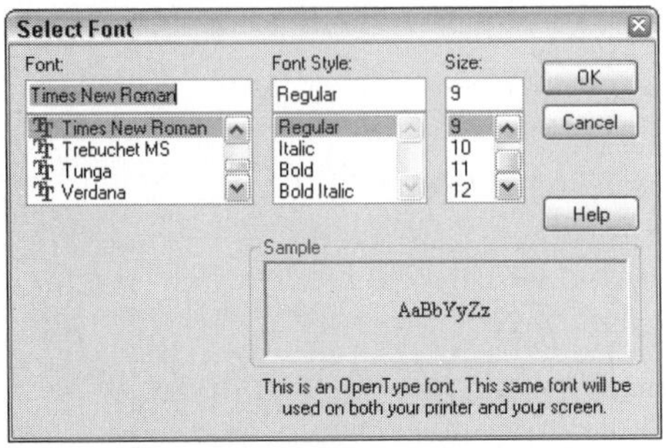

Figure 5-12:
The Select
Font dialog
box.

Experiment for a while with the font, font style, and type size settings. For example, if you have a bookstore, choose the Bookman font (maybe using bold for your company's name and address); if you run a messenger service, choose Courier; Italian mathematicians can use Times Roman (just kidding). You can see what your choices look like in the Sample box.

When you finish fooling around, click the OK button to go back to the Printer Setup dialog box.

8. Click the Partial Page tab of the Printer Setup dialog box and then choose a Partial Page Printing Style.

Fortunately, some graphics appear; otherwise, you wouldn't have a clue what these options are, would you? These options are for the environmentally friendly among you. Suppose that you feed two checks to the printer, but the check sheets have three checks each. You have a leftover check.

Thanks to this option, you can use the extra check. Click one of the options to tell QuickBooks Simple Start how you plan to feed the check to the printer — vertically on the left (the Left option), vertically in the middle (the Centered option), or horizontally (the Portrait option). You feed checks to the printer the same way that you feed envelopes to it.

9. (Optional) Click the Logo button and then enter a company logo or some clip art.

In the Logo dialog box, click File and find the directory and BMP (bitmapped) graphic file that you want to load. Click OK. Only graphics that are in BMP format can be used on your checks.

10. Click OK when you're finished.

That setup was no Sunday picnic, was it? But your checks are all ready to be printed, and you'll probably never have to go through that ordeal again.

Printing a Check

You can print checks one at a time from the Write Checks window. Or you can print a whole batch of checks by using the File menu's Print Checks command. I describe both methods in the following sections.

Printing a check as you write it

If you're in the Write Checks window and you've just finished filling out a check, you can print it. Here's how:

1. Fill out your check.

Yes, I strongly recommend filling out the check before printing it. Flip back to the start of the chapter to the section, "Recording Your Bills by Writing Checks," for information about how to do this.

2. Click the Print button in the Write Checks window.

You see the Print Check dialog box, shown in Figure 5-13.

Figure 5-13:
The Print
Check
dialog box.

3. Enter a check number in the Printed Check Number text box and click OK.

You see the similarly named Print Checks dialog box, shown in Figure 5-14. The settings that you see in this dialog box are the ones that you chose when you first told QuickBooks Simple Start how to print checks. If you change the settings in the Print Checks dialog box, the changes affect only this particular check. The next time you print a check, you'll see your original settings again.

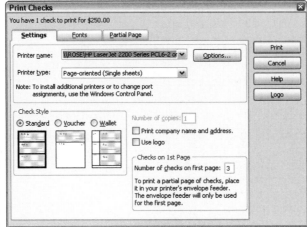

Figure 5-14:
The other
Print Checks
dialog box.

4. **Either click Print to accept the default settings, or make changes in the dialog box and then click Print.**

   In the Printer Name box, specify which printer you want to print to. In the Check Style area, indicate whether you want to print a Standard, Voucher, or Wallet-sized check.

   If you're printing a partial page of forms on a laser printer, use the Partial Page tab to indicate both the number of check forms on the partial page and how you'll feed them through your printer.

   If you want your company's name and address to appear on the check, select the Print Company Name and Address check box.

   See how the Number of Copies text box is grayed out? If you want to change this setting, you need to go back to the Printer Setup dialog box (choose File⇨Printer Setup).

   After you click Print, QuickBooks Simple Start prints the check, and you see the Did Check(s) Print OK? dialog box (not shown).

5. **If the check didn't come out right, type the number of the incorrectly printed check in the Did Check(s) Print OK? dialog box and click OK. Then click the Print button again, enter the new check number, and click Print again.**

   For example, if check number 1005 printed incorrectly, type **1005**. Then click the Print button again, enter the new check number, and click Print again. If preprinted check form 1005 is still usable (say, because you accidentally printed check 1005 on blank paper instead of on the form), you can reprint the check on check form 1005 by typing **1005** in the

Print Check dialog box (refer to Figure 5-14). If the incorrectly printed check ruined check form 1005 (say, because you loaded the form upside down), load your printer with a fresh check form and verify the new check number, in this case probably 1006.

QuickBooks Simple Start doesn't automatically keep track of incorrectly printed check forms, so you have to. If you botch a check form, be sure to write the word *VOID* in large letters and permanent ink across the face of the check. Then file the check away for your reference. Don't throw the check away.

If you still have questions about how to check any mistakes, see the section "What if I make a mistake?" later in this chapter.

6. **If your check looks good, click OK.**

   You return to the Write Checks window. Don't forget to sign the check.

Printing checks by the bushel

What if you write a mess of checks and then decide to print them? That's how the process is usually done. Here's how to print a bushel of checks:

1. **Choose File⇨Print Forms⇨Checks.**

2. **Click the check marks next to the checks that you don't want to print and then click OK.**

   All the checks are selected at first. If you want to print them all, fine. If not, click the check marks next to the checks that you don't want to print so that QuickBooks Simple Start removes the check marks. Or, if you want to print only a few of the checks, click the Select None button and then click next to the checks that you want to print so that QuickBooks Simple Start places a check in the column.

   When only the checks that you want to print are selected, click OK to continue with this crazy little thing called check printing. QuickBooks, happy with your progress, displays the Print Checks dialog box. Here you see the settings that you chose when you first told QuickBooks Simple Start how to print checks.

3. **Either click Print to accept the default settings, or make changes in the dialog box and then click Print.**

   You can change the settings in this dialog box if you want them to be different. Any changes that you make for a particular batch of checks don't affect the default settings. The next time you print a check, your original settings appear again.

In the Check Style box, indicate whether you want to print Standard, Voucher, or Wallet-sized checks. If you're printing a partial page of checks, enter the number of checks on the first page in the Number of Checks on First Page text box.

If you want your company's name and address to appear on the checks, select the Print Company Name and Address check box.

Note that the Number of Copies text box is grayed out. If you want to change these settings, you need to choose File➪Printer Setup.

QuickBooks Simple Start prints the checks, and then you see the Did Check(s) Print OK? dialog box.

4. **Review the checks that QuickBooks Simple Start printed. Then do one of the following:**

   - If QuickBooks Simple Start printed the checks correctly, answer the Did Check(s) Print OK? message box by clicking OK. (QuickBooks, apparently thinking that you now want to do nothing but print checks, redisplays the nearly exhausted Write Checks window.)

   - If QuickBooks Simple Start didn't print a check correctly, type the number of the first incorrectly printed check in the text box and then click OK. In this case, repeat the steps for check printing. Note, though, that you need to reprint only the first bad check and the checks that follow it. You don't need to reprint good checks that precede the first bad check.

     Don't forget to write the word *VOID* in large letters and permanent ink across the front of incorrectly printed check forms. Then file the checks for safekeeping. (Don't throw them away.) To record the voided check in QuickBooks, see the next section, "What if I make a mistake?"

   If your checks came out all right, take the rest of the day off. Give yourself a raise while you're at it.

5. **Sign the printed checks.**

   Then — and I guess you probably don't need my help here — put the checks in the mail.

If the numbers of the checks you need to reprint aren't sequential and are, in fact, spread all over creation, make it easy on yourself. Click OK to clear the list of checks to be printed, go into the Checking register, and enter **T** in the Number line of the checks you need to reprint. QuickBooks Simple Start automatically fills these with To Print. Then choose File➪Print Forms➪Checks, as in Step 2, and continue from there.

What if I make a mistake?

If you discover a mistake after you print a check, the problem might not be as big as you think.

If you've already mailed the check, however, you can't do much. You can try to get the check back (if the person you paid hasn't cashed it already) and replace it with a check that's correct. (Good luck on this one.)

If the person has cashed the check, you can't get the check back. If you overpaid the person by writing the check for more than you should have, you need to get the person to pay you the overpayment amount. If you underpaid the person, you need to write another check for the amount of the underpayment.

If you printed the check but haven't mailed it, void the printed check. This operation has two parts. First, write *VOID* in large letters across the face of the check form. (Use a ballpoint pen if you're using multipart forms so that the second and third parts also show as VOID.) Second, display the Checking register, highlight the check, and then choose Edit⇨Void Check. (This option marks the check as one that has been voided in the system so that QuickBooks Simple Start doesn't use the check in calculating the account balance.) If you're voiding an incorrectly printed check, you need to first create a transaction for the check number that printed incorrectly and then void that transaction.

Of course, if you want to reissue a voided check, just enter the check all over again — only this time, try to be more careful.

If you notice only after clicking OK in the Did Checks Print OK? dialog box that a check printed incorrectly, you can tell QuickBooks Simple Start you want to reprint the check in one of two ways. If you have the register window

---

A big bad warning concerning check voiding

In general, you shouldn't void checks from a previous year (you do this by using the Void command in the Edit menu). If you do, you'll adjust the previous year's expenses, which sounds okay, but you don't want to do this because (a) it means you can no longer prepare income statements and balance sheets that correspond to your financial statements and tax returns and (b) because you've already presumably included the check in your deductions for the previous year. If you do have a check that should be voided — say it's outstanding and has never been cashed or was a mistake in the first place — record a journal entry into the current year that undoes the effect of the check. Or have your accountant record a journal entry.

displayed, you can change the check's number from 007, for example, to To Print. If you have the Write Checks window displayed, you can select the To Be Printed box.

Oh where, oh where do unprinted checks go?

Unprinted checks — those that you entered by using the Write Checks window but haven't yet printed — are stored in the Checking register. To identify them as unprinted checks, QuickBooks Simple Start puts To Print in the Number line. What's more, when you tell QuickBooks Simple Start to print the unprinted checks, what it really does is print the checks in the register that have To Print in the Number line. All this knowledge is of little practical value in most instances, but it results in several interesting possibilities.

For example, you can enter the checks that you want to print directly into the register — all you need to do is enter **To Print** in the Number line.

Expense Recordkeeping Suggestions

Can I make a handful of easy-to-implement suggestions for your expense recordkeeping? If you follow the suggestions, you'll not only get better information out of QuickBooks, but you'll also find it easier to more accurately prepare your federal and state income tax returns.

Here are my ideas:

- ✔ Don't commingle your personal and business expenses. Do that, and it'll be just about impossible to figure out what expenses are business and what are personal. By losing track of what your business expenses are, you'll thereby also be prevented from figuring out what your business profits are. Ugh.

- ✔ If you must commingle — for example, if you've got a sole proprietorship — create a new personal expenses category for your nonbusiness expenses. And then, anytime you pay for some item that's not a business expense, stick the expense into this personal expenses category.

In the case of corporations, legal reasons exist for not commingling. Ask your attorney for the details, but here's the short version of the story: If you commingle personal and business funds, you might lose the liability protection that you set up the corporation to get. One of my attorney friends tells me about the law school class discussion where the professor explained why commingling is so dangerous. In some court case having to do with a poor drycleaner who commingled, the judge said, "Hey bozo, here's the deal . . . if you're not going to respect the corporation as a single legal entity, there's no reason for the creditors to have to do so."

✔ Use the QuickBooks Simple Start standard expense categories as much as possible. These expense categories all tie to the federal and state income tax returns that you'll need to use for preparing your income tax return. You make your end-of-year accounting much easier, therefore, if you use just the standard categories.

✔ If you use a credit card to charge expenses, don't create an expense category for "credit card charges." That's not enough detail. Instead, record individual credit card charges and then correctly identify the expense category or categories for each charge.

Chapter 6

Reeling in the Dough

*Y*ou need to record the amounts customers pay you when they fork over cash, whether at the time of a sale or after you invoice them. In this chapter, I describe how to record these payments and explain how to make bank deposits. I also share a few words on the subject of tracking the amounts that customers owe and pay.

If you've been using QuickBooks to prepare customer invoices, you're ready to begin recording payments. You'll have no problem. If you haven't been invoicing customers, you need to make sure that you have a couple of things ready to go before you can record cash sales.

First, you need to make sure that your lists are up-to-date. (I describe updating these lists in Chapter 3.) And second, if you want to print sales receipts, you need to have your printer set up to print them. You do so by choosing File⇨Printer Setup and then selecting Sales Receipt from the Form Name drop-down list box. Setting up your printer to print sales receipts works just like setting it up to print invoices and credit memos (as I describe in Chapter 4).

Recording a Sales Receipt

You record a *sales receipt* when a customer pays you in full for the goods or services at the point of sale. Sales receipts work similarly to regular invoiced sales (for which you first invoice a customer and then later receive payment on the invoice). In fact, the big difference between the two types of sales is that sales receipts are recorded in a way that changes your cash balance rather than your accounts receivable balance.

In the following steps, I describe how to record sales receipts for products, which are the most complicated type of cash sale. Recording sales receipts for services works basically the same way, however. You simply fill in fewer fields.

1. **Click the Sales Receipts New hyperlink.**

   Alternatively, click the Sales Receipts icon and choose New.

   The Enter Sales Receipts window appears, as shown in Figure 6-1.

   Your Enter Sales Receipts window might not look exactly like mine for a couple of reasons. QuickBooks Simple Start slightly customizes its forms to fit your particular type of business.

   Customizing sales receipt forms works in a similar way to customizing invoices and credit memos, as I describe in Chapter 4. For example, you can add a logo. You can also make other modest changes.

2. **Identify the customer.**

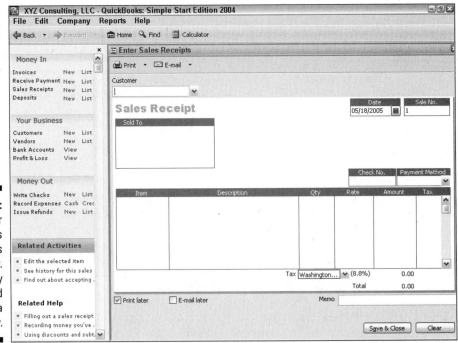

Figure 6-1: The Enter Sales Receipts window. Strangely empty and perhaps a bit lonely.

Click the down arrow to the right of the Customer drop-down list. Scroll through the Customer List until you see the customer name that you want and then click it. Note that unlike invoices, the Customer field is not required for cash sales.

3. **Date the sales receipt.**

   Press Tab to move the cursor to the Date text box. Then type the correct date in MM/DD/YY format. You can change the date by using any of the date-editing codes. (You can find these codes in Chapter 4 and on the Cheat Sheet at the front of the book.)

4. **(Optional) Enter a sale number.**

   QuickBooks Simple Start suggests a cash sale number by adding 1 to the last cash sale number you used. Use this number, or tab to the Sale No. text box and change the number to whatever you want.

5. **Fix the Sold To address, if necessary.**

   QuickBooks Simple Start grabs the billing address from the Customer List and uses the billing address as the Sold To address. You can change the address for the cash sale, however, by replacing the appropriate part of the usual billing address.

6. **Record the check number.**

   Enter the customer's check number in the Check No. text box. If the customer is paying you with cold hard cash, you can leave the Check No. text box empty.

7. **Specify the payment method.**

   To specify the payment method, click the Payment Method drop-down list and select something from it: cash, check, VISA, MasterCard, or whatever. If you don't see the payment method that you want to use, you can add the method to the Payment Method List. Choose Add New to display the New Payment Method dialog box. Enter a description of the payment method in the text box and click OK.

8. **Describe each item that you're selling.**

   Move the cursor to the first row of the Item/Description/Qty/Rate/Amount/Tax list box. When you do, QuickBooks Simple Start turns the Item field into a drop-down list box. Click the Item drop-down list of the first empty row in the list box and then select the item. When you do, QuickBooks Simple Start fills in the Description and Rate text boxes with whatever sales description and sales price you entered in the Item List. (You can edit this information if you want, but that probably isn't necessary.) Enter the number of items sold in the Qty text box. (QuickBooks Simple Start then calculates the amount by multiplying the quantity by the rate.) Describe each of the other items you're selling by filling in the next empty rows of the list box.

If you've already read the chapter on invoicing customers (see Chapter 4), what I'm about to tell will seem very familiar: You can put as many items on a sales receipt as you want. If you don't have enough room on a single page, QuickBooks Simple Start adds as many pages as you need to the receipt. The sales receipt total, of course, goes on the last page.

9. **Describe any special items that the sales receipt should include.**

If you didn't set up the QuickBooks Simple Start item file, you have no idea what I'm talking about. But here's the scoop: QuickBooks Simple Start thinks that anything that you stick on a receipt (or an invoice, for that matter) is something that you're selling. If you sell blue, yellow, and red thingamajigs, you obviously need to add each of these items to the Item List. But if you add a subtotal to your receipt, QuickBooks Simple Start thinks that the subtotal is just another thingamajig and requires you to enter another item in the list. The same is true for a volume discount that you want to stick on the receipt. And if you add sales tax to your receipt, well, guess what? QuickBooks Simple Start thinks that the sales tax is just another item that needs to be included in the Item List. (For more information about working with your Item List and adding new items, refer to Chapter 3.)

To include one of these special discount or subtotal items, move the cursor to the next empty row in the Item box, click the arrow on the right side of the drop-down and then select the special item. After QuickBooks Simple Start fills in the Description and Rate text boxes, you might need to edit this information. Enter each special item — subtotals or discounts — that you're itemizing on the receipt by filling in the next empty rows of the list box.

If you selected the Taxable check box when you added the item to the Item List, the word *Tax* appears in the Tax column to indicate that the item will be taxed.

If you want to include a discount item (so that all the listed items are discounted), you need to stick a subtotal item on the receipt after the inventory items or other items you want to discount. Then stick the discount item directly after the subtotal item. In this way, QuickBooks Simple Start calculates the discount as a percentage of the subtotal.

10. **Specify the sales tax.**

If you specified tax information when you created your company file during the EasyStep Interview, remember how QuickBooks Simple Start asked whether you charge sales tax? QuickBooks Simple Start fills in the default tax information by adding together the taxable items (which are indicated by the word *Tax* in the Tax column) and multiplying by the percentage you indicated when you created your company file. If the information is okay, move on to Step 13. If not, move the cursor to the

Tax box that's to the right of the Customer Message box, activate the drop-down list box, and select the correct sales tax. For more information about setting a default sales tax for a customer on the Customer List, refer to Chapter 3.

11. (Truly optional and probably unnecessary for cash sales) Add a memo in the Memo text box.

You can include a memo description with the cash sale information. This memo isn't for your customer. It doesn't even print on the cash receipt, should you decide to print one. The memo is for your eyes only. Memo descriptions give you a way to store information that's related to a sale with the sales receipt information.

12. Decide whether you're going to print the receipt.

If you're not going to print the receipt, make sure that the Print Later check box is empty — if not, deselect it.

Figure 6-2 shows a completed Enter Sales Receipts window.

13. Click Save & Close to save the sales receipt.

QuickBooks Simple Start saves the sales receipt that's on-screen.

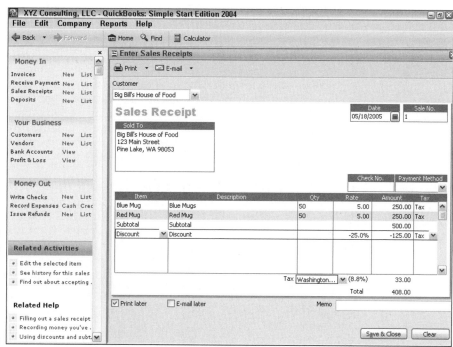

Figure 6-2:
The completed Enter Sales Receipts window.

Printing a Sales Receipt

To print a single sales receipt as you're recording the information, click the Print button in the Enter Sales Receipts window. The Print One Sales Receipt dialog box appears, as shown in Figure 6-3. The following steps tell you how to complete this dialog box:

1. **Select the type of sales receipt form.**

   If you're using a different sales receipt form type than you described for the invoice/PO printer setup, select the type of form that you want to print on by clicking an option button in the Print On box. You can choose Intuit Preprinted Forms, Blank Paper, or Letterhead. (See Chapter 4 for more on these printer options.)

   You shouldn't have to worry about printing test receipts or fiddling with form alignment problems if you addressed these issues during the invoice printer setup, so I'm not going to talk about the Align button here. If you want to print a test receipt or need to change the alignment, refer to Chapter 4 for information on how to proceed.

2. **Print that puppy!**

   Click the Print button to send the form to the printer. QuickBooks Simple Start prints the sales receipt.

3. **Review the sales receipt and reprint the form, if necessary.**

   Review the sales receipt to see whether QuickBooks Simple Start printed it correctly. If the form doesn't look okay, fix whatever problem fouled up the printing; perhaps you forgot to include the company name and address, for example. Then reprint the form by clicking the Print button (in the Enter Sales Receipts window) again, selecting the form on which you want to print (again), and then clicking the Print button in the Print One Sales Receipt dialog box (you got it — again).

To print a batch of receipts, make sure that you select the Print Later check box on each receipt that you want to print and then display the Enter Sales Receipts window — such as by clicking the Sales Receipts New hyperlink, and then click the arrow beside the Print button, and choose Print Batch from the drop-down list. QuickBooks Simple Start displays the Select Receipts to Print dialog box, which enables you to choose which receipts to print. Choose the desired receipts by putting a check in the first column, and then click OK. The Print Sales Receipts dialog box appears. This dialog box resembles the Print One Sales Receipt dialog box in just about every way, and the instructions work in exactly the same manner. For help with this dialog box, refer to the sections on printing invoices and credit memos in batches in Chapter 4.

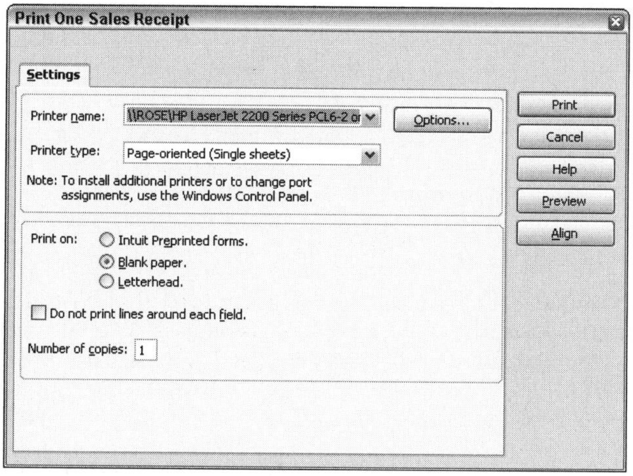

Figure 6-3:
The Print
One Sales
Receipt
dialog box.

Special Tips for Retailers

Are you a retailer? If so, you're probably saying to yourself, "Hey idiot, what you just described is way too much work to do every time someone walks into the store and buys, for example, some $3 item."

You know what? You're right. So here's what retailers do to record their sales. Retailers record the day's sales using one, two, or three sales receipt transactions. Retailers don't record each individual sales receipt transaction.

For example, suppose that some coffee mug retailer had sold 300 blue coffee mugs for the day and given everybody a 10-percent discount. (Perhaps the discount was given because of a storewide sale or something.) In that case, at the end of the day, the retailer would need to record total sales of $300, a $30 discount, and then the sales tax (in our example, sales tax equals 8.8 percent). Using these example numbers, the *daily* sales would be recorded using a sales receipt transaction like the one shown in Figure 6-2.

Pretty straightforward, right? And that's not too much work, all things considered.

Let me share a handful of other tips for recording retail sales:

✔ You probably want to record a sales receipt transaction for each deposit you make. In this manner, you can indicate that a particular sales receipt transaction (really a batch of sales) is deposited at one time into your bank account — which will make reconciling your bank account relatively easy.

✔ You probably want to separate cash sales from credit card sales because often credit card sales are handled differently. Your credit card processing company, for example, might hold onto credit card sales for a few days, or it might deduct a fee before depositing the money into your bank account. You want to record a separate sales receipt transaction for each deposit you make (or some other company makes) into the bank account — again to make reconciling the bank account easier.

✔ Because in QuickBooks Simple Start you don't actually use the Item List to monitor your inventory (because you have way too many items to store in the QuickBooks Item List), you'll probably want to use catchall items. For example, you might use a single item called something like "merchandise." Or, if you're segregating your merchandise into two groups — often called departments — you might use items that correspond to these departments. You might, for example, use a Dept-A and a Dept-B item. By the way, when you don't track inventory in your items file, your CPA handles the inventory and cost of goods sold calculations on your tax return. He or she probably also records a journal entry transaction to get your account balances right as of the end of your fiscal year. Chapter 17 talks in more detail about how you can use the QuickBooks Simple Start program in a retail setting.

✔ You might want to look at the QuickBooks Point of Sale system. The QuickBooks Point of Sale system makes it easy to quickly record cash register sales. In fact, the more expensive version of the QuickBooks Point of Sale system comes with a scanner, a receipt printer, and a cash drawer. When you use the QuickBooks Point of Sale system, the software automatically records your sales and the effect on inventory and cost of goods sold when you ring up a sale.

Correcting Sales Receipt Mistakes

If you make a mistake in entering a cash sale, don't worry. Here's a list of common problems and how to fix them:

✔ **If the sales receipt is still displayed on-screen:** If the sales receipt is still on-screen, you can move the cursor to the box or button that's wrong and then fix the mistake. Most of the bits of information that you enter in the Enter Sales Receipts window are fairly short or are entries that you've selected from a list. You can usually replace the contents of a field by typing over whatever's already there or by making a couple of quick clicks. If you really messed up and want to start over from scratch, you can click the Clear button. To save a receipt after you've entered it correctly, click Save & Close.

If you need to insert a line in the middle of a sales receipt, right-click where you want to insert the line and choose Insert Line from the shortcut menu that appears. To delete a line, right-click it and then choose Delete Line from the shortcut menu.

✓ **If the sales receipt isn't displayed on-screen:** If the sales receipt isn't on-screen and you haven't yet printed it, click the Sales Receipts List hyperlink. QuickBooks Simple Start displays the Sales Receipts You've Created window (see Figure 6-4). Double-click the sales receipt you want to edit. Then, fix the error as I describe in the preceding bullet. If you make a mistake while editing a receipt, you can click the Revert button to go back to the saved receipt and not save your changes.

Even if you've printed the customer's receipt, you can make the sort of change that I just described. For example, you can locate the sales receipt using the Sales Receipts You've Created window. And you can correct the error and print the receipt again. I'm not so sure that you want to go this route, however. Your whole life will be much cleaner if you void the cash sale by displaying the sales receipt and choosing Edit➪Void Sales Receipt. Then enter a new, correct cash sales transaction.

✓ **If you don't want the sales receipt:** You usually won't want to delete sales receipts, but you can delete them. (You'll almost always be in much better shape if you just void the sales receipt.) To delete the receipt, display it in the Enter Sales Receipts window and then choose Edit➪Delete Sales Receipt. When QuickBooks Simple Start asks you to confirm the deletion, click Yes.

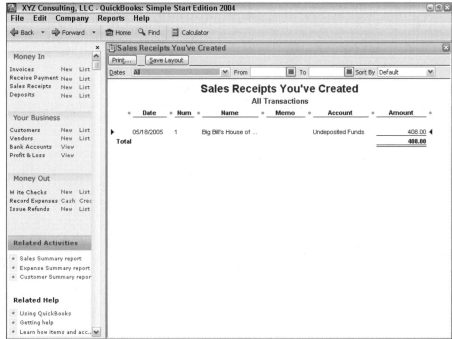

Figure 6-4:
The Sales Receipts You've Created window.

Recording Customer Payments

If your customers don't always pay you up front for their purchases, you need to record another type of payment — the payments that customers make to pay off or pay down what you've invoiced them. To record the payments, of course, you need to first record invoices for the customer. If you issue credit memos that customers can use to reduce the amounts they owe, you also need to first record credit memos for the customer. (Check out Chapter 4 for how to record these invoices and credit memos.) The rest is easy.

To display the Receive Payments window, click the Receive Payments New hyperlink. Or click the Receive Payment icon and choose New. When QuickBooks Simple Start displays the Receive Payments window, describe the customer payment and the invoices paid. If you want the gory details, read through the following steps:

1. **Click the Receive Payment New hyperlink.**

   The Receive Payments window appears, as shown in Figure 6-5. (You might be asked whether your company accepts credit cards — click Yes or No to close the dialog box.)

2. **Identify the customer.**

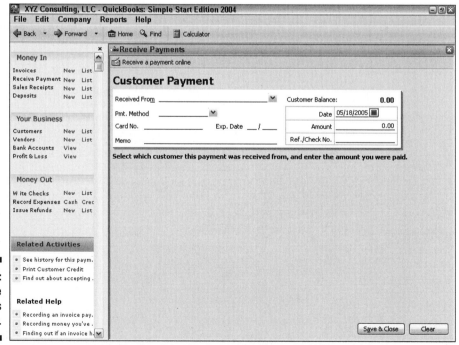

Figure 6-5:
The Receive
Payments
window.

Activate the Received From drop-down list and select the customer by clicking it. QuickBooks Simple Start lists the open, or unpaid, invoices for the customer in the big Unpaid Invoices for This Customer list box at the bottom of the window.

3. Specify the payment date.

Press Tab to move the cursor to the Date text box and type the correct date in MM/DD/YY format. To edit the date, you can use the secret date-editing codes that I describe in Chapter 4 and on the Cheat Sheet at the front of the book.

4. Enter the amount of the payment.

Move the cursor to the Amount line and type the customer payment amount.

5. (Optional) Specify the payment method.

Activate the Pmt. Method drop-down list and select the payment method.

6. (Optional) Give the check number.

You can guess how this works, right? You move the cursor to the Ref./ Check No. line. Then you type the check number from the customer's check. Do you need to complete this step? Naw. But this bit of information might be useful if you or the customer later have questions about what checks paid for what invoices. So I'd go ahead and enter the check number.

7. (Optional) Add a memo description.

Use the Memo description for storing some bit of information that will help you in some way. Note that this field prints on the Customer Statement.

8. If the customer has any outstanding credits, decide whether to apply them in this payment.

QuickBooks Simple Start totals the amounts of any of the customer's existing credits. They could be anything from an overpayment on a previous invoice to a return credit or anything else.

If you want to apply a credit memo to a specific open invoice, select the invoice and then click the Apply Unused Credits button. When QuickBooks Simple Start displays the Credits tab of the Discount and Credits dialog box, as shown in Figure 6-6, click the credit memo you want to apply and then click Done.

9. Identify which open invoices the customer is paying.

By default, QuickBooks Simple Start automatically applies the payment to the open invoices, starting with the oldest open invoice. You can change which invoices are paid with a payment by marking the paid invoices with a check mark. (The check mark goes in the first column of the Unpaid invoices for this customer list.) You can also change this application by entering amounts in the Payment column. Simply click the open invoice's payment amount and enter the correct amount.

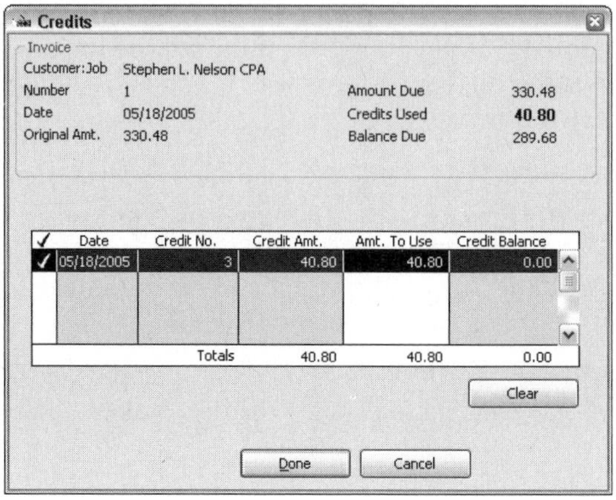

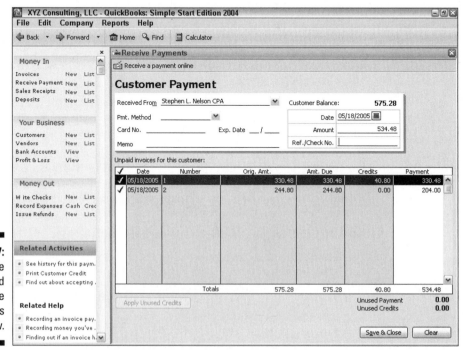

Figure 6-6:
The Credits
dialog box.

10. Record the customer payment information.

After you identify which invoices the customer is paying — the unapplied amount should probably show as zero — you're ready to record the customer payment information. You can do so by clicking Save & Close. QuickBooks saves the customer payment shown on-screen. Figure 6-7 shows a completed Receive Payments window.

Figure 6-7:
The completed Receive Payments window.

You can see a list of the customer payments you've recorded by clicking the Receive Payments List hyperlink or by clicking the Receive Payments icon and then choosing List.

Correcting Mistakes in Customer Payments Entries

You can correct mistakes you make in entering customer payments in basically the same way that you correct mistakes you make in entering cash sales.

First, you display the window you used to enter the transaction. In the case of customer payments, you click Receive Payments List hyperlink to display the Payments You've Received window (see Figure 6-8). Scroll through the list of payments (if you need) and then double-click the payment you want to edit. Then you make your changes. Then you click Save & Close. Pretty straightforward, right?

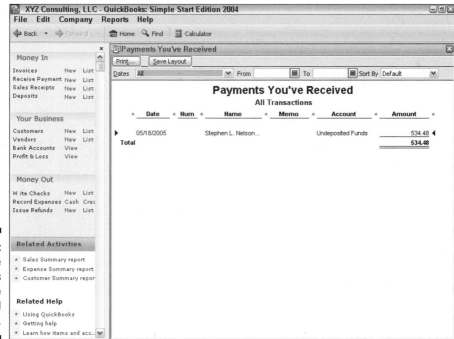

Figure 6-8: The Payments You've Received window.

In the Bank

Whenever you record a cash sale or a customer payment on an invoice, QuickBooks adds the cash to its list of undeposited funds. These undeposited funds could be a bunch of checks that you haven't yet deposited, or they could consist of currency and coins.

Eventually, though, you'll want to take the money out from under your mattress and deposit it in the bank. To do so, follow these steps:

1. **Click the Deposits New hyperlink.**

   Or, alternatively, click the Deposits icon and then choose New.

   The Payments to Deposit dialog box appears, as shown in Figure 6-9. This dialog box lists all the payments, regardless of the payment method. Amounts from sales receipts are listed as RCPT (such as the first transaction listed in Figure 6-9), and amounts from invoice payments are listed as PMT (such as the second transaction lists in Figure 6-9).

2. **Select the payments that you want to deposit.**

   Click a payment or cash receipt to place a check mark in front of it, marking it for deposit. If you want to deselect a payment, click it again. To deselect all the payments, click the Select None button. To select all the payments, click the Select All button.

3. **Click OK.**

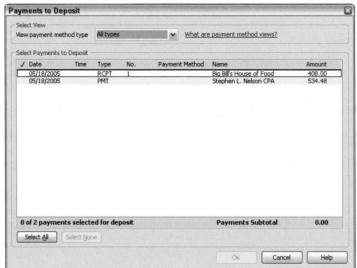

Figure 6-9:
The
Payments to
Deposit
dialog box.

After you indicate which payments you want to deposit, click OK. QuickBooks displays the Make Deposits window, as shown in Figure 6-10.

4. Tell QuickBooks into which bank account you want to deposit the money.

Activate the Deposit To drop-down list and select the bank account in which you want to place the funds.

5. Specify the deposit date.

Press Tab to move the cursor to the Date text box and type the correct date in MM/DD/YY format. Use the secret date-editing codes if you need to edit the date. (Get these codes from Chapter 4 or the Cheat Sheet at the front of the book if you don't know them.)

6. (Optional) Add a memo description, if you want.

I don't know what sort of memo description you would add for a deposit. Sorry. A bank deposit is a bank deposit. At least to me.

If you need to redisplay the Payments to Deposit dialog box — maybe you made a mistake or something, and now you need to go back and fix it — click the Choose Payments to Deposit button. Note, though, that QuickBooks won't display the Payments to Deposit dialog box unless the undeposited funds list still has undeposited payments in it.

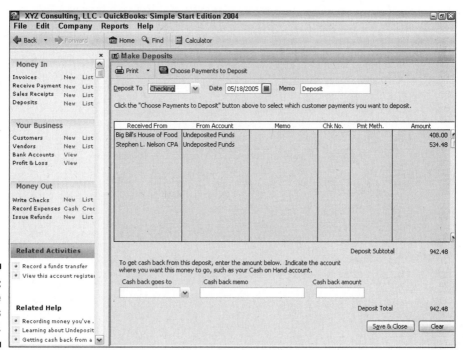

Figure 6-10:
The Make Deposits window.

7. **Specify the cash back amount.**

   If you want cash back from the deposit, activate the Cash Back Goes To drop-down list box and select a cash account. Then enter a memo in the Cash Back Memo text box and the amount of cash back you're taking in the Cash Back Amount text box.

8. **Record the deposit.**

   Click Save & Close.

Tracking What Your Customers Owe

You can track what a customer owes in a couple of ways. Probably the simplest method is by using the Customer Balances report. To do so, choose Reports➪Customer Balances. QuickBooks whips up a page that lists open invoices grouped by customer and recent payments received from the customer. Figure 6-11 shows the Customer Balances report.

QuickBooks also provides a nifty Invoices That Haven't Been Paid report. You produce this report by choosing Reports➪Invoices that haven't been paid (see Figure 6-12).

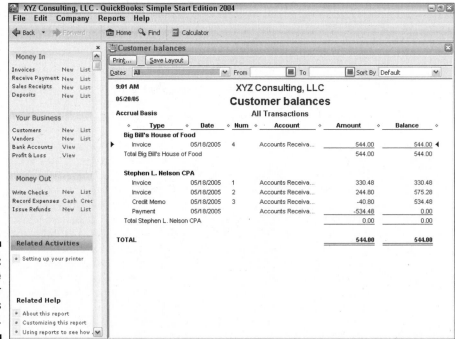

Figure 6-11: The Customer Balances report.

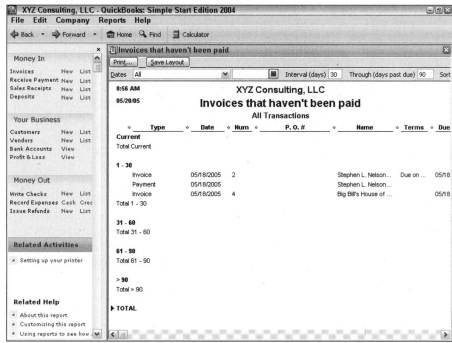

Figure 6-12:
The Invoices
That Haven't
Been Paid
report.

On the Invoices that haven't been paid report, QuickBooks groups invoices by age: current invoices, those due in the past 30 days, those due from 31 to 60 days ago, and so on.

In Chapter 13, I describe, in general terms, how you go about producing and printing QuickBooks reports. So see Chapter 13 if you have questions. You can't hurt anything or foul up your financial records just by displaying and printing reports. So go ahead and noodle around.

The full-fledged versions of QuickBooks include two useful tools for better managing the amounts that customers owe: a customer statements generator and a finance charge calculator. Customer statements are a handy way to remind forgetful customers or clients about overdue amounts. You don't, by the way, need to send statements to everybody or every month. In my CPA practice, I send out statements a couple of times a year to clients with past-due accounts. This friendly reminder always produces a handful of quick payments and friendly apologies. A finance charge calculator automatically calculates finance charges, creates finance charge invoices, and then adds finance charges to customer statements. Finance charges tend to improve your cash flow because some people will pay earlier just to avoid the charges. I mention this business about customer statements and finance charges because if you have a delinquent accounts problem, you might want to upgrade to QuickBooks or QuickBooks Pro.

A word of advice from an accountant

While I'm on the subject of tracking what your customers owe you, let me share a thought about collecting this money. You should have firm collection procedures that you follow faithfully. For example, as soon as an invoice is a week or so past due, it's very reasonable to place a friendly telephone call to the customer's accounts payable department and verify that the customer has received the invoice and is in the process of paying. You have no reason to be embarrassed because some customer is late in paying you! What's more, you might find out something surprising and essential to your collection. You might discover, for example, that the customer didn't receive the invoice. Or you might find out that something was wrong with the gizmo you sold or the service you provided.

As soon as an invoice is a month or so past due, you need to crank up the pressure. A firm letter asking that the customer call you to explain the past due amount is very reasonable — especially if the customer assured you only a few weeks ago that payment was forthcoming.

When an invoice is a couple of months past due, you need to get pretty serious. You'll probably want to stop selling the customer anything more because it's unclear whether you'll be paid. And you might want to start a formal collection process. (Ask your attorney about starting such a process.)

Chapter 7

Cash Management

• •

In This Chapter

▶ Writing checks from the Write Checks window

▶ Writing checks from the bank register

▶ Recording deposits

▶ Adding new bank accounts

▶ Voiding and deleting transactions

▶ Searching for transactions

• •

*Y*ou need to know how to handle your bank accounts in QuickBooks Simple Start. And that's what I describe in this chapter. Specifically, I cover how to record checks and enter other transactions directly into a bank account register, how to record deposits that aren't from customers, and how to handle account transfers.

Because I want to do right by you in this chapter, I also describe some of the tools that you'll want to use when you work with bank accounts, including the commands you use to set up additional bank accounts, the commands you use to clean up bank account registers by voiding or deleting bogus transactions, and the Find button, which you can use to search for specific transactions within a bank account.

Writing Checks

Chapter 5 shows you one way to write checks: by using the Write Checks window. But you can also write checks another way, and that is, directly from the bank account register. I'm going to briefly describe (again) how to use the Write Checks window . . . and then describe in more detail how you use the bank account register.

Writing checks from the Write Checks window

You can record handwritten checks and other checks that you want to print with QuickBooks Simple Start by describing the checks in the Write Checks window.

To write a check from the Write Checks window, follow these steps:

1. **Click the Banking View hyperlink.**

   Or click the Banking icon and choose View from the menu. QuickBooks Simple Start displays the Write Checks window, shown in Figure 7-1

2. **Click the Bank Account drop-down list at the top of the window and choose the account from which you want to write this check.**

   If you've set up multiple bank accounts, this step is really important and is something you should always check before you write a check.

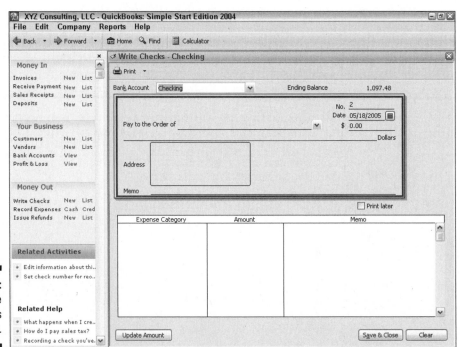

Figure 7-1: The Write Checks window.

3. **Enter a check number or mark the check for printing.**

   Select the Print Later check box if you plan on printing the check with QuickBooks Simple Start, using your printer and preprinted check forms that you've purchased. (I describe this process in Chapter 5.) If you're recording a check you wrote by hand, enter the check number you used for the check in the No. box.

4. **Fill in the check.**

   If you've written a check to this person or party before, the AutoFill feature fills in the name of the payee in the Pay to the Order Of line for you after you start typing the name. QuickBooks Simple Start compares what you've typed so far with names on your lists of customers, employees, and other names. As soon as QuickBooks Simple Start can match the letters you've typed with a name on one of these lists, it grabs the name.

   If you haven't written a check to this person or party before, QuickBooks Simple Start asks you to add the payee name to the Vendor List. Do that. (If you're not sure whether you want to add a payee or how to add a payee, refer to Chapter 3.)

   Enter the amount of the check next to the dollar sign and press Tab. QuickBooks Simple Start writes out the amount for you on the Dollars line. It also writes out the address if it has been filled out in the payee's master file.

5. **Fill in the Expense Category information.**

   Don't know what this is? Chapter 5 explains them in minute detail.

6. **Click Save & Close to finish writing the check.**

   There you have it. Your check is written, is entered in the bank account register, and is ready to be printed and mailed.

Recording a check into the Checking register

You can also use the register window to record checks you've written. The advantage of using the bank account register is that you can enter a bunch of transactions at one time — and even different sorts of transactions at one time. (Remember that when you record checks by using the Write Checks window, you kind of do so one check at a time.)

Paying for items with cash

To track petty cash purchases, you need a petty cash account. You can set up a petty cash account (which works just like a bank account) by following the steps in "Adding New Bank Accounts," later in this chapter. To record purchases you make from the money in that coffee can beside your desk, use the petty cash register. You can record cash purchases just as you record checks. (Of course, you don't need to worry about using the correct check numbers when you record cash purchases — you can just use the numbers 1, 2, 3, and so on.) To record cash withdrawals to be used for petty cash in the office, just record the withdrawal as a transfer to your petty cash account, as I describe later in the chapter.

To record a check by using the Checking register, follow these steps:

1. **Open the bank account register.**

   Click the Bank Accounts View hyperlink on the navigation bar, or click the Banking icon and choose View from the menu. If you have more than one bank account, QuickBooks Simple Start displays the Use Register dialog box (see Figure 7-2).

Figure 7-2:
The Use
Register
dialog box.

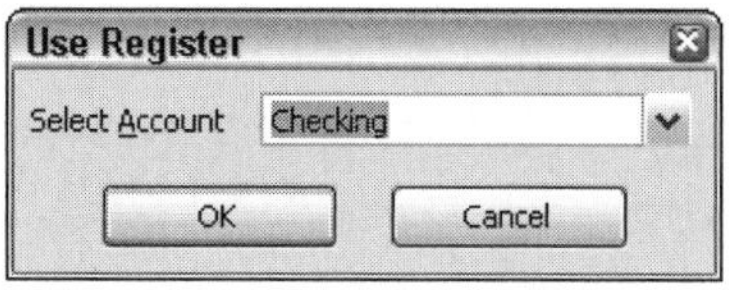

From the drop-down list, choose the checking account against which you want to write the check and click OK. You see the bank account register window. (See Figure 7-3.) The cursor is at the end of the register, ready for you to enter check information. (QuickBooks Simple Start automatically fills in the date.)

2. **Fill in the information for your check.**

   Notice that the entries you make in this register are the same ones that you would make in the Write Checks window. You just go from field to field and enter the information in the register. Again, use the drop-down lists to enter the Payee and Account names. If you enter a Payee or Account name that QuickBooks Simple Start doesn't recognize, the program asks you to give more information.

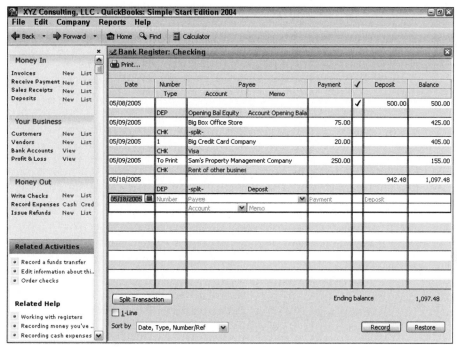

Figure 7-3:
The Bank
Register
window.

To split a check among several expense categories, click the Split
Transaction button.

3. Click Record.

If you write checks by hand as opposed to printing them with QuickBooks
Simple Start, make sure that the check numbers in the Checking register and
the check numbers in your checkbook match up. You might need to go into the
QuickBooks Simple Start bank account register and change numbers in the
Number column. When your bank statement comes, reconciling your bank
statement and your checkbook is much easier if you entered check numbers
correctly.

Changing a check that you've written

What if you need to change a check after you've already entered it? Perhaps
you made a terrible mistake, such as recording a $52.50 check as $25.20. Can
you fix it? Sure. Just go into the bank account register and find the check that

you want to change. Go to the Payment field and make the change. When you finish, click Record.

Packing more checks into the register

Usually, QuickBooks Simple Start displays two rows of information about each check register transaction — checks, deposits, and transfers — that you enter. If you want to pack more transactions into a visible portion of the register, select the 1-Line check box at the bottom of the bank account register window. When you select this check box, QuickBooks Simple Start uses a single-line format to display all the information in the register except the Memo field.

Compare Figures 7-3 and 7-4 to see what the 1-Line display looks like. Bank account registers can get awfully long, and the 1-Line display is helpful when you're looking through a long register for a check, deposit, or transfer.

Figure 7-4:
The Bank Register window when using the single-line display.

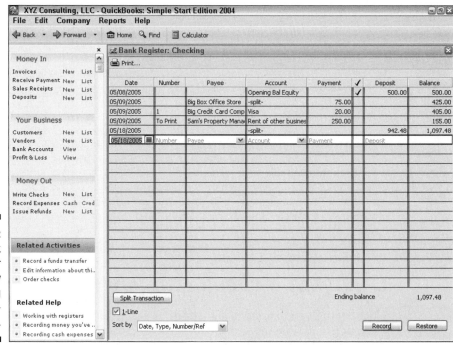

Depositing Money into a Checking Account

Although most of the deposits you make into a checking account get recorded automatically when you record a payment from a customer (see Chapter 6 for the dirty lowdown), you can also record deposits directly into a bank account register.

Why would do you record a deposit directly into the register? Well, first, you would not record a customer payment directly into the register. But not all your money comes from customers. You might, especially in the early stages of the business, be depositing personal funds into the business (to subsidize losses or to fund the start-up stage.) You will also occasionally receive payments from vendors, such as refunds and rebates.

If you have a simple deposit to make — again a sum of money that didn't come from one of your customers — here's how you record the deposit directly into the bank account register.

For example, suppose that your elderly Aunt Iris sends you $100 with a note explaining how, more than 80 years ago, Great-uncle Bert started his hammock manufacturing business with only $100, and for good luck, she's sending you $100 to help you along.

Recording deposit transactions

Recording a simple deposit is, well, pretty simple. Follow these steps:

1. **Open the bank account register.**

   Click the Bank Accounts View hyperlink. Or click the Banking icon and choose View from the menu. If you have more than one bank account, QuickBooks Simple Start displays the Use Register dialog box. Select the bank account into which you want to make the deposit and click OK. QuickBooks Simple Start displays the bank account register window. (Refer to Figure 7-3 or 7-4.)

2. **Enter the date on which you made the deposit in the Date column.**

3. **In the Payee column, enter the name of the person or business that sent you money.**

Don't worry if QuickBooks Simple Start adds a check number in the Number field when you move to the Payee column. When you enter a deposit amount, QuickBooks Simple Start changes the Number field to DEP (for deposit, of course).

4. **Enter the amount that you're depositing.**

Move the cursor to the Deposit column and enter the amount.

5. **Enter an account for this deposit.**

Move to the Account field, click the down arrow, and choose an account from the list. This is the only tricky step. Typically, you'll find yourself facing one of three situations:

- If you're receiving funds that represent an additional investment of capital, you select an owners equity account — something like "contributed capital" or "owner investments" to show that the money represents an additional contribution of capital. (Which account you use will depend on the type of entity you set up to operate the business.)

- If you're receiving funds that represent a refund of some expense you've previously paid, you select the expense account that needs to be adjusted.

- If you're receiving funds that represent some sort of miscellaneous, non-customer-related income (maybe interest income on a bank account), you select an income account — something like "interest income" or "sale of assets."

6. **Click the Record button.**

Your deposit is entered, and your bank account's balance is fattened accordingly. Note that all entries in the bank account register are made in chronological order, with deposits first and checks next.

You don't use the method described in the preceding paragraphs to record deposits of money that you receive from customers. See Chapter 6 for information about how to record those sorts of deposits.

Changing a deposit transaction that you've already entered

Changing a deposit transaction works just like changing a check. First, you find the deposit in the account register. Then you select it. Then you make your changes and click Record.

Adding New Bank Accounts

As soon as your business is stable and profitable, you'll probably want to set up additional bank accounts. You might want to set up a savings account or money market account, for example, to store excess cash someplace where it can earn interest. (Many business bank accounts don't pay interest, as you're probably painfully learning.) And you might have other reasons for wanting to set up a separate bank account. (Often businesses like to use a separate bank account for payroll checks, just to keep those funds separate.)

Fortunately, setting up new bank accounts is easy. Just follow these steps:

1. **Display the Chart of Accounts window.**

   Choose the Company⇨Lists⇨Chart of Accounts command. Alternatively, you can also press the secret key code combination for the Chart of Accounts command, which just happens to be Ctrl+A. QuickBooks Simple Start displays the Chart of Accounts window, which simply lists the accounts you've set up (or that QuickBooks Simple Start has set up) for your business (see Figure 7-5).

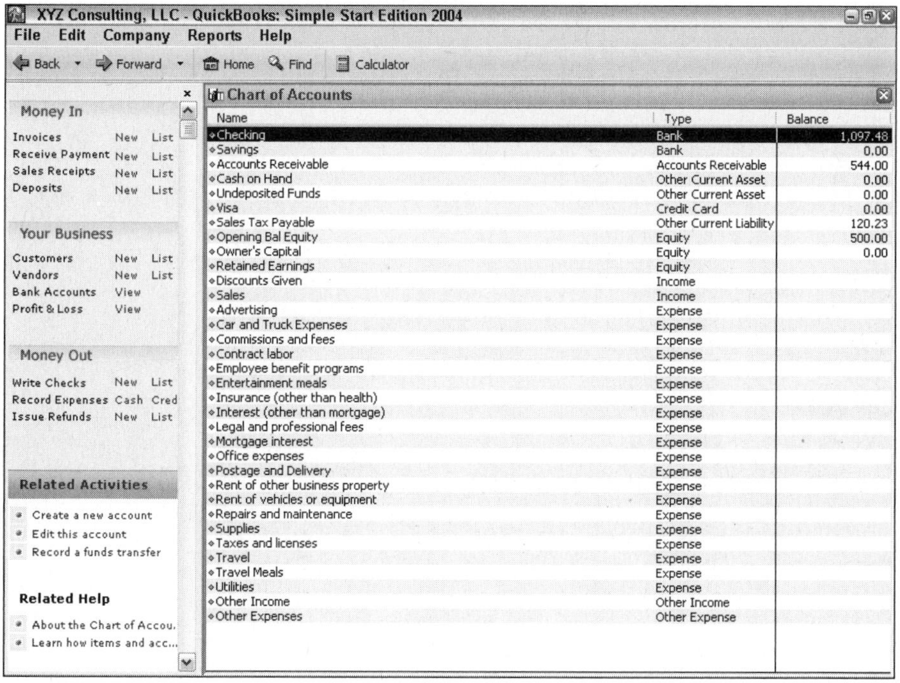

Figure 7-5:
The Chart of
Accounts
window.

2. Tell QuickBooks Simple Start you want to add a new account.

Right-click the Chart of Accounts window and choose New from the shortcut menu that appears. QuickBooks Simple Start displays the New Account window (see Figure 7-6).

3. Verify that Bank is shown in the Type drop-down list box.

If the Type drop-down list box doesn't show Bank, select Bank from the list box.

4. Name the account using the Account Name box.

In the pages of this book, I'm using names such as "Checking" and "Savings." But in real life, you might want to use actual bank names or even account numbers, especially if you've got a bunch of different bank accounts. Using descriptive names makes it easier for you to identify and choose the right bank account.

5. (Highly optional) Provide additional information.

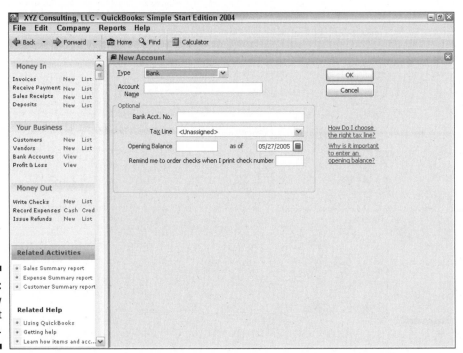

Figure 7-6:
The New Account window.

You can store the full bank account number in the Bank Acct. No. box, for example. You can also identify the tax form line on which this bank account gets reported (this is only relevant for larger corporations and partnerships — not sole proprietorships). You can even specify when QuickBooks Simple Start should remind you to order more checks by specifying a check number.

You don't want to enter an opening balance using the New Account window. That sloppy and ultimately destructive approach results in a one-sided entry that doesn't tell you where the cash actually came from: additional owner investment, a refund, some non-customer, and so on. If you have a bank account that you need to set up that does have a cash balance, use a deposit transaction to set the opening balance. See the earlier section, "Depositing Money into a Checking Account," for more information.

Transferring Money between Accounts

Account transfers occur when you move money from one account to another — for example, from your savings account to your checking account. But, jeepers, why am I telling you this? If you have one of those combined savings and checking accounts, you probably do this sort of thing all the time.

Oh, now I remember why I brought this up — QuickBooks Simple Start makes quick work of account transfers as long as you've already set up both accounts.

You record an initial transfer by completing the following steps:

1. **Display the bank account register for one of the accounts.**

   You know how to do this by now, right? Oh, what's that? The man in the back row wants a quick review? No problem. Click the Bank Accounts View link and choose the bank account from the Use Register dialog box. QuickBooks Simple Start displays the bank account register (see Figure 7-7).

2. **Enter the transfer date into the Date column.**

   By the way, all the usual date entry tricks work here, of course. See the Cheat Sheet for details.

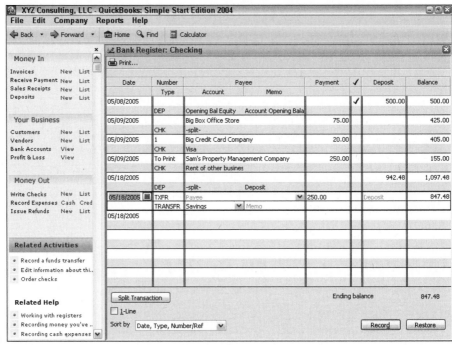

Figure 7-7:
The bank
register with
a transfer
transaction
selected.

3. **(Optional) Enter a short abbreviation for transfer into the Number column.**

   For fun, take a look back at what I did in Figure 7-7. See that? See how I entered TXFR?

4. **Leave the payee field blank.**

   There's no payee for a transfer, right?

5. **Specify the transfer amount.**

   If you're moving money from this account, enter the transfer amount into the Payment column. If you're moving money into this account, enter the transfer amount into the Deposit column.

6. **Identify the transfer account.**

   Use the Account box to specify the other account involved in the transaction. In Figure 7-7, for example, you can see I specify the transfer account as "Savings." That's the name of the other account.

7. (Optional but a good idea) Provide a memo description.

Someday, you'll wonder why you transferred this money. Filling in the Memo box solves this little mystery beforehand.

8. Click the Record button.

QuickBooks Simple Start records the transfer.

Here's the cool thing about transfer transactions: QuickBooks Simple Start automatically records the other half of the transfer for you. Figure 7-8 shows the other half of the transfer from Figure 7-7.

You can jump to the "other half" of a transfer transaction by selecting a transfer transaction and then choosing the Edit⇨Go To Transfer command.

Changing a transfer that you've already entered works just like changing a check or deposit. Find the transaction, make your changes, and click Record.

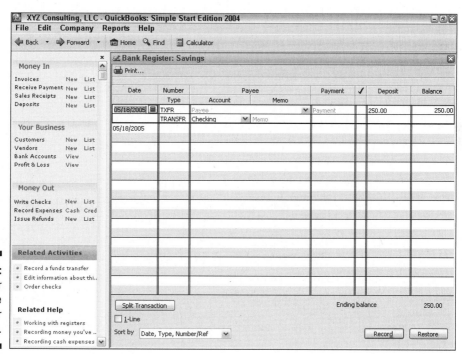

Figure 7-8: The other half of the transfer transaction.

To Delete or to Void?

What happens if you put a transaction — a deposit, a check, or a transfer payment — in a bank account register and later decide that it shouldn't be there? You have two ways of handling this situation. If you want to keep a record of the transaction but render it moot, meaningless, or nada, then you void the transaction. But if you want to obliterate the transaction from the face of the earth as though it never happened in the first place, you delete it.

Decide whether you want to void or delete the transaction and then follow these steps:

1. **Find the transaction in the register.**

   In the following section, I tell you some quick ways to find transactions.

2. **Choose either Edit⇨Delete Check or Edit⇨Void Check and click the Record button.**

   There, the deed is done. Figure 7-9 shows a bank account register window with a voided check. The voided transaction is the one selected. Notice the word VOID in the Memo column. If this check had been deleted, it wouldn't even show up in the register.

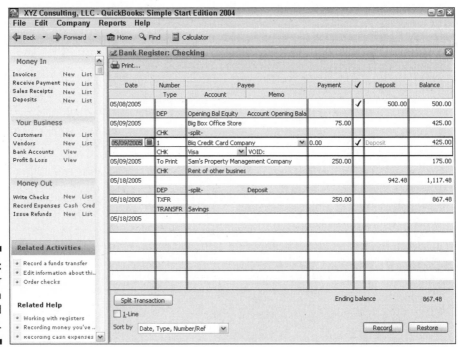

Figure 7-9: The register shows a voided check.

The Edit menu changes depending on what kind of transaction shows or is selected in the open window (that is, Void Deposit, Void Check, and so on).

The Big Register Phenomenon

If you start entering checks, deposits, and transfers into your registers, you soon find yourself with registers that contain hundreds, and even thousands, of transactions. You can still work with one of these big registers by using the tools and techniques that I talk about in the preceding paragraphs. Nevertheless, let me give you some more help for dealing with . . . (drumroll, please) . . . the big register phenomenon.

Moving through a big register

You can use the Page Up and Page Down keys to page up and down through your register, a screen full of transactions at a time. Some people call this activity *scrolling*. You can call it whatever you want.

You can also use the Home key to move through the register. Press the Home key once to move to the front of the field you're currently in. Press the Home key twice to move to the first field of the transaction you're on (the Date field), or press it three times to move to the first transaction in the register.

The End key works in a similar fashion. Bet you can guess how this works. Press the End key once to move to the end of the field you're in, press it twice to move to the last field of the transaction you're on (the Memo field), or press it three times to move to the last transaction in the register.

Of course, you can use the vertical scroll bar along the right edge of the bank account register, too. Click the arrows at either end of the vertical scroll bar to select the next or previous transaction. Click either above or below the square scroll box to page back and forth through the register. Or, if you have no qualms about dragging the mouse around, you can drag the scroll box up and down the scroll bar.

QuickBooks Simple Start lets you sort your register in different ways, which makes scrolling through and finding transactions much easier. To sort your register the way you prefer, choose an option from the Sort By drop-down list box in the lower-left corner of the bank account register window.

Finding that darn transaction

Want to find that one check, deposit, or transfer? No problem. I discuss this technique earlier in the book, but it's appropriate here, too. The Edit menu's Find command provides a handy way for doing just such a thing. Here's what you do:

1. **Click the Find button.**

   QuickBooks Simple Start, with restrained but obvious enthusiasm, displays the Find window (see Figure 7-10). You use this window to describe — in as much detail as possible — the transaction that you want to find by using the transaction type, customer or job name, date, number, and amount.

2. **Choose the type of transaction you're looking for.**

   Figure 7-10 shows the transaction type as Check, but you know what? You can use the Find window to look for just about any type of transaction.

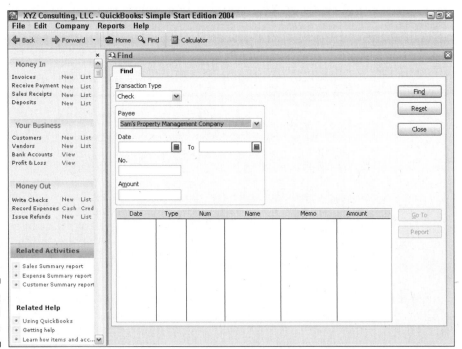

Figure 7-10:
The Find window.

3. **Specify the payee you're looking for.**

   You select a payee from the Payee drop-down list box.

4. **Select a range of dates if appropriate.**

   You make this selection, predictably, using the Date and To boxes. *Note:* These date boxes accept all those handy little date codes. Also note that you can click the tiny calendar button at the end of each box to display a pop-up calendar that you can use to select a date.

5. **Specify the transaction number.**

   For example, if you know which check number you want to find, specify the check number. (I guess obviously if you're looking for some other type of transaction, you don't use check numbers. If you're looking for invoices, for example, you probably use invoice numbers, right?)

6. **Describe the transaction amount.**

   Just enter the transaction amount into the Amount box.

7. **Let the search begin.**

   Click the Find button to begin looking.

   If QuickBooks Simple Start finds transactions that match the one you described, QuickBooks Simple Start lists them in the bottom half of the window.

Part III

Month-End and Year-End Routines

The 5th Wave   By Rich Tennant

"Great! Now that we're using QuickBooks Simple Start, we can find out where all the money around here is going."

In this part . . .

After you start using QuickBooks Simple Start, you need to complete some tasks at the end of every week, month, or year. This part describes these tasks: reconciling bank accounts, paying sales taxes, measuring your profits, assessing your financial condition. . . . The list goes on and on.

Chapter 8

The Balancing Act

I want to start this chapter with an important point: Balancing a bank account in QuickBooks Simple Start is easy and quick.

I'm not just trying to get you pumped up about an otherwise painfully boring topic. I don't think that balancing a bank account is any more exciting than you do.

My point is simply this: Because bank account balancing can be tedious and boring, use QuickBooks Simple Start to speed up the drudgery.

Balancing a Bank Account

Balancing a bank account is remarkably easy in QuickBooks Simple Start. In fact, I'll go so far as to say that if you have any problems, they stem from . . . well, sloppy recordkeeping that preceded your use of QuickBooks Simple Start.

Enough of this blather; I'll get started by describing how you reconcile a bank account.

Giving QuickBooks Simple Start information from the bank statement

As you probably know, in a *reconciliation,* you compare your records of a bank account with the bank's records of the same account. You should be able to explain any difference between the two accounts — usually by pointing to checks that you've written but that haven't cleared. (Sometimes deposits fall into the same category; you've recorded a deposit and mailed it, but the bank hasn't yet credited your account.)

The first step, then, is to supply QuickBooks Simple Start with the bank's account information. You get this information from your monthly statement. Supply QuickBooks Simple Start with the figures it needs, as follows:

1. **Tell QuickBooks Simple Start you want to reconcile an account.**

   You can do this by choosing Company⇨For Your Accountant⇨Reconcile. QuickBooks Simple Start displays the Begin Reconciliation dialog box, shown in Figure 8-1.

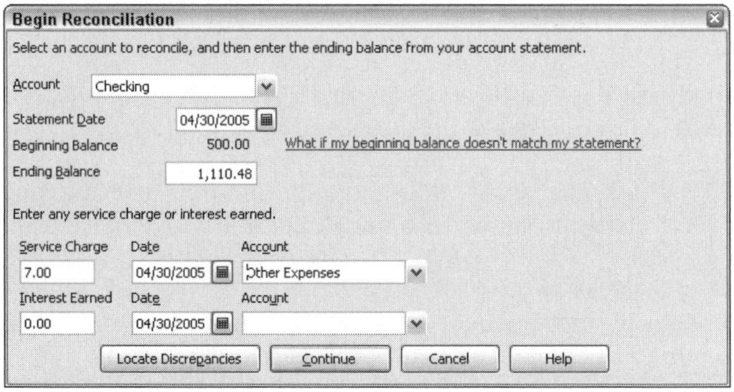

Figure 8-1:
The Begin Reconciliation dialog box.

2. **Tell QuickBooks Simple Start which account you want to reconcile.**

   Verify that the bank account shown in the Account list box is correct. If it isn't — and it might not be if you have several bank accounts — open the Account list box and select the correct account.

3. **Enter the bank statement date into the Statement Date box.**

   Remember that you can adjust a date one day at a time by using the plus (+) and minus (–) keys. You can also click the Calendar button on the right side of the text box to select a date from the calendar. See the Cheat Sheet at the front of this book for a list of other secret date-editing tricks.

4. **Verify the bank statement opening balance.**

   QuickBooks Simple Start displays an amount in the Beginning Balance text box. (Refer to Figure 8-1.)

If the opening balance isn't correct, see the sidebar "Why isn't my opening balance the same as the one in QuickBooks Simple Start?" elsewhere in this chapter.

5. Enter the ending balance.

What is the ending, or closing, balance on your bank statement? Whatever it is, move the cursor to the Ending Balance text box and enter the ending balance.

6. Enter the bank's service charge.

If the bank statement shows a service charge and you haven't already entered it, move the cursor to the Service Charge text box and type the amount.

7. Enter a transaction date for the service charge transaction.

QuickBooks Simple Start adds one month to the service charge date from the last time you reconciled. If this date isn't correct, type the correct one.

8. Assign the bank's service charge to an account.

Enter the expense account to which you assign bank service charges in the first Account text box — the one beside the Date text box. Activate the drop-down list by clicking the down arrow, highlight the category by using the arrow keys, and press Enter.

9. Enter the account's interest income.

If the account earned interest for the month and you haven't already entered this figure, type an amount in the Interest Earned text box (for example, type **9.17** for $9.17).

10. Enter a transaction date for the interest income transaction.

You already know how to enter dates. I won't bore you by explaining it again (but see Step 3 if you're having trouble).

11. Assign the interest to an account.

Enter the category to which this account's interest should be assigned in the second Account text box. I bet that you record this one under the interest Income account, which is near the bottom of the Account drop-down list. To select a category from the Account list, activate the drop-down list by clicking the down arrow, highlight the category, and press Enter.

12. Click Continue.

After you supply the information that the Begin Reconciliation dialog box asks for, click the Continue button. QuickBooks Simple Start displays the Reconcile window, shown in Figure 8-2.

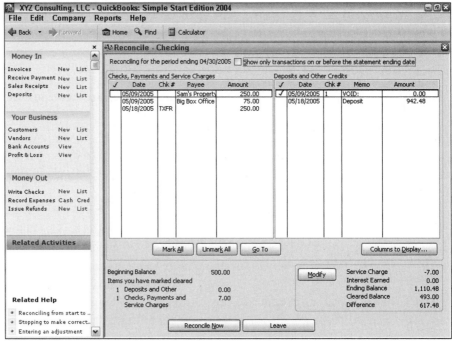

Figure 8-2:
The
Reconcile
window.

Marking cleared checks and deposits

Using the Reconcile window shown in Figure 8-2, you tell QuickBooks Simple Start which deposits and checks have cleared at the bank. (Refer to your bank statement for this information.)

1. **Identify the first deposit that has cleared.**

   You know how to do so, I'm sure. Just leaf through the bank statement and find the first deposit listed.

2. **Mark the first cleared deposit as cleared.**

   Scroll through the transactions listed in the Deposits and Other Credits section of the Reconcile window, find the deposit, and then click it. You also can highlight the deposit by using the Tab and arrow keys and then pressing the spacebar. QuickBooks Simple Start places a check mark in front of the deposit to mark it as cleared and updates the cleared statement balance.

If you have a large number of deposits to make and you can identify them quickly, click the Mark All button and then simply unmark the transactions that aren't on the bank statement. To deselect a transaction, click it. The check mark disappears.

3. **Record any cleared, but missing, deposits.**

   If you can't find a deposit, you haven't entered it into the Checking register yet. I can only guess why you haven't entered it. Maybe you just forgot. Close or deactivate the Reconcile window by clicking Leave. Now open the Checking register and enter the deposit in the register in the usual way. To return to the Reconcile window, either reopen it or reactivate it.

4. **Repeat Steps 1 through 3 for all deposits listed on the bank statement.**

   Make sure that the dates match and that the amounts of the deposits are correct. If they're not, go back to the transactions and correct them. To get to a transaction, click the Go To button. You see the Write Checks or Make Deposits window where the transaction was originally recorded. Make the corrections there and click Save & Close. You return to the Reconcile window.

5. **Identify the first check that has cleared.**

   No sweat, right? Just find the first check or withdrawal listed on the bank statement.

6. **Mark the first cleared check as cleared.**

   Scroll through the transactions listed in the Checks, Payments, and Service Charges section of the Reconcile window, find the first check, and then click it. You also can highlight it by pressing Tab and an arrow key. Then press the spacebar. QuickBooks Simple Start inserts a check mark to label this transaction as cleared and updates the cleared statement balance.

7. **Record any missing, but cleared, checks.**

   If you can't find a check or withdrawal — guess what? — you haven't entered it in the register yet. Close or deactivate the Reconcile window by clicking its Leave button or activating another window. Then display the Checking register and enter the check or withdrawal. To return to the Reconcile window, reopen or reactivate it.

8. **Repeat Steps 5 through 7 for all withdrawals listed on the bank statement.**

These steps don't take very long. Reconciling my account each month takes me about two minutes. And I'm not joking or exaggerating. By two minutes, I really mean two minutes.

If the difference equals zero

After you mark all the cleared checks and deposits, the difference between the Cleared Balance for the account and the bank statement's Ending Balance should equal zero (see Figure 8-3 for an example where everything is perfect). Notice, though, that I said "should," not "will." Oftentimes your records don't balance with the bank's.

If the difference does equal zero, you're finished. Just click the Reconcile Now button. QuickBooks Simple Start displays a congratulatory message box telling you that the reconciliation is complete. As a reward for being such a good boy or girl, the message box asks you whether you want to print a free, all-expenses-paid Summary or Full reconciliation report. Click Summary or Full and click OK if you want to print the report. Otherwise, just click OK.

Can't decide whether to print the reconciliation report? Unless you're a business bookkeeper or an accountant who is reconciling a bank account for someone else — your employer or a client, for example — you don't need to print the reconciliation report. All printing does is prove that you reconciled the account. (Basically, this proof is the reason why you should print the report if you're a bookkeeper or an accountant. The person for whom you're reconciling the account will know that you did your job and will have a piece of paper to come back to later with any questions.)

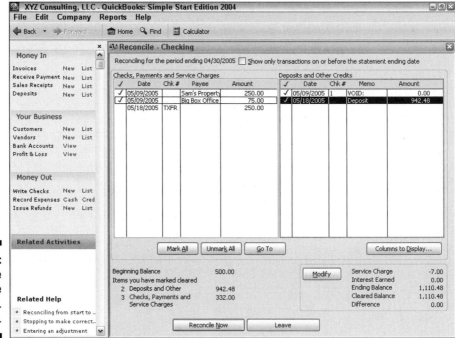

Figure 8-3:
The
Reconcile
window.
Again.

Why isn't my opening balance the same as the one in QuickBooks Simple Start?

An opening balance that isn't the same as the one shown in the Opening Balance text box can mean a couple of things.

First, you might have mistakenly cleared a transaction the last time you reconciled. If you cleared a transaction last month that didn't go through until this month, your opening balance is wrong. Go back to the Checking register and start examining transactions. Each one that's cleared has a check mark next to it in the narrow column between the Payment and Deposit columns. If one of the checks that appears on this month's statement has a check mark, you made a boo-boo last month. From the Checking register, click the check mark to remove it. You're asked to confirm

your actions. The check now appears in the Reconcile window.

The other reason why the opening balance is different can be that a transaction that you cleared in the past got changed. If you deleted a transaction that occurred before this reconciliation period, for example, it threw your balance off. Why? Because the transaction that you deleted helped balance your account the last time around, but now that transaction is gone.

Whatever happens, don't fret. If you can't track down the faulty transaction, you can just have QuickBooks Simple Start adjust the balance for you, which I explain elsewhere in this chapter.

Now each deposit, withdrawal, and check that you just cleared is marked with a check mark in your register. If you don't believe me, open the register and find out.

If the difference doesn't equal zero

If the difference doesn't equal zero, you have a problem. If you click Reconcile Now, QuickBooks Simple Start shows you the Reconcile Adjustment dialog box, shown in Figure 8-4. This dialog box tells you how unbalanced your account is and asks whether you want to adjust your maladjusted account.

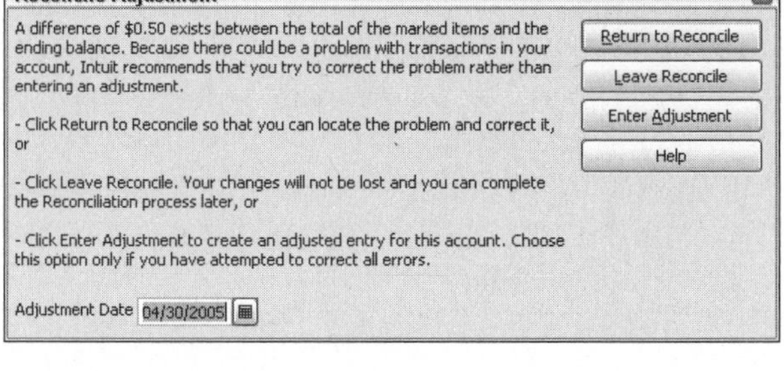

Figure 8-4: The Reconcile Adjustment dialog box.

Reconcile Adjustment

A difference of $0.50 exists between the total of the marked items and the ending balance. Because there could be a problem with transactions in your account, Intuit recommends that you try to correct the problem rather than entering an adjustment.

- Click Return to Reconcile so that you can locate the problem and correct it, or

- Click Leave Reconcile. Your changes will not be lost and you can complete the Reconciliation process later, or

- Click Enter Adjustment to create an adjusted entry for this account. Choose this option only if you have attempted to correct all errors.

Adjustment Date 04/30/2005

Return to Reconcile
Leave Reconcile
Enter Adjustment
Help

Click Return to Reconcile if you want to go back to the Reconcile window and start the search for the missing or incorrectly entered transaction.

If you want to force the two amounts to agree, click OK. Forcing the two amounts to agree isn't a very good idea. To do so, QuickBooks Simple Start adds a cleared transaction equal to the difference. (I talk about this transaction a little later in the chapter.)

Postponing a reconciliation (by clicking Leave Reconcile) and not choosing to adjust the bank account balance is usually the best approach because you can then locate and correct problems. (The following section contains some ideas that can help you determine what the problem is.) Then you can restart the reconciliation and finish your work. (You restart a reconciliation the same way that you originate one.)

Eleven Things to Do if Your Offline Account Doesn't Balance

I want to give you some suggestions for reconciling an account when you're having problems. If you're sitting in front of your computer wringing your hands, try the tips in this section:

- ✔ **Make sure that you're working with the right account.** Sounds dumb, doesn't it? If you have several bank accounts, however, ending up in the wrong account is darn easy. So go ahead and confirm, for example, that you're trying to reconcile your checking account at Mammoth International Bank by using the Mammoth International Bank checking account statement.

- ✔ **Look for transactions that the bank has recorded but you haven't.** Go through the bank statement and make sure that you've recorded every transaction that your bank has recorded. You can easily overlook cash machine withdrawals, special fees, or service charges (such as charges for checks or your safe-deposit box), automatic withdrawals, direct deposits, and so on.

  If the difference is positive — that is, the bank thinks that you have less money than you think that you should have — you might be missing a withdrawal transaction. If the difference is negative, you might be missing a deposit transaction.

- ✔ **Look for reversed transactions.** Here's a tricky one: If you accidentally enter a transaction backward — a deposit as a withdrawal or a withdrawal as a deposit — your account doesn't balance. And the error can be difficult to find. The Reconcile window shows all the correct transactions, but a transaction amount appears in the wrong list. (The amount appears in the Deposits, Interest, and Other Credits list if it belongs in the Checks, Payments, and Service Charges list, or vice versa.) The check that you wrote to Acme Housewreckers for the demolition of your carport appears in the Deposits, Interest, and Other Credits list, for example.

✓ **Look for a transaction that's equal to half the difference.** One handy way to find the transaction that you entered backward — if you have only one — is to look for a transaction that's equal to half the irreconcilable difference. If the difference is $200, for example, you might have entered a $100 deposit as a withdrawal or a $100 withdrawal as a deposit.

✓ **Look for a transaction that's equal to the difference.** While I'm on the subject of explaining the difference by looking at individual transactions, I'll make an obvious point: If the difference between the bank's records and yours equals one of the transactions listed in your register, you might have incorrectly marked the transaction as cleared or incorrectly left the transaction unmarked (shown as uncleared). I don't know. Maybe that was too obvious. Naaaah.

✓ **Check for transposed numbers.** Transposed numbers occur when you flip-flop two digits in a number. For example, you enter $45.89 as $48.59. These turkeys always cause headaches for accountants and bookkeepers. If you look at the numbers, detecting an error is often difficult because the digits are the same. For example, when you compare a check amount of $45.89 in your register with a check for $48.59 shown on your bank statement, both check amounts show the same digits: 4, 5, 8, and 9. They just show them in different orders.

Transposed numbers are tough to find, but here's a trick that you can try. Divide the difference shown in the Reconcile window by 9. If the result is an even number of dollars or cents, chances are good that you have a transposed number somewhere.

✓ **Use the Locate Discrepancies button.** Would you mind, terribly, taking a peek back at Figure 8-1? The dialog box shown in that figure includes a Locate Discrepancies button, which you can click to display another dialog box that prints reports that might help you reconcile your account. In particular, the dialog box lets you view a report of changes made to previously cleared transactions (which would be pretty suspicious bookkeeping activity and would definitely foul up your reconciliation). It also lets you view a report that lists transactions marked as cleared during previous reconciliations (which might be interesting because maybe you erroneously marked a transaction as cleared before it really was cleared).

✓ **Have someone else look over your work.** This idea might seem pretty obvious, but I'm amazed at how often a second pair of eyes can find something that I've been overlooking. Ask one of your coworkers or employees (preferably that one person who always seems to have way too much free time) to look over everything for you.

✔ **Be on the lookout for multiple errors.** If you find an error by using this laundry list and you still have a difference, start checking at the top of the list again. You might, for example, discover after you find a transposed number that you entered another transaction backward or incorrectly cleared or uncleared a transaction.

✔ **Try again next month (and maybe the month after that).** If the difference isn't huge in relation to the size of your bank account, you might want to wait until next month and attempt to reconcile your account again.

Before my carefree attitude puts you in a panic, consider the following example: In January, you reconcile your account, and the difference is $24.02. Then you reconcile the account in February, and the difference is $24.02. You reconcile the account in March and, surprise, surprise, the difference is still $24.02. What's going on here? Well, your starting account balance was probably off by $24.02. (The more months you try to reconcile your account and find that you're always mysteriously $24.02 off, the more likely that this type of error is to blame.) After the second or third month, I think that having QuickBooks Simple Start enter an adjusting transaction of $24.02 is pretty reasonable so that your account balances. (In my opinion, this circumstance is the only one that merits your adjusting an account to match the bank's figure.)

If you've successfully reconciled your account with QuickBooks Simple Start before, your work might not be at fault. The mistake might be (drumroll, please) the bank's! And in this case, you should do something else. . . .

✔ **Get in your car, drive to the bank, and beg for help.** As an alternative to the preceding idea — which supposes that the bank's statement is correct and that your records are incorrect — I suggest asking the bank to help you reconcile the account. Hint that you think the mistake is probably the bank's, but in a very nice, cordial way. Smile a lot. And one other thing — be sure to ask about whatever product the bank is currently advertising in the lobby (which encourages the staff to think that you're interested in that 180-month certificate of deposit, causing them to be extra nice to you).

In general, the bank's recordkeeping is usually pretty darn good. I've never had a problem either with my business or personal accounts. (I've also been lucky enough to deal with big, well-run banks.) Nevertheless, your bank quite possibly has made a mistake, so ask for help. Be sure to ask for an explanation of any transactions that you discover only by seeing them on your bank statement. By the way, you'll probably pay for this help.

A Few Words about Online Banking

In the realm of QuickBooks Simple Start, online banking means using your computer to transmit payment instructions to your bank (so that your bank, rather than you, writes a check) and using your computer to grab electronic versions of your bank statements.

Online banking isn't available in QuickBooks Simple Start. But it is available in the regular, more fully featured versions of QuickBooks such as QuickBooks Pro and QuickBooks Premium. And so I want to tell you something about online banking. Although a regular manual reconciliation is quick, as you've seen in the preceding paragraphs, online bank account reconciliations are even quicker. In an online banking situation, QuickBooks automatically matches transactions you've entered with transactions shown on the electronic version of your bank statement. Therefore, if you find that reconciling an account the usual way is too much work, you might, just might want to consider upgrading to QuickBooks Pro.

And that's all I have to say about that.

Chapter 9

Paying Sales Taxes

• •

In This Chapter

▶ Finding out how sales tax works

▶ Paying your sales tax bill

• •

A s you know or are now finding out, your state and local governments have a bunch of tasks they want you to perform. You are, after all, a business. Never mind that you make, create, or sell useful products or services. Never mind that you provide jobs. Never mind that economic growth rests on your shoulders — and those of your fellow small business brothers and sisters. Yes, in spite of all this, your state and local governments have one or two other, minor tasks for your "Honey Do" list. This short chapter describes how QuickBooks Simple Start helps with one such task: collecting and then remitting sales tax. More specifically, the chapter explains how sales tax accounting works in QuickBooks Simple Start. And then the chapter describes the steps for paying your sales tax bill.

How Sales Tax Works

If you understand how sales tax accounting works and how QuickBooks Simple Start handles sales tax accounting, skip ahead to the "Paying the Sales Tax Bill" section.

If you're a wee bit confused about how this sales tax stuff works, take the time to read through this short introductory discussion. I want to describe how sales tax is calculated and how QuickBooks Simple Start handles sales tax.

Calculating sales tax

As you might already know, your state and local governments probably levy sales taxes when businesses sell certain products and, in some cases, services. The tax is calculated as a percentage of the sale amount. For example, if you sell a $100 box of rocks and the sales tax percentage equals 8.8 percent, the sales tax amount equals $8.80 — $8.80 is 8.8 percent of $100.

Figure 9-1 shows an invoice where this calculation is made.

Okay, so far so good. In the paragraphs that follow, I make a handful of hopefully relevant observations about this calculation and how it's controlled.

Telling QuickBooks Simple Start you're subject to sales tax

When you set up QuickBooks Simple Start, you told it whether your firm is subject to sales tax, the sales tax percentage, and to whom you remit any sales tax you collect. (Whether you are or aren't subject to sales tax depends on your state and local governments' sales tax laws.)

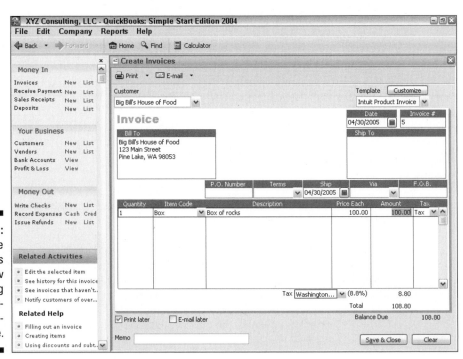

Figure 9-1: The Create Invoices window showing a subject-to-sales-tax sale.

If you goofed up that setup task, you can fix your mistake by choosing File⇨ Preferences to display the Preferences dialog box (see Figure 9-2). To specify whether you are or aren't subject to sales tax, mark the appropriate "yes" or "no" answer button for the question "Do you charge sales tax when you make a sale?" To specify to whom you remit sales tax, enter the tax agency name into the Tax Name box. To specify when you, technically speaking, owe the sales tax, select the Upon Receipt of Payment option or the As of Invoice Date option. (Often, you owe the sales tax liability when you invoice, and in that case you select the As of Invoice Date option. But you should check your local laws and not rely on some author who's talking only in gross generalities.)

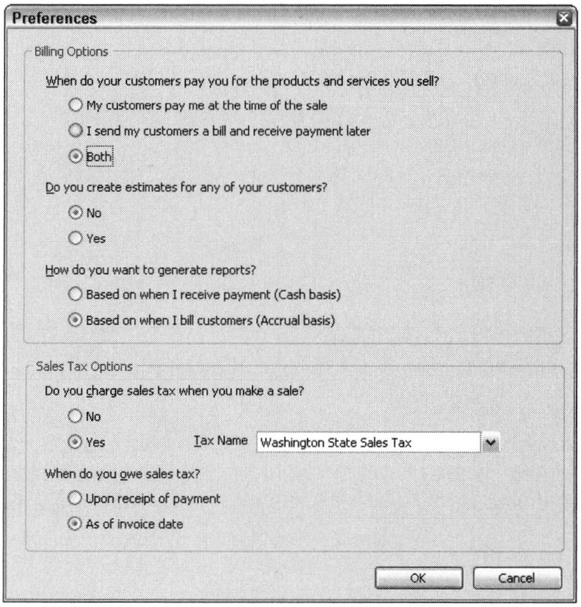

Preferences

Billing Options

When do your customers pay you for the products and services you sell?

○ My customers pay me at the time of the sale

○ I send my customers a bill and receive payment later

◉ Both

Do you create estimates for any of your customers?

◉ No

○ Yes

How do you want to generate reports?

○ Based on when I receive payment (Cash basis)

◉ Based on when I bill customers (Accrual basis)

Sales Tax Options

Do you charge sales tax when you make a sale?

○ No

◉ Yes   Tax Name Washington State Sales Tax

When do you owe sales tax?

○ Upon receipt of payment

◉ As of invoice date

[OK]   [Cancel]

Figure 9-2:
The
Preferences
dialog box.

Specifying the sales tax percentage

When you set up QuickBooks Simple Start, you specified what sales tax percentage you should pay when you record a sale subject to sales tax. But you can change the percentage if you made a mistake. To fix the sales tax rate, choose Company⇨Lists⇨Item List to display the Item List window. Then, right-click the sales tax item that's incorrectly set up and choose Edit from the shortcut menu that QuickBooks Simple Start displays. When QuickBooks Simple Start displays the Edit Item window, edit the percentage value shown in the Tax Rate box (see Figure 9-3).

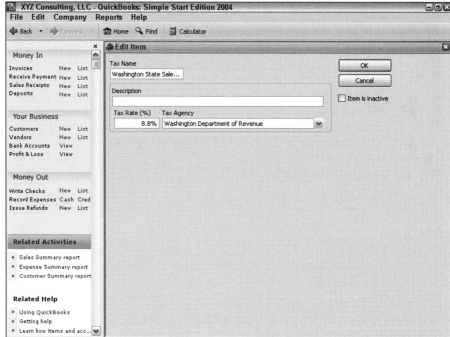

Figure 9-3:
The Edit
Item
window.

Flagging subject-to-tax sales

To tell QuickBooks Simple Start that some item shown on the invoice is
subject to tax, you select Tax from the Tax column. The Tax column appears
on the Create Invoices window. (Refer to Figure 9-1 for just a moment if you
wouldn't mind.)

Specifying a default sales tax rule for an item

You can tell QuickBooks Simple Start whether an item is or isn't usually
subject to sales tax. To do this, choose Company⇨Lists⇨Item List to display
the Item List window. Then, right-click the item that's incorrectly set up and
choose Edit from the shortcut menu that QuickBooks Simple Start displays.

When QuickBooks Simple Start displays the Edit Item window, make sure
that the code shown in the Tax Code box is correct (see Figure 9-4). If an item
is usually subject to tax, make sure the Tax Code box shows "Tax." If an item
usually is not subject to tax, make sure the Tax Code box shows "Non." I think
this is French for "No."

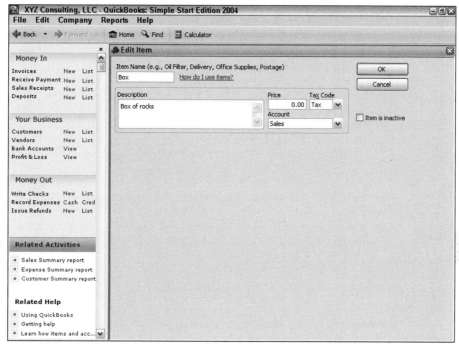

Figure 9-4:
The Edit
Item
window.
Yes, again.

Adding new sales tax items

If you want to add a new sales tax item to the Item List, you can. But you need to use a trick. Take another peek at the Create Invoices window shown in Figure 9-1. At the bottom of the window, notice the Tax drop-down list box. That shows the sales tax item used to calculate the sales tax for the invoice.

You can activate that drop-down list box and choose Add New. QuickBooks Simple Start then displays a New Item window for adding sales tax items to the Item List. This baby basically mirrors the Edit Item window, shown in Figure 9-3, so I'm not going to show it here as a figure. You use this New Item window to add additional sales items to the Item List.

If you have multiple sales tax items, you need make sure that the sales tax item used on an invoice is correct. You can do this by verifying that the sales tax item shown in the Tax drop-down list box is correct. If the sales tax item shown isn't correct, activate the drop-down list box and select the correct one.

Accounting for sales tax

You need to know how QuickBooks Simple Start accounts for sales tax. Look back at Figure 9-1 again.

See how the invoice total equals $108.80, but $8.80 of that is sales tax? QuickBooks Simple Start only counts as income the $100. In other words, it excludes the sales tax from your revenue totals. If you run an income statement for the day of the sale and no other invoices were created on that day, the income statement report shows total income equal to $100 (see Figure 9-5).

I discuss income statements and how to produce them in Chapter 11. So don't start thinking, "Income statements? What the heck! Did I miss something in this chapter? !#%#@" But, just so you know, to produce an income statement report like the one shown in Figure 9-5, you choose Reports⇨ Accountant Reports⇨Profit & Loss Standard.

So, the $8.80 question is "Where's the beef?" Or, restated in technical sales tax accounting terms, "What happens to that $8.80 of sales tax?"

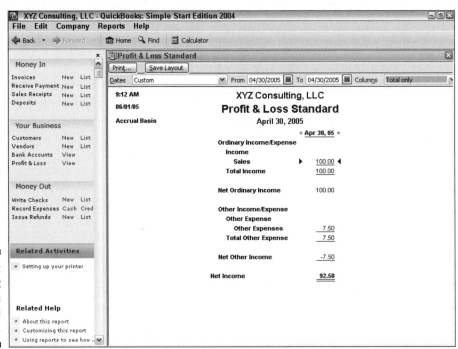

Figure 9-5:
A Profit
& Loss
Standard
report.

The answer goes like this: That sales tax, at some point, becomes a liability of the business. And liabilities, as you might know already or as you can find out from the appendix, appear on the balance sheet.

Figure 9-6 shows a balance sheet report at the day of the sale the invoice shown in Figure 9-1 was recorded. If you look down to the LIABILITIES & EQUITY section, you can see an area of the balance sheet report labeled, "Current Liabilities." Dig a little deeper into the details of this report, and you'll see an Other Current Liabilities amount equal to $8.80. There's your sales tax liability.

I discuss balance sheets and how to produce them in Chapter 11. To produce a balance sheet like the one shown in Figure 9-6, you choose Reports➪ Accountant Reports➪Balance Sheet Summary.

By the way, truly obsessive readers might also want to note that the accounts receivable balance shown in the balance sheet in Figure 9-6 appears as $108.80. That includes both the amount the business will get (the $100 for the box of rocks item shown in Figure 9-1) and the $8.80 of sales tax that the business will collect but owes to the tax agency.

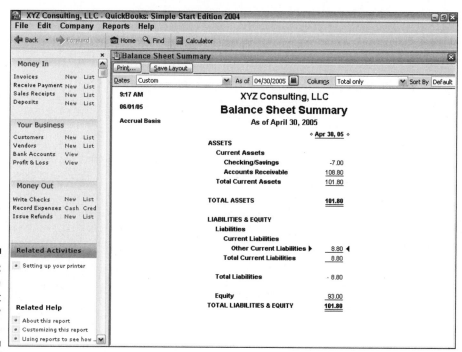

Figure 9-6:
The Balance
Sheet
Summary
report.

Paying the Sales Tax Bill

Periodically, perhaps monthly or quarterly, you remit the sales tax amounts you've collected or will collect to the appropriate tax agency. (The tax agency tells you how often you must make this payment. You don't, for example, do it according to your own ideas or accounting schedule.)

Payment mechanics

To remit sales tax amounts, you follow these steps:

1. **Tell QuickBooks Simple Start you want to remit.**

   Choose the Company⇨Pay Sales Tax command. QuickBooks Simple Start displays the Pay Sales Tax dialog box (see Figure 9-7).

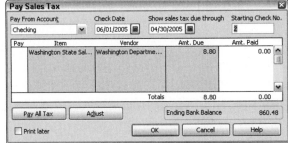

Figure 9-7:
The Pay
Sales Tax
dialog box.

2. **Choose a bank account for making the payment.**

   To do this, select a bank account from the Pay From Account dialog box.

   If sales taxes add up to a big number relative to your profits or cash, you might want to use a separate bank account to segregate your sales tax collections. The "separate accounts" approach might make it easier to come up with money needed to pay your sales tax. With a separate sales tax account, for example, you might be less likely to spend the sales tax money on business or personal expenses.

3. **Specify the check date.**

   You can figure this one out yourself, right? All you need to do is enter the check date into the Check Date box.

4. **(Important!) Specify the "as of" date for the sales tax liability.**

   Use the Show sales tax due through box to specify the date as of which you want to calculate the sales tax liability and, presumably, pay the liability owed. For example, if you're paying the liability you owed as of the end of April, you might enter April 30th into the Show Sales Tax Due Through box.

5. **Give a check number.**

If you haven't yet guessed it, QuickBooks Simple Start is actually going to record and possibly write a check to pay your sales tax bill. So some of the information that it's collecting is data needed to write the check. The check number is one such bit of check-writing information.

6. **Identify the sales tax liabilities you'll pay.**

Select the listed sales tax liabilities you want to pay by clicking them with the mouse. QuickBooks Simple Start places a check mark in front of sales tax liabilities.

7. **(Optional and perhaps dangerous) Adjust the amount.**

QuickBooks Simple Start assumes that you want to pay the entire sales tax liability — which is probably correct — but you can click the Adjust button to display the Sales Tax Adjustment dialog box (see Figure 9-8). To use this dialog box, you select the tax agency from the Sales Tax Vendor drop-down list box, specify the account that QuickBooks Simple Start should use to record the adjustment transaction using the Adjustment Account box, as appropriate mark either the Increase Sales Tax By or Reduce Sales Tax By buttons, and then enter the adjustment amount into the Amount text box.

When you adjust the sales tax liability owed to some tax agency, you're essentially saying that either the starting balance you set for the liability is wrong (which is quite possible) or that the sales tax amount that QuickBooks Simple Start has calculated for your invoices is wrong (which is quite unlikely if you've carefully set up QuickBooks Simple Start). For this reason, you want to be very careful when fooling around with the sales tax liability adjustment stuff. For example, if QuickBooks Simple Start is incorrectly calculating sales tax, you need to fix the bad inputs that are causing the incorrect outputs.

Figure 9-8:
The Sales
Tax
Adjustment
dialog box.

Further, note, too, that you want to think carefully about the appropriate adjustment account to use. (QuickBooks Simple Start actually adjusts two accounts when you adjust sales tax liability — the actual sales tax liability account and the offsetting debit or credit to balance the liability adjustment.) If you're adjusting the sales tax liability for an incorrect starting balance, you might be able to adjust an owners equity account. If you're adjusting the sales tax liability for any other reason, however, you'll want to adjust an income or expense account. (An old accountant's trick, by the way, is to flush your adjustment through a large expense account like cost of goods sold so that any effect is muted.)

8. **Indicate whether you want to print the check.**

   To print the check with QuickBooks Simple Start, select the Print Later check box.

   For information on how to print regular old checks refer to Chapter 5.

9. **Click OK.**

   QuickBooks records the check that pays the sales tax liability and adjusts the sales tax liability balance accordingly. Figure 9-9 shows the bank account register after I've recorded a check to pay the $8.80 of sales tax liability accrued because of that crazy transaction I showed you at the beginning of the chapter in Figure 9-1. It's a lot of work for $8.80, isn't it?

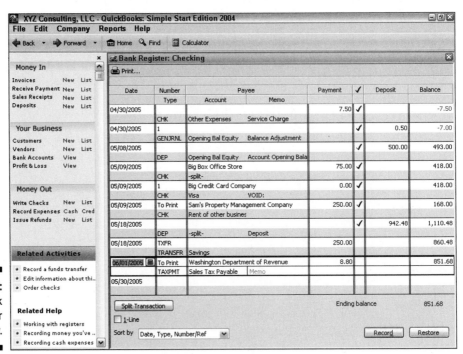

Figure 9-9: The bank register window.

If you told QuickBooks Simple Start that you will print a check later, you need to remember to do that. Refer to Chapter 5 for the gory details.

Sales tax returns

Can I make a brief but hopefully obvious point as I close this chapter? You don't simply send in a check to the state or local government tax agency with, for example, a sticky note that says, "Hi guys, here's my sales tax payment for the month."

You will need to prepare and file a sales tax return. The sales tax return reports your sales for the reporting period (probably a month or a quarter) and the sales taxes you should have collected. It's this amount — the sales taxes that you should have collected — that you'll need to remit. Fortunately, the sales tax amount shown on the sales tax return will agree with your QuickBooks Simple Start record if you've set up your sales tax calculations correctly.

Chapter 10

Measuring Your Profits

*I*n my opinion, this chapter is the most important one in the book. Here's why: If you're going to operate a small business, you absolutely must know whether you're making a profit or incurring a loss. And this short chapter explains how, in QuickBooks Simple Start, you measure your profits (or, ugh, your losses).

Closing the Accounting Period

Most of the data entry that you need to do in order to measure profits or losses occurs naturally. If you write a check to pay a bill, for example, you indirectly record the expense the bill pays. And if you produce an invoice or enter a sales receipt, you record the income the business earns from the sale.

However, in order to accurately (or more accurately) measure your profits or losses, you should typically perform some end-of-accounting-period accounting. For reasons having to do with the mechanics of old manual accounting systems, this process is called "closing the books" or "closing the month" or "closing the year."

I want to briefly describe the stuff you should do in QuickBooks Simple Start to "close the books" and thereby get a more accurate measurement of the profits or losses for the accounting period.

Step 1: Get caught up on your invoicing

This seems like an obvious point, I guess, but in order to accurately measure your income for a month or year, you have to enter all of the invoices and sales receipts for the month or for the year.

This probably makes sense, right? QuickBooks Simple Start totals all the invoices and sales receipts for a month to get the month's income. QuickBooks Simple Start totals all the invoices and sales receipts for a year to get the year's income.

So, Step 1 is to get caught up on your invoicing and the recording of any sales receipts.

Step 2: Get caught up on your bill paying

Another obvious point: In order to accurately measure your expenses, you have to enter all the checks and credit card charges for the month or year. QuickBooks Simple Start totals all your checks and charges for a month in order to get the month's expenses. It also totals all the checks and charges for a year to get the year's expenses.

Step 3: Reconcile the bank accounts

The third step you should probably take to close an accounting period is reconciling your bank accounts for the month or year. All of them.

I describe the mechanics of reconciling your bank accounts in Chapter 8, so I won't repeat that discussion here. But let me make a quick point about the importance of bank account reconciliations and profit calculations: By reconciling your bank accounts, you tend to catch errors that you've made in recording deposits and withdrawals. Because most deposits affect income and most withdrawals affect expenses, when you catch (and then fix) deposit and withdrawal errors, you fix the related income and expense errors.

Step 4: Record any special transactions

This fourth and final step is sort of a catchall, but if there are other special transactions that need to get recorded in order to fairly tally income and expenses for a month, you need to record those transactions, too.

"Special transactions?" you say. "How the heck am I supposed to know what these are?"

Actually, I don't want to be argumentative, but I think you probably can identify what these other transactions are. For example, are there assets that you've purchased and which, therefore, need to be depreciated? In that case, you need to record (or you need to get your accountant to record) depreciation expense transactions. And an amortization expense (you might be recording this if you purchased intangible assets for your business) needs to be handled in roughly the same way as depreciation.

If you've sold some asset at a gain or loss, you need to record (or you need to get your accountant to record) the gain or loss on the sale as well as the actual disposal.

If you're carrying inventory, you need to (at least at year-end) make an adjustment so that the QuickBooks Simple Start inventory balance matches the results of a physical count of your inventory.

You can usually get help from your accountant. Typically, CPAs figure out which special transactions need to be recorded to "close the books" simply as part and parcel of preparing a business's tax return.

If you have questions about how to handle inventory accounting, refer to Chapter 17.

Producing the Profit and Loss Statement

After you close the accounting period (as described in the preceding section), you're ready to produce a profit and loss statement. Here are the steps you follow:

1. **Tell QuickBooks Simple Start you want to produce a profit and loss statement.**

   Choose the Company⇨Accountant Reports⇨Profit & Loss Standard command. QuickBooks Simple Start displays the Profit & Loss Standard report in the report window (see Figure 10-1).

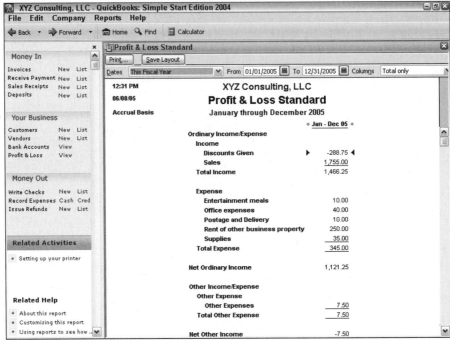

Figure 10-1:
The Profit
& Loss
Standard
report.

2. Verify the reporting interval.

Take a peek at Figure 10-1 again. See the Dates box? That box controls the time period for which QuickBooks Simple Start measures your profits. You can open the Dates drop-down list box to see the available reporting options. But the list of reporting options is pretty predictable: this month, last month, this fiscal year, last fiscal year, and so on. If you don't see a reporting interval that matches the period for which you want to calculate profits, you can also specify a range of dates using the From and To boxes.

The "fiscal year" is just the accounting year you use to measure annual profits. Small businesses, including sole proprietorships, partnerships, LLCs and S corporations usually use a fiscal year that matches the calendar year. Large businesses (and especially C corporations) often use a fiscal year that doesn't match a calendar year. For example, a big corporation might use a fiscal year that runs from July 1 through June 30.

3. (Optional) Describe the reporting columns you want.

Normally, you'll just want to see income and expense totals for the reporting period you've selected. This is what I did for Figure 10-1, for example. You can, however, break the income and expense data down using some other classification method. To do this, open the Columns drop-down list box (this box appears in the upper-right corner of the report window) and choose the method you want to use to further analyze the data. The Columns drop-down list box lets you view the data using shorter reporting intervals (by the day, the week, for two-week intervals, so on), by customer, vendor, item, and so on. For fun, I show a Profit & Loss Standard report with customer columns in Figure 10-2.

Many of these Column options — such as the "columns by class" or "columns by customer:job" — don't make much sense in QuickBooks Simple Start because QuickBooks Simple Start doesn't let you break down the data into the hinted-at columns. Why does QuickBooks Simple Start provide such "Column" options then? That's a good question and one that I don't know the answer to. But it's probably because the fully-featured versions of QuickBooks do let you work at these more granular levels of detail.

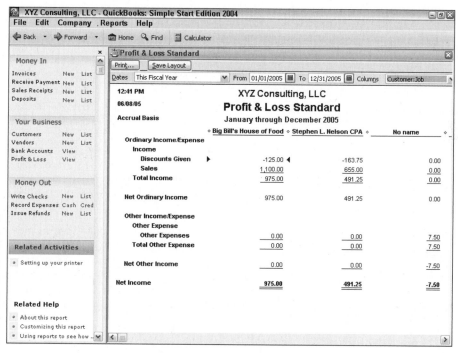

Figure 10-2:
The Profit
& Loss
Standard
report with
columns for
customers.

If you add columns to the Profit & Loss Standard report, you'll almost surely need to use the report window's scroll bars to move the report around within the report window.

4. **Verify the accounting method.**

   When you set up QuickBooks Simple Start — perhaps assisted by my instructions in Chapter 1 — you indicated to QuickBooks Simple Start whether you wanted reports prepared on an accrual basis or on a cash basis. It identifies the accounting method used in the upper-left corner of the report window. Therefore, you should briefly verify that QuickBooks Simple Start uses the right accounting method. If QuickBooks Simple Start isn't using the right accounting method, choose File➪Preferences. When QuickBooks Simple Start displays the Preferences dialog box (see Figure 10-3), change your answer to the How Do You Want to Generate Reports? question.

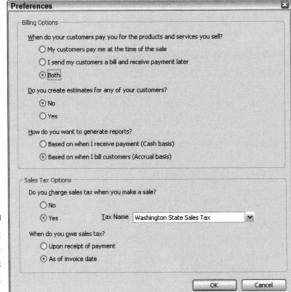

Figure 10-3:
The
Preferences
dialog box.

The difference between accrual-basis and cash-basis reports in QuickBooks Simple Start boils down to a single feature: When revenue from invoiced amounts is counted. With accrual-basis accounting, QuickBooks Simple Start counts revenue when you invoice some amount. With cash-basis accounting, QuickBooks Simple Start counts revenue when you collect the previously invoiced amount. For all practical purposes, no other differences exist between accrual-basis and cash-basis accounting in QuickBooks Simple Start.

5. **Print your profit and loss report.**

To print a copy of your profit and loss report, click the Print button (which appears in the upper-left corner of the report window). QuickBooks Simple Start might display a message that tells you it'll do a bang-up job of printing — in which case you need to click the "OK now stop bugging me" button. QuickBooks Simple Start eventually displays the Print Reports dialog box (see Figure 10-4).

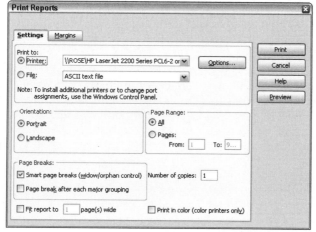

Figure 10-4:
The Print
Reports
dialog box.

If you truly need blow-by-blow descriptions of the steps for using the Print Reports dialog box, check out Chapter 12. If you just want to print a report, however, click the Print button. QuickBooks Simple Start then prints you a hard copy of the profit and loss statement.

For many small businesses, all the information you need to prepare your profit and loss statement can come right off of the Profit & Loss Standard report.

6. **(Optional) Save your report layout.**

If you want, you can click the Save Layout button to tell QuickBooks Simple Start that the next time you produce the Profit & Loss Standard report that you want it to look the same way. The next Profit & Loss Standard report will use the same reporting interval and the same column setting.

7. (Not optional) Save the hard copy report.

I am not someone who thinks you need to hoard accounting documents. Most of the reports you produce with QuickBooks Simple Start can be discarded (or, better yet, shredded) after you produce and view them. But absolutely you want to save paper copies of your annual Profit & Loss Standard reports. The annual reports explain the numbers on your tax returns. You probably also want to save paper copies of your monthly or quarterly Profit & Loss Standard reports because these reports probably explain the numbers on your sales tax returns.

Reviewing Profit and Loss Statements

A while back — oh, say 20 years ago — I would have been inclined to end this chapter after the preceding paragraph. My thinking would have gone something like this: Well, the reader has now read how to generate a profit and loss statement and that's as good a place as any to leave them and jump on to the next topic.

But a couple of decades of working in and with small businesses have changed me. In the following sections, I share some thoughts on how you should review the profit and loss statement and throw out one or two ideas about how you can use the information provided in the profit and loss statement.

Auditing the numbers

Here's my first thought about reviewing the profit and loss statement. I think that your very first step should be to take a critical look at the numbers, especially the total revenue, the total expenses, and the bottom-line profit figure.

Do they all make sense? Are they what you expect? For example, if it's been a good month or year, sales should probably be up as compared to last year, right? If it's been a really tough year, you might expect to see sales down, expenses up, and very possibly, a nasty loss.

I'm not going to spend a bunch of time on this subject, but especially in a small business, you should be able to eyeball your profit and loss report and know, at a gut level, whether it makes sense or not.

If the report doesn't make sense, you've got errors in your data and you'll need to fix those errors so you can rely on the report.

QuickZooming individual numbers

One helpful tool provided by QuickBooks Simple Start is QuickZoom. If you point to a number on a report and QuickBooks Simple Start turns the mouse-pointer into a magnifying glass with a kooky "Z" on it, you can double-click the number to see a QuickZoom report.

Take a peek at the report shown in Figure 10-5, for example. Suppose that the number reported as the sales for the year, $1,105, seems suspicious.

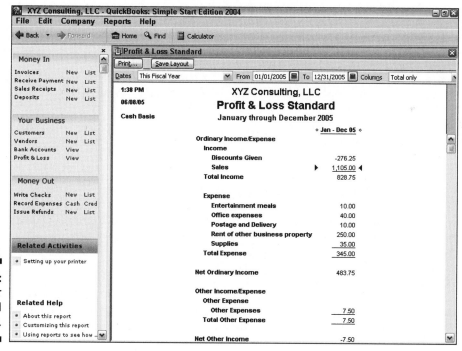

Figure 10-5:
Another profit and loss report.

By double-clicking that number, QuickBooks Simple Start displays a QuickZoom report that lists all of the individual transactions that make up the total (see Figure 10-6).

You can even QuickZoom a number on a QuickZoom report, and in that case, QuickBooks Simple Start typically displays the transaction that supplies the number (see Figure 10-7).

QuickZoom lets you double-check report values, find errors, and increase your understanding of the information shown in a report. In short, QuickZoom rocks.

If during your auditing of reports or your QuickZooming you find errors, you'll need to fix them. Obviously. To do that, you use the same window that you used to originally enter the transaction that was incorrectly entered.

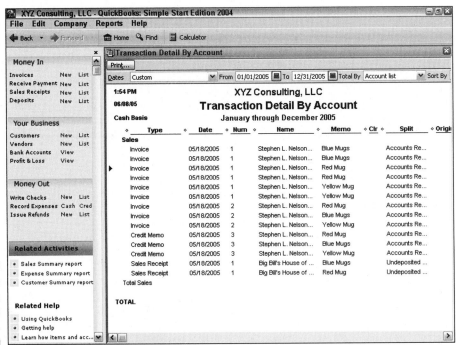

Figure 10-6:
A
QuickZoom
report.

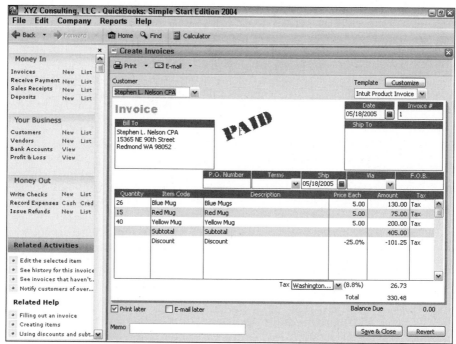

Figure 10-7:
QuickZoom
ultimately
takes
you to the
transaction.

Benchmarking

I want to close with a final but important point.

You can and should compare your profit and loss statement to other firms in your industry. By knowing how much similar firms make and spend, you can plan appropriately. And you'll have a much better understanding of what you're doing right and of what you're doing wrong. (Hey, seriously, stop and think about this for a minute: Wouldn't you just *love* to know what your competitors spend on advertising or salaries or rent? And wouldn't it be super-useful to really know what firms like yours make?)

Okay, so I've convinced you that this benchmarking sounds pretty good. Who wouldn't want to know this stuff? But what's a guy supposed to do? Break into competitors' offices? Well, fortunately, you don't have to do anything that Tony Soprano-ish. You can probably get such info either right online (if you've got an Internet connection) or at your local public library.

First stop: The Internet

Your first stop should be a visit to the BizStats.com Web site (www.bizstats.com), shown in Figure 10-8. You can find tons of interesting business statistics about businesses just like yours. Figure 10-8 shows the home page for the BizStats.com Web site. (To use the site, you select your industry from the list box and enter your revenue into the text box.) Figure 10-9 shows an example profit and loss statement for a small CPA firm. Hmmm. That's interesting. I think I better compare my advertising to the averages.

Second stop: The local library

You can also often get great information at your local public library. You can, for example, ask for the RMA (Risk Management Association) survey, the Dun & Bradstreet survey, or the Troy's survey. All of these resources are useful.

- ✔ The **RMA** surveys bank-lending officers, creates a summary of the information these bankers receive from their customers, and publishes the results.

- ✔ **Troy** (who's actually a business Ph.D.) collects Internal Revenue Service data and publishes the same sort of financial results.

- ✔ **Dun & Bradstreet** collects and summarizes its own proprietary financial information.

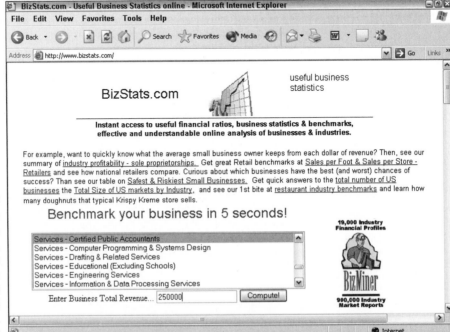

Figure 10-8: The BizStats. com Web site is a great site for small businesses.

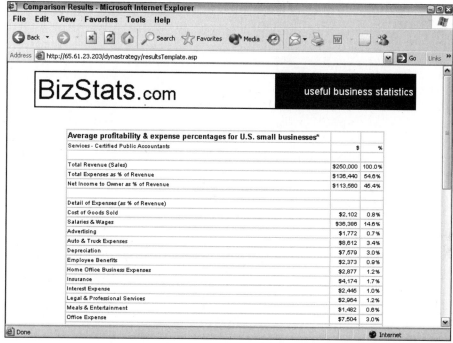

Figure 10-9:
An example
profit and
loss state-
ment from
the Biz
Stats.com
Web site.

The figure shows a browser window titled "Comparison Results - Microsoft Internet Explorer" displaying the BizStats.com Web site with the following table:

Average profitability & expense percentages for U.S. small businesses*

Services - Certified Public Accountants	$	%
Total Revenue (Sales)	$250,000	100.0%
Total Expenses as % of Revenue	$136,440	54.6%
Net Income to Owner as % of Revenue	$113,560	45.4%
Detail of Expenses (as % of Revenue)		
Cost of Goods Sold	$2,102	0.8%
Salaries & Wages	$36,386	14.6%
Advertising	$1,772	0.7%
Auto & Truck Expenses	$8,612	3.4%
Depreciation	$7,579	3.0%
Employee Benefits	$2,373	0.9%
Home Office Business Expenses	$2,877	1.2%
Insurance	$4,174	1.7%
Interest Expense	$2,446	1.0%
Legal & Professional Services	$2,964	1.2%
Meals & Entertainment	$1,482	0.6%
Office Expense	$7,504	3.0%

In each of the mentioned surveys, you can get really useful information about what businesses like yours spend, make, and own. For example, you can look up what percentage of sales the average tavern spends on beer and peanuts, the average profit your CPA makes, and the sales a car dealership generates. (Isn't that all kind of interesting stuff?)

Neither the BizStats.com Web site nor the aforementioned surveys actually has a line on the tavern's page labeled "beer and peanuts." It'll be called "cost of goods sold" or some similarly vague accounting term.

Chapter 11

Assessing Your Financial Condition

In This Chapter

▶ Explaining what a balance sheet is

▶ Producing a balance sheet

▶ Reviewing balance sheets

*A*n important part of prudently managing your business is monitoring the firm's financial condition using a balance sheet. In this chapter, therefore, I explain what balance sheets are, provide the steps for producing a balance sheet, and give you a handful of tips about how to use their information to monitor and better understand the financial condition of the business you're running.

Explaining What a Balance Sheet Is

First things first. I want to quickly describe what a balance sheet is:

✔ A balance sheet lists and totals the assets that a business owns. The balance sheet uses the amounts originally paid for the assets for the report values.

✔ A balance sheet lists and totals the liabilities a business owes.

✔ A balance sheet either calculates the difference between these two totals (the total assets less the total liabilities) or explains the difference between the two totals. The difference is the firm's equity, sometimes also known as its net worth or net book value.

The balance sheet report might sound complicated. But here's a weird little curiosity. Business balance sheets, and especially small business balance sheets, usually aren't very complicated. Figure 11-1 shows an example balance sheet for XYZ Consulting, LLC, the imaginary business I've been using in the pages of this book.

Notice that in the assets portion of the balance sheet (by long convention, this appears at the top of the page or window), the report shows as assets the cash balances of $1,101.68 and the total accounts receivable of $652.80, and then sums these two amounts to produce a total assets value equal to $1,754.48.

In many small businesses, these assets might be the only ones listed. In other businesses, you might also have a couple of other numbers, though: inventory held for resale and fixtures (which is stuff like machinery, furniture, and equipment).

At the bottom of the page or window, the report lists the liabilities and the equity. In the simple report shown in Figure 11-1, the liabilities include a credit card balance of $20 and a mysterious other current liabilities balance of $120.23. (This happens to be for sales tax payable.) Small business' liabilities might also, in other situations, include trade accounts payable (which are for amounts owed to vendors), loans payable, and wages payable.

The bottom portion of the report also shows the equity, also sometimes known as the owners equity. In this report, the equity value is calculated as the difference between the total assets and the total liabilities.

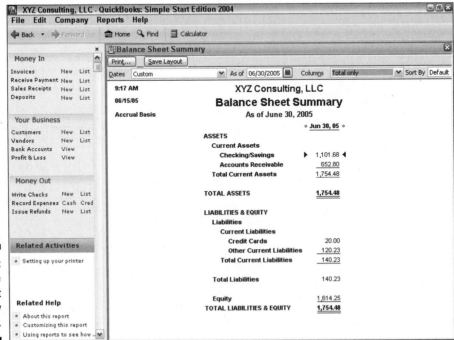

Figure 11-1:
The Balance Sheet Summary report.

The very last line of the report shows the total liabilities and total equity value. This amount will always agree with, or *balance to,* the total assets value. (This is why a balance sheet is called a balance sheet.)

If you look at a balance sheet and see numbers that don't make any sense — cash balances that are negative even though you know you've got money in the bank, for example — that means that somewhere, something in your account-ing is goofed up. Because of the goofed-up-ness, you can't rely on your balance sheet. And you probably shouldn't rely on your profit and loss statement. In a way, then, balance sheets don't just show you your financial condition. They also (in some cases) alert you to problems in your accounting or bookkeeping.

A Few Words About Closing the Accounting Period

A slight digression: In Chapter 10, I talk about the process of closing the accounting period. Mostly, "closing the accounting period" means you catch up on and double-check your data entry for the month or year.

I'm not going to talk about this "closing" business again in this chapter. But do note that in order to get a good, reliable, and meaningful balance sheet, you should have "closed" the accounting period.

You should also be producing a balance sheet using an "as of" for the last day of the accounting period. Just to beat this last point to death, you typically only get a good balance sheet report for the last day of a month or year when you've gone to the work of formally and officially "closing" the month or year. That's the point at which you're caught up on your data entry. You've done whatever error-checking you can do.

Producing the Balance Sheet

After you close the accounting period (as discussed in the preceding sec-tion), you're ready to produce a balance sheet summary. Here are the steps you follow:

1. **Tell QuickBooks Simple Start you want to produce a balance sheet summary.**

Choose the Company⇨Accountant Reports⇨Balance Sheet Summary command. QuickBooks Simple Start displays the Balance Sheet Summary report in the report window (see Figure 11-1).

2. **Verify the reporting interval.**

   Take a peek at Figure 11-1 again. See the As Of box? That box specifies the date that QuickBooks Simple Start looks at and tallies your assets and liabilities. You should specify the As Of date as the last day of the accounting period: the last day of the month, the last day of the quarter, or the last day of the year. Do you remember that QuickBooks Simple Start provides one-character codes that you can use to change the date in the selected date box? I didn't think so. Here they are:

Code	What It Does
T or t	Changes date to today's date
M or m	Changes date to first day in month
H or h	Changes date to last day in month
Y or y	Changes date to first day in year
R or r	Changes date to last day in year

3. **(Optional) Describe the reporting columns you want.**

   Normally, you'll just want to see balance sheet totals for the reporting period you've selected. This is what I did for Figure 11-1. You can also break the data down using some additional reporting interval. To do this, open the Columns drop-down list box (this box appears in the upper-right corner of the report window) and choose the columns you want to use to further analyze the data. The Columns drop-down list box lets you view the data using a bunch of shorter reporting intervals, including: by the day, the week, for two-week intervals, and so on.

Just because QuickBooks Simple Start lets you create a balance sheet that shows values by the day or week doesn't mean the reported values are accurate. Values reported as of a specified date will probably only be accurate if you've "closed" the books through that day or week. See my earlier discussion in this chapter, "A Few Words About Closing the Accounting Period," for more information.

If you add columns to the balance sheet summary report, you'll almost surely need to use the report window's scroll bars to move the report around within the report window.

4. Verify the accounting method.

When you set up QuickBooks Simple Start — perhaps assisted by my instructions in Chapter 1 — you indicated to QuickBooks Simple Start whether you wanted reports prepared on an accrual basis or on a cash basis. QuickBooks Simple Start identifies the accounting method used in the upper-left corner of the report window. Therefore, you should briefly verify that QuickBooks Simple Start is using the correct accounting method. If it isn't, choose File➪Preferences. When QuickBooks displays the Preferences dialog box (see Figure 11-2), change your answer to the How Do You Want to Generate Reports? question.

In order to see accounts receivable on your balance sheet report, you need to be using accrual-basis accounting. The difference between accrual-basis and cash-basis reports in QuickBooks Simple Start boils down to a single feature: when revenue from invoiced amounts is counted. With accrual-basis accounting, QuickBooks Simple Start counts revenue when you invoice some amount — and that's what creates an accounts receivable amount. With cash-basis accounting, QuickBooks Simple Start counts revenue when you collect the previously-invoiced amount, which means accounts receivable is not an option when you use cash-basis accounting.

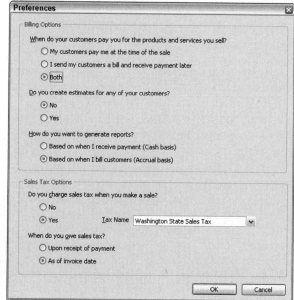

Figure 11-2:
The
Preferences
dialog box.

5. **Print your balance sheet summary.**

To print a hard copy of your balance sheet report, click the Print button (which appears in the upper-left corner of the report window). QuickBooks Simple Start might display a message that tells you it'll do a bang-up job of printing — in which case you need to click OK. QuickBooks Simple Start will eventually display the Print Reports dialog box (see Figure 11-3).

If you truly need blow-by-blow descriptions of the steps for using the Print Reports dialog box, flip to Chapter 12. If you just want to print a report, however, click the Print button. QuickBooks Simple Start then prints you a hard copy of the balance sheet report.

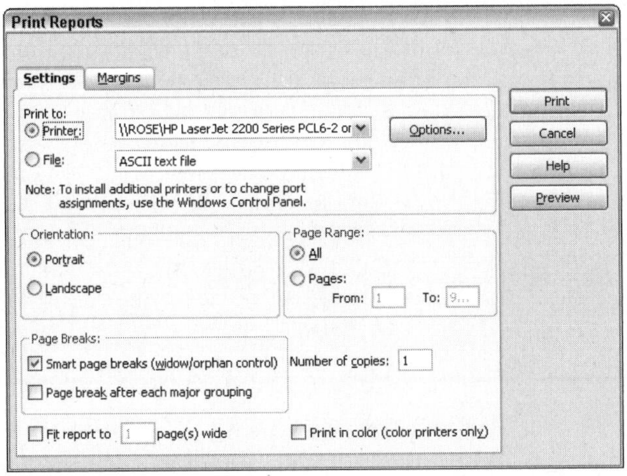

Figure 11-3:
The Print
Reports
dialog box.

6. **(Optional) Save your report layout.**

Click the Save Layout button to tell QuickBooks Simple Start that the next time you produce the balance sheet summary, you want it to look the same way. This means that the next balance sheet summary report will use the same report date and the same column setting.

7. **(Not optional) Save the hard copy report.**

You want to save paper copies of your annual balance sheet summary reports. The annual reports might explain the numbers on your tax returns. (Partnership and corporation tax returns typically include balance sheets, which is one reason these returns are more complicated than regular, old sole proprietorship returns.)

Reviewing Balance Sheet Summary Reports

Before you and I finish up this short chapter, I want to share a handful of tips about working with and using balance sheet reports and their information. I apologize up front for the laundry-list nature of this information:

- ✔ **Auditing and QuickZooming the numbers:** In Chapter 10, I briefly talk about why and how you should audit your numbers. Everything I say there about the profit and loss statement applies to balance sheets. If you haven't perused that discussion, I respectfully suggest you do so now.

- ✔ **Benchmarking:** In Chapter 10, I also talk a bit about how and when to benchmark your business's financial statistics against firms similar to yours. You should try to benchmark balance sheet data, too. Remember that a balance sheet reports on the financial condition of a firm — practically speaking, that means a balance sheet shows a firm's economic strength or its weakness. Hey, that's important stuff to know. What's more, benchmarking can also suggest what assets (cash, inventory, fixtures, and so on) you need to operate your business. And what outside funding through liabilities (accounts payable, bank loans, and so on) you can reasonably expect.

- ✔ **Trend analysis:** Beware that because a balance sheet shows only a snapshot at a point in time, a balance sheet isn't very good about suggesting the direction a business is headed, whether it's getting stronger or if it's getting weaker. For example, a business might have an ugly balance sheet that shows lots of debt and razor-thin equity. But you know what? Maybe that's okay if the core business is in pretty good shape and the firm's debt is steadily decreasing. As another example, a business with a solid-looking balance sheet (a balance sheet that shows lots of cash and a big equity value) might actually be in deep trouble if losses are not only occurring but steadily growing. To make sure that you get all the information you can from a balance sheet, compare one month's balance sheet to the previous month's balance sheet and this year's balance sheet to last year's balance sheet. Look for trends either good or bad. Also be aware that sometimes things that superficially look good (like growing assets) might really be bad when you dig a little deeper (maybe the assets are growing because you've got more and more unsaleable inventory).

Chapter 12

More Reporting on Reporting

In This Chapter

▶ Reviewing the other reports
▶ Customizing reports
▶ Taking a crash course on printing and printers

*I*n Chapters 10 and 11, I introduce the subject of QuickBooks Simple Start reports. I also discuss the two most important reports that QuickBooks Simple Start provides: the profit and loss statement (also known as an income statement) and the balance sheet.

QuickBooks Simple Start provides several other useful and interesting reports, however. In this chapter, I describe these reports. In some detail, in fact.

But that's not all this chapter does. I needed a chapter in which to plunk down a discussion of what (modest) report customization opportunities QuickBooks Simple Start provides. And I want to provide a thorough discussion of how report printing works in QuickBooks Simple Start. So I'm going to sneak that information into this chapter as well.

Reviewing the Other Reports

Figure 12-1 shows the Reports menu. As you can see, the menu provides nine commands: Total Sales by Customer, Total Sales By Item, All Activity By Customer, Customer Balances, Invoices that Haven't Been Paid, Total Expenses by Payee, All Transactions By Vendor, Tax Reports, and Accountant Reports. Fortunately, you need to know only two things about the Reports menu commands in order to pass the test I'm giving at the end of the chapter.

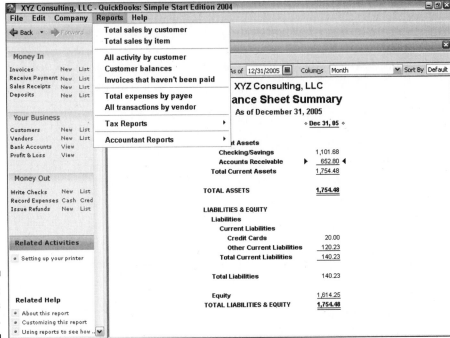

Figure 12-1:
The Reports
menu.

Reports menu commands are self-descriptive

The command name identifies the contents of the report in the first seven reports. For example, if you choose the first command, the one labeled Total Sales by Customer, QuickBooks Simple Start provides a report that summarizes the sales you've booked by customer (see Figure 12-2).

Similarly, if you choose the second command listed — the one titled Total Sales By Item — you get a report that shows how much of each item you've sold.

Tax reports and accountants reports are for accountants (mostly)

The second thing to know about the Reports menu (see Figure 12-1) is this: The eighth and ninth commands — the commands labeled Tax Reports and Accountant Reports — display submenus of commands you use to produce more specialized reports — and these specialized reports are mostly just for accountants.

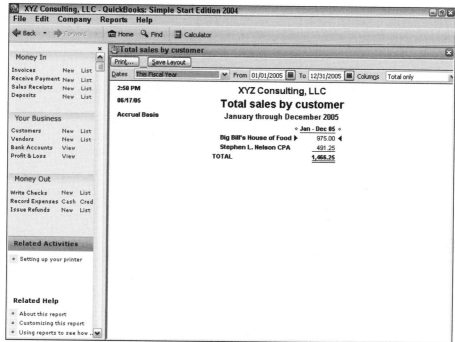

Figure 12-2:
An example
Total Sales
by Customer
report.

The Tax Reports menu, for example, lists commands for producing reports
that summarize your income and expenses the same way your tax returns
do, that provide detailed income about your taxable income and deductions,
and that report on the sales tax liabilities you owe. I'm not even sure you need
to look at these reports. But your accountant or tax preparer will (especially
if he or she suspects that you've fouled up your bookkeeping and tax recordkeeping over the year).

The Accountants Report command, which not surprisingly displays the
Accountants Report submenu, lists commands for producing a profit and
loss statement, a balance sheet, a general ledger, and a journal. As I mention
in Chapters 10 and 11, the profit and loss statement and the balance sheet are
really important. You need to produce those reports regularly to see how your
business is doing and where it's headed. But the general ledger and journal
report? Whew. Don't go there. Really.

Summarizing reports

Table 12-1 lists each of the reports and describes in a very general way what
information the report supplies.

Table 12-1	The QuickBooks Simple Start Reports
Report	**Description**
Total sales by customer	Tallies the total sales by customer for the current month.
Total sales by item	Tallies the total sales by item for the current month.
All activity by customer	Shows invoice, sales receipt, and payment transactions grouped by customer.
Customer balances	Shows open invoices by customer. A good report to see who owes what.
Invoices that haven't been paid	Identifies those deadbeat customers who think you don't care if they don't pay you.
Total expenses by payee	Shows what you've paid in total to everybody you've written checks to.
All transactions by vendor	Lists the checks and credit card charges for each vendor.
Income tax summary	Summarizes your income and expense amounts by tax form line.
Income tax detail	Provides a detailed listing of all the transactions that get reported on a tax form line. No kidding, this is the report the IRS examining agent will ask to see.
Sales tax due	Identifies the sales taxes payable amounts you owe. The state department of revenue agent will ask to see this one.
Profit & Loss Standard	Produces a standard profit and loss statement so you can see how your business is doing. Read more about this report in Chapter 10.
Balance Sheet Summary	Produces a standard balance sheet report so you can see what financial condition your business is in. Read more about this report in Chapter 11.
General Ledger	Oh man. What should I say here? The General Ledger report summarizes the debits and credits that have been posted to an account. Does that make sense? If not, you probably shouldn't be using this report. Sorry.
Journal	A chronological list of the transactions you've recorded in QuickBooks Simple Start.

Customizing Reports

QuickBooks Simple Start doesn't provide you with a ton of report customization opportunities. But you still have a surprising amount of flexibility available to you. I'll quickly go through your options.

Setting the report dates or date

Every QuickBooks Simple Start report has date-related boxes. On any report that shows totals for a period particular period of time, you see a Dates box, and a From and To box. Figure 12-3, for example, shows the All Activity by Customer report. In the upper-left corner of the report window, you see a Dates box, a From box, and a To box. You use these boxes to control the time interval for which the report shows data.

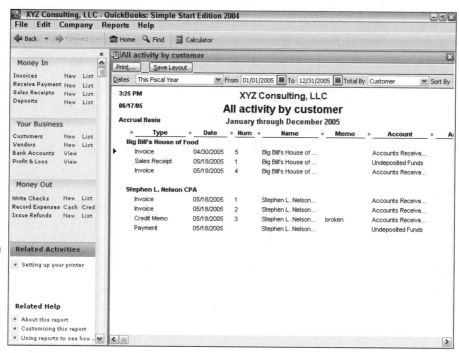

Figure 12-3:
An example
All Activity
by Customer
report.

The Dates drop-down list box, for example, lists report interval options: This month-to-date, This fiscal quarter, This fiscal quarter-to-date, and so on. If you want a report for a time interval you see listed, you just pick an option from the Dates drop down list box.

The From and To boxes let you control the time interval by specifying some weird starting and ending date. You only have to enter the date using the normal MM/DD/YYYY format. For example, November 26, 2020 (my antici-pated retirement date) should be entered as 11/26/2020.

Do you remember the one-character codes you can type to enter a date into a date-input box? You do? Great. Well, know that the codes work in the From and To boxes, too. For example, press t or T to enter today's date, m or M to enter the first day of the month, h or H to enter the last day of the month, y or Y to enter the first day of the year, and r or R to enter the last day of the year. You can also adjust the date already shown one day at a time by pressing the – and + keys.

Note: The balance sheet doesn't report on an interval of time. Rather, the report shows account balances at a specific point in time. For this reason, for a balance sheet report you enter only a single "as of" date.

Customizing columns

Some report windows provide a Columns box that lets you break down your data into more granular detail. Columns often let you see report information by smaller time intervals (for example, a report that shows data for the year can also, by using columns, break the data down into monthly, weekly, or even daily totals). When you're not busy sometime — or even better yet, when you want to really dig down into your data — go ahead and noodle around with the Columns box. Sometimes, the extra detail makes your reports more useful.

Sorting report data

Some report windows provide a Sort By box that lets you tell QuickBooks Simple Start how it should sort, or arrange, the information shown on the report. The sorting options available depend (not surprisingly) on the infor-mation presented in a report. But you can often sort by transaction number, transaction type, date, number, name, memo, account, and even by debits and credits.

Totaling report data

A few report windows provide a Total By box that lets you tell QuickBooks Simple Start how it should subtotal the information shown on the report. As you would guess, the sorting options available depend on the information presented in a report. But you can (sometimes) subtotal by customer, vendor, customer type, vendor type, item, time intervals, and a bunch of other stuff as well.

Fooling with column spacing

If you take a close look at Figure 12-4, you'll see small diamonds between the labels that identify each column of data.

You can drag those diamonds to resize a column. In other words, if you need a larger column so you can see all the data, drag the diamond one way. And if you want to shrink a column perhaps because you don't care about the data, drag the diamond the other way.

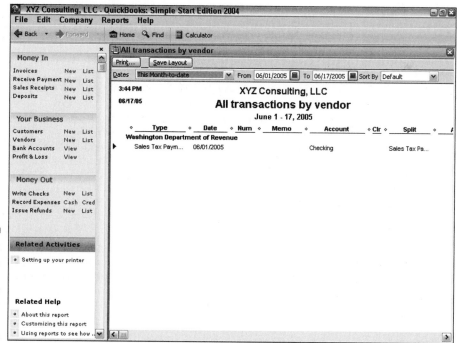

Figure 12-4:
An example All Trans-actions by Vendor report.

Moving report columns

If you point to a column label, QuickBooks Simple Start changes the mouse pointer into a karate-chop-shaped hand. When you see this pointer, you can drag the column label to a new location, thereby moving the column's data. I admit it, this is very hard to understand from a poorly written paragraph. So just try this on your own. Point, chop, and drag.

Saving report layouts

If you make the sorts of customizations described in the preceding paragraphs, you might want to save your handiwork. You can do so by clicking the Save Layout command. By clicking Save Layout, you tell QuickBooks Simple Start to use the same customizations for the next report.

Getting rid of reports

If you see an on-screen report that you want to get rid of, just close the report window. (Do this by clicking the small box marked with an "X" in the upper-right corner of the report window.)

Crash Course on Printer and Printing

You can control the way your printers work from within QuickBooks Simple Start. You can also, at the time you tell QuickBooks Simple Start to print, control the actual printing. If you can't get reports that look just the way you want, knowledge about how to exercise this control is really useful. For that reason, I'm going to describe in detail both how you control the printing setup and the printing process.

Printer setup stuff

If you choose the File⇨Printer Setup command, QuickBooks Simple Start displays the Printer Setup dialog box (see Figure 12-5). This dialog box lets you control which printer QuickBooks Simple Start uses (if you have more than one printer available) and some other, basic printing settings as well.

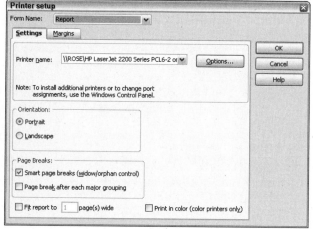

Figure 12-5:
The Settings
tab of the
Printer
Setup
dialog box.

To use the Printer Setup dialog box, follow these steps:

1. **Tell QuickBooks Simple Start which form or report you want to specify the printer setup for.**

   Printer setup varies based on the thing that you're printing. So the first thing you need to do is use the Form drop-down list box — this appears at the top of the Printer Setup dialog box — to specify which printed thing you want the new printer setup options to apply to. You click the arrow at the right end of the drop-down list box and select the specific form or the catchall selection for reports, *report.*

   In this chapter, I'm talking about printer setup in the context of report printing. But as you know if you've read the preceding step, printer setup also applies to the forms you print for invoices, sales receipts, and even checks.

2. **Choose your printer.**

   The Printer Name box lets you select a printer. If you have only one printer, of course, this box (when opened) lists only the single printer. But if you've got several printers, you can select one from the Printer Name drop-down list box.

   The Printer Setup dialog box lets you make general changes to the way a printer works, but it doesn't let you fiddle with any of a printer's specific-to-that-printer features, like paper tray selection (if a printer has multiple paper trays) or print speed-versus-quality tradeoffs. If you click the Options button, which appears to the right of the Printer Name drop-down list box, however, QuickBooks Simple Start opens the selected printer's properties dialog box. The printer's properties dialog box does let you change the way the specific printer's features work.

3. **Select the page orientation.**

   You can use the Portrait and Landscape buttons to specify whether QuickBooks Simple Start prints on 8.5-inch-by-11-inch pages or 11-inch-by-8.5-inch pages.

4. **Specify how pages should break.**

   The Page Breaks check boxes let you control, to a degree, how QuickBooks Simple Start breaks a report into pages. If neither box is marked, QuickBooks Simple Start just fills up each report page with as much stuff as it can fit. If you check the Smart page breaks box, QuickBooks Simple Start breaks pages in a way that minimizes any widows or orphans. A *widow* or *orphan* is just a chunk of text that really belongs with something on the preceding or next page. If you check the Page break after each major grouping box, QuickBooks Simple Start breaks pages whenever a major grouping of data ends. For example, if you produce a report of all activity by customer, QuickBooks Simple Start would break the report between each customer.

5. **Fit the report onto a specified number of pages.**

   You can check the Fit report to [X] page(s) wide box to tell QuickBooks Simple Start to scrunch your report onto a specified number of pages. If you check this box, you can either accept the default scrunch setting — which is a single page — or you can enter some new scrunch-to-this-number-of-pages value into the text box. Keep in mind that QuickBooks Simple Start is a great piece of software, but is still constrained by the laws of physics.

6. **Specify if you want to use color.**

   If your printer prints in color, check the Print in Color box to use color on your reports.

7. **Adjust the report page margins.**

   If you click the Margins tab, QuickBooks Simple Start displays the Margins tab. Go figure. (see Figure 12-6). The Margins tab lets you specify the margins QuickBooks Simple Start leaves around the edges of the report pages. You specify the margins you want by entering values into the Top Margin, Left Margin, Bottom Margin, and Right Margin boxes.

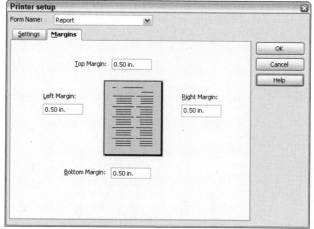

Figure 12-6:
The Margins
tab of the
Printer
Setup
dialog box.

A curious bit of QuickBooks Simple Start Printer Setup trivia: If you enter a value, QuickBooks Simple Start assumes that you're using inches as your units of measurement. You can also use points and in this case, you enter a value followed by the letter *p*. A point equals $\frac{1}{72}$ of an inch, and therefore 72 points equals an inch. So if you enter 72p, you're setting a 1-inch margin. Fortunately, QuickBooks Simple Start does convert margins entered in points to inches, just to keep the American campaign against the metric system alive and well.

8. Click OK to set your settings.

When you finish fiddling with the Printer Setup dialog box, you click OK to make your changes. Of course you can also click Cancel to cancel your changes and leave the printer setup stuff unchanged.

Printing: The unabridged story

If you click the Print button, which appears at the top of every report window, QuickBooks Simple Start displays the Print Reports dialog box (see Figure 12-7). This dialog box lets you both print the displayed report and control the printer.

Note: Just in case you've just read the preceding chapter section, "Printer setup stuff," let me mention that many of the printing options available when you click the Print command mirror options available when you choose the File⇨Printer Setup command. Keep in mind that when you use the Printer

Setup command, you control how the printer is setup and how printing works whenever printing any report or form. When you use the Print dialog box, you control how the printer is setup and how printing works for the specific report you're in the process of printing.

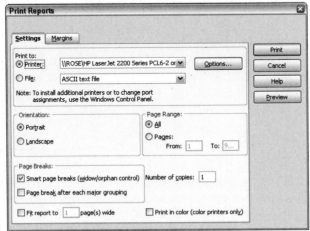

Figure 12-7:
The Print
Reports
dialog box.

Printing on paper

To use the Print dialog box to print a hard copy (paper) version of a report, follow these steps:

1. **Choose your printer.**

   If the Printer button is marked — and by default it is — the Printer Name box lets you select a printer. If you have only one printer, of course, you don't need to worry about this box because it'll list and show only the single printer. But if you've got several printers, the world is your oyster, and you can select any of the printers listed in the Printer Name drop-down list box.

   The Printer Setup dialog box doesn't let you fiddle with any of a printer's specific-to-that-printer features like paper tray selection (if a printer has multiple paper trays) or print speed-versus-quality tradeoffs. To do that sort of stuff, click the Options button, which appears to the right of the Printer Name drop-down list box. QuickBooks Simple Start then opens the selected printer's Properties dialog box where you can change the way the specific printer's features work.

2. **Select the page orientation.**

   You can use the Portrait and Landscape buttons to specify whether QuickBooks Simple Start prints on 8.5-inch-by-11-inch pages or 11-inch-by-8.5-inch pages.

3. **Specify how pages should break.**

   The Page Breaks check boxes let you control how QuickBooks Simple Start breaks a report into pages. Without your supervision, QuickBooks Simple Start just fills up each report page as best it can. If you check the Smart page breaks box, however, QuickBooks Simple Start breaks pages in a way that minimizes any widows or orphans — chunks of text that really belong on the preceding or next page. If you check the Page break after each major grouping box, QuickBooks Simple Start breaks pages whenever a major grouping of data ends. For example, if you produce a report of all expenses by payee, QuickBooks Simple Start would break the report at payee between each payee.

4. **Fit the report onto a specified number of pages.**

   Check the Fit report to [X] page(s) wide box to tell QuickBooks Simple Start to scrunch your report onto a specified number of pages. If you check this box, you can either accept the default scrunch setting — which is a single page — or you can enter some new scrunch-to-this-number-of-pages value into the text box.

5. **Color you beautiful.**

   If your printer prints in color, select the Print in Color check box to tell QuickBooks to use color on your reports.

6. **Select a page range.**

   If you want only a page or a few pages of a long report, mark the Page Range Pages button and then use the From and To boxes to specify the page range.

7. **Specify the number of copies you want.**

   See the Number of Copies text box? Enough said.

8. **Adjust the report page margins.**

   If you click the Margins tab, QuickBooks displays the Margins tab (see Figure 12-8). The Margins tab lets you specify the margins QuickBooks leaves around the edges of the report pages using the Top Margin, Left Margin, Right Margin, and Bottom Margin boxes.

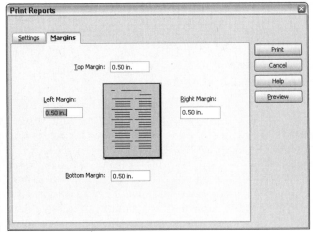

If you enter a value, QuickBooks assumes that you're using inches as
your units of measurement. You can also use points by entering a value
followed by the letter *p*. A point equals $\frac{1}{72}$ of an inch, and therefore
72 points equals an inch. So if you enter 72p, you're setting a 1-inch
margin.

9. **Preview the Report.**

    You can click the Preview button to see what your report will look like
    when it prints. QuickBooks displays the Print Preview window when you
    do this (see Figure 12-9). The Print Preview window provides Prev Page
    and Next Page buttons you can use to page through a long report. The
    Zoom In button "zooms in" or magnifies the report shown in the window
    so you can actually read the information shown on the report's pages.
    The Help and Close buttons — well, wait a minute, you don't need me
    to tell you what those buttons do.

10. **Click Print to print your settings.**

    You can print from the Print dialog or the Print Preview window. Just
    click Print. Either way, you'll (usually only briefly) see a "printing"
    message. And then you'll hear and see the printed report spewing
    out of the printer.

Printing to a file

You can also print a report to a file. And you'll want to do this at least occasionally. By printing a report to a file, you can use the report's information in
programs (like your word processor or spreadsheet).

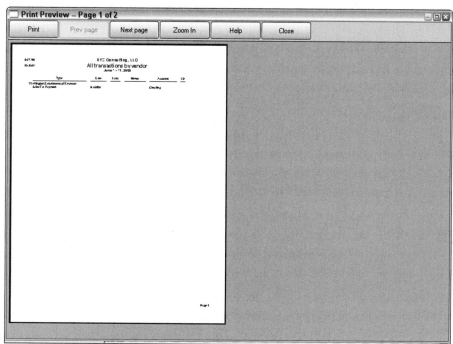

Figure 12-9:
The Print
Preview
window.

To use the Print dialog box to print a file (electronic) version of a report, follow these steps:

1. Specify what you want to print to a file.

Mark the File button to tell QuickBooks that you want to print the report as a file.

2. Choose the file format.

Select the file format from the File drop-down list box. You have only three format choices and you choose a format based on what you want to do later on with the file. Choose ASCII text file if you want to later use the report in a word-processing program. Choose the Comma delimited file format or the Tab delimited file format — it really doesn't matter which — to use the report in a spreadsheet program.

Want to work with QuickBooks information in Microsoft Excel or some other spreadsheet? Here's how: First, produce a report that shows the information you want to analyze or chart with Excel. Next, print the report as a comma-delimited file. Then open the new comma-delimited file by using Excel. As they say in France, "Voilà."

3. **Select a page range.**

   If you want only a page or a few pages of a report, mark the Page Range Pages button and then use the From and To boxes to specify the page range.

4. **Adjust the report page margins.**

   If you click the Margins tab, QuickBooks displays the Margins tab (see Figure 12-8). The Margins tab lets you specify the margins QuickBooks leaves around the edges of the report pages. You can specify the margins you want by entering values in inches into the Top Margin, Left Margin, Right Margin, and Bottom Margin boxes.

5. **(Optional) Preview the report.**

   You can click the Preview button to see what information your report file will contain. QuickBooks displays the Print Preview window when you do this (see Figure 12-9). The Print Preview window provides Prev Page and Next Page buttons you can use to page through the report. The Zoom In button "zooms in" or magnifies the report shown in the window so you can actually read the information shown on the report's pages.

6. **Tell QuickBooks to create the report file.**

   Click Print to create the report file from the Print dialog box or the Print Preview window. QuickBooks displays the Create Disk File dialog box (see Figure 12-10).

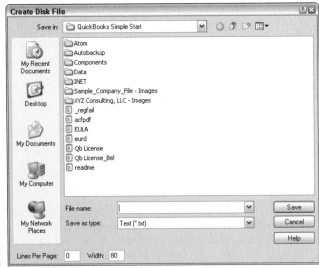

Figure 12-10:
The Create
Disk File
dialog box.

7. Specify the filename and location.

Use the Create Disk File dialog box's Save In drop-down list box to specify where you want to locate the report file. Use the File Name box to name the report file.

8. (Optional) Control "page breaking" within the report file.

You can use the Lines Per Page and Width boxes to specify (roughly) how QuickBooks breaks report information with the file into "pages." A Lines per page setting of 0 (the default) tells QuickBooks not to break information into pages. You can break the report information into pages by setting some other Lines Per Page value. A width box setting tells QuickBooks how wide (measured in characters) the report's information can be.

If you want to fool around with the Lines per page and Width settings, your best bet is probably to experiment a bit. That experimentation will help you figure out more quickly than I can how different setting values control the appearance and arrangement of information in the output report file.

9. Save the report file.

Click Save to create the report file in the location you specified using the name you specified.

10. Use the file.

After you create the report file, you're ready to use it someplace else. Typically, such use just means you open the new file with another application program. For example, if you want to use a report's information in Microsoft Excel, you would open the new report file using Excel.

Chapter 13

Housekeeping Matters

. . . .

. . . .

*O*kay, you don't need to worry about chasing dust bunnies in QuickBooks Simple Start, but you do have a handful of important housekeeping tasks to take care of. For example, you need to know how to work with the data files, especially how to back up and restore your data. You might want to know how to change the company-level information (such as your business name and address) and accounting preferences (such as the accounting method you use). And, just to keep the "insides" of your data files accurate, you'll also want to know how to make a general journal entry. In this chapter, I describe these chores and how to do them correctly with minimal hassle.

Backing Up Is (Not That) Hard to Do

Sure, I can give you some tricky, technical examples of fancy backup strategies, but they have no point here. You want to know the basics, right?

The guiding rule is that you back up anytime you work on something that you wouldn't want to redo. Some people think that a week's worth of work is negligible, and others think that a month's worth of work is negligible.

So here's what I do to back up my files. I back up every week after I enter my data for the week. Then I stick the disk (you may use any removable disk, such as a Zip disk or writable CD or a Memory Stick) in my briefcase so that if something terrible happens (like a tornado hits my office building), I don't lose both my computer and the backup disk with the data. (I carry my briefcase around with me — a sort of middle-age security blanket — so that it won't get destroyed in some after-hours disaster.) Sounds like a pretty good system, huh? Actually, I admit that my strategy has its problems:

- ✔ Because I'm backing up weekly, I might have to re-enter as much as a week's worth of data if the computer crashes toward the end of the week. In my case, I wouldn't lose all that much work. However, if you're someone with heavy transaction volumes — if you prepare hundreds of invoices or write hundreds of checks each week, for example — you probably want to back up more frequently, perhaps every day.

- ✔ A second problem with my strategy is only remotely possible but still worth mentioning: If something bad does happen to the QuickBooks Simple Start files stored on my computer's hard drive and the files stored on the backup floppy disk, CD-R, CD-RW, or Zip disk, I'll be up the proverbial creek without a paddle. (I should also note that a removable disk [especially a floppy] is far more likely to fail than a hard drive.) If this worst-case scenario actually occurs, I'll need to start over from scratch from the beginning of the year.

TIP

Backing up files online

You can quickly and easily back up your data online. By doing so, you no longer need to remember to make backups and take them off-site. To find out more about online backup, click the Tell Me More button on the Back Up Company File tab of the QuickBooks Backup dialog box. (Refer to Figure 13-1.) To back up online, click the Online option button shown in Figure 13-1 and then click OK.

The Online Backup service is a pretty good idea if you have a fast Internet connection, but the service isn't cheap. You pay at least $80 a year and as much as $240 a year depending on the level of service. But you can set up the service so that QuickBooks Simple Start automatically backs up your data on a regular basis.

Just for the record, I don't think you need to worry about the security. You can read more about the security measures at the QuickBooks Web site, but your data is as secure online as it is in your office.

To prevent this scenario from happening, some people who are religiously careful circulate three sets of backup disks to reduce the chance of this mishap. They also regularly move one copy off-site, such as to a safe-deposit box. In this scenario, whenever you back up your data, you use the oldest set of backup disks.

Suppose that you back up your data every week, and your hard drive not only crashes but also bursts into a ball of flames rising high into the night. To restore your files, you use the most recent set of backups — one week old, max. If something is wrong with those, you use the next recent set — two weeks old. If something is wrong with those, you use the last set — three weeks old. This way, you have three chances to get a set that works — a nice bit of security for the cost of a few extra disks. I should also add that, generally, a backup file doesn't fit on a single floppy disk, so you probably want to have a high-density removable disk for your backups such as a writable CD or a Zip disk — especially if you're maintaining multiple backup copies of the QuickBooks Simple Start file.

You know what else? All backup files are condensed to save disk space. If you're so inclined (I'm not), open Windows Explorer or My Computer and look in the `Program Files\Intuit\QuickBooks` folder for your company's file. (The backup file is, of course, on the disk you specify in the backup procedure, which I describe in the following section.) If you set Windows Explorer to show file size — click the Views button and choose Details from the drop-down menu to do so — you'll notice that your backup file (the one with the `.QBB` extension displayed, if you don't have your file extensions hidden) is a fraction of the size of its regular company file counterpart (the one with the `.QBW` extension). QuickBooks Simple Start shrinks the backup file to keep the disk from getting too crowded.

If you can't fit your backup QuickBooks Simple Start file on a single floppy and you want to use floppy disks, you can back up across multiple floppies.

Backing up the quick-and-dirty way

You're busy. You don't have time to fool around. You just want to do a passable job of backing up, and you've decided how often you plan to do it. Sound like your situation? Then follow these steps:

1. **Insert a blank disk in your drive.**

   You can back up to any removable disk, including floppy disks, Zip disks, Memory Sticks, and writable CDs.

Heck, I should admit that you can back up to any fixed drive, such as your hard drive or a network drive, but the advantage of a removable drive is that you can store it in some other location. As a compromise, you can also use a network drive. You typically don't want to use your hard drive (although this is better than nothing) because one of the disasters that might befall your data is hard drive failure.

2. **If you store data for more than one company, make sure that the company whose data you want to back up is the active company.**

Yes, I know that all your companies are active — I'm hoping they're not dead in the water. My point is that you want to back up the right company. To find out whether the right company is active, just look at the QuickBooks application window's title bar, which names the active company. (If you don't remember setting up multiple files, don't worry. You probably have only one file — the usual case. If you do remember setting up multiple files but that's all you remember, refer to the later chapter section, "Working with Multiple Data Files.")

3. **Choose File⇨Maintenance⇨Back Up to begin the backup operation.**

QuickBooks displays the Back Up Company File tab of the QuickBooks Backup dialog box, as shown in Figure 13-1.

Figure 13-1:
The Back Up Company File tab of the Backup dialog box.

4. **To identify the backup drive, click the Disk option button and then click the Browse button.**

   QuickBooks displays the Back Up Company To dialog box (see Figure 13-2).

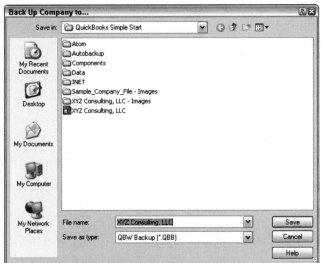

Figure 13-2:
The Back Up
Company To
dialog box.

5. **Click the Save In drop-down list and select the letter of the drive that you stuffed the disk into.**

   QuickBooks Simple Start includes two special backup options — Verify Data Integrity and Format Each Floppy During Backup — which appear as check boxes on the Back Up Company File tab of the QuickBooks Backup dialog box (refer to Figure 13-1). You can select these check boxes to have QuickBooks double-check the data it copies to the backup disk and, if necessary, to have QuickBooks first format the backup floppy disk. As the Back Up Company To tab indicates, however, these options do slow down the backup process.

6. **Click Save.**

   QuickBooks returns to the Back Up Company File tab of the QuickBooks Backup dialog box (refer to Figure 13-1).

7. **Click OK.**

   QuickBooks backs up your company file. When it finishes, it displays a message telling you that the backup worked.

Getting back the data you've backed up

What happens if you lose all your QuickBooks Simple Start data? First of all, I encourage you to feel smug. Get a cup of coffee. Lean back in your chair. Gloat for a couple of minutes. You, my friend, have no problem. You have followed instructions.

Okay, you might have one or two problems, but you probably can blame PC gremlins for those. If the disaster that caused you to lose your data also trashed other parts of your computer, you might need to reinstall QuickBooks Simple Start. You also might need to reinstall all your other software.

After you've gloated sufficiently (and pieced your computer back together again if it was the cause of the disaster), carefully do the following to reinstate your data:

1. **Get your backup disk.**

    Find the backup disk you created and carefully insert it into one of the disk drives.

2. **Start QuickBooks Simple Start and choose File⇨Maintenance⇨Restore.**

    QuickBooks closes the company file you have open. QuickBooks displays the Restore Company Backup dialog box (see Figure 13-3).

Figure 13-3:
The Restore
Company
Backup
dialog box.

```
Restore Company Backup                                          [x]

 Get Company Backup From:

        ⤴     If you are restoring from a 3.5-inch disk or other removable storage
      [===]   media, put the disk in the drive before clicking Restore.

      ⦿ Disk:  Filename:  [XYZ Consulting, LLC.QBB              ]
                Location:  [C:\Program Files\Intuit\QuickBooks ...]  [ Browse ]

      ○ Online:  To restore an online backup, click Restore, retrieve the file using the
                 online backup service, then open the file in QuickBooks.

 Restore Company Backup To:

        ↪⌷    Select the location and name to restore your company to.

         Filename:  [XYZ Consulting, LLC.QBW                           ]
         Location:  [C:\Program Files\Intuit\QuickBooks Simple Start\ ]  [ Browse ]

                    [ Restore ]    [ Cancel ]    [ Help ]
```

3. **Use the Filename and Location boxes in the Get Company Backup From area to identify the backup file you want to use.**

If you know the company filename and location, you can enter this information in the boxes provided. If you don't know this information, click the Browse button. QuickBooks Simple Start displays the Restore From dialog box (see Figure 13-4). Use the Look in box to identify the drive that contains the file you want to back up. Then select the file you want to restore and click Open.

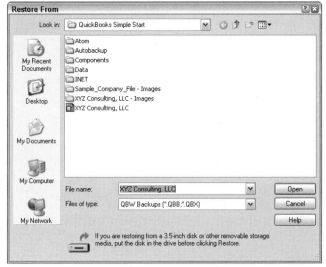

Figure 13-4:
The Restore
From dialog
box.

4. **Use the Filename and Location boxes in the Restore Company Backup To area to identify the file you want to replace.**

   If you know the company filename and location, you can enter this information in the boxes provided. If you don't know this information, click the Browse button. QuickBooks Simple Start displays the Restore To dialog box. Use the Save In drop-down list box to make sure that you place the restored file in the correct folder on the correct drive.

5. **Click the Restore button.**

   If the file you're trying to restore already exists, you see a message box telling you so. Either click Yes to overwrite or replace the file with the one stored on the floppy disk, or click No to keep the original copy.

QuickBooks Simple Start might ask you for your password to verify that you have administrative permission to restore the file. Then, if everything goes okay, you see a message box that says so. Breathe a deep sigh of relief and give thanks.

Oops. I almost forgot:

- ✔ When you restore a file, you replace the current version of the file with the backup version stored on the floppy disk. Don't restore a file for fun. Restore a file only if the current version is trashed and you want to start over by using the version stored on the backup disk.

- ✔ You need to re-enter everything you entered since you made the backup copy. I know. You're bummed out. Hopefully, it hasn't been all that long since you backed up.

Working with Multiple Data Files

You can set up and work with more than one data file. For example, suppose you have two businesses: a little sole proprietorship that does consulting and a cool little retail business that operates as a corporation. In this case, you have two businesses (obviously). And you need to keep two sets of books (perhaps slightly less obviously). But that's okay because QuickBooks Simple Start lets you keep the books for more than one company (fortunately). You simply need to set up more than one data file.

Setting up another data file

To set up another data file, you choose the File⇨New Company command. QuickBooks Simple Start then starts up the Setup Interview, which is the way that you (or someone) set up your first data file. Chapter 1 describes how you set up the first data file. You follow the same procedures to set up other data files, so refer to Chapter 1 if you have questions.

Flipping between your data files

QuickBooks Simple Start allows you to have only a single data file open at a time. To work with a data file, then, the data file needs to be opened. To open a data file, you choose the File⇨Open Company command. QuickBooks Simple Start displays the Open a Company dialog box (see Figure 13-5). If you know the company filename and location, you can enter this information in the Filename box. If you don't know this information, use the Look In box to identify the drive and folder that contains the file you want to open. Then select the file you want to open from the list that appears in the middle of the dialog box and click Open.

Two points about flipping between files should be made: First, before you open a new file, QuickBooks Simple Start closes the previously open file. Second, when you start QuickBooks Simple Start, it opens automatically whatever file was open when you last exited from QuickBooks Simple Start.

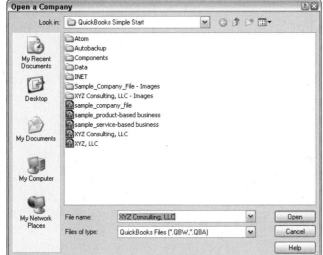

Figure 13-5:
The Open a
Company
dialog box.

Using the File Maintenance Tools

Observant readers compulsively following along with this chapter's preceding discussions of backing up and restoring data files will have noticed something slightly suspicious about the submenu that QuickBooks Simple Start displays when you choose the File⇨Maintenance command. The Maintenance submenu not only displays a Backup and Restore command, the submenu also displays a Verify Data and Rebuild Data. A few explanatory words are in order concerning these two commands. . . .

Verifying your data

The Verify Data command looks through your data file for errors and, if it finds errors, writes up a little description of the error for the error log file. As a practical matter, you don't really need to think about this command. Oh sure, the name "Verify Data" sounds pretty important. But you're only going to use this command when someone like a QuickBooks technical support engineer you've called tells you to. You're not going to use this command for hoots or because you're bored.

If you find yourself with a compelling reason to use the Verify Data command with no adult supervision, use the QuickBooks Simple Start Help feature. The Help file information gives you the name and location of the log file and tells you what to do if you run the Verify Data command only to discover the hard cold truth that your data is corrupt. (Basically, the procedures are to back up your corrupted copy of the data file and then use the Rebuild Data command. But don't take my word for it: Read through the Help file discussion and instructions.)

Rebuilding your data

The Rebuild Data command attempts to rebuild and repair a corrupted data file. Typically, you choose this command after you have chosen the Verify Data command and gotten bad news.

I don't want to sound like a broken record, but you shouldn't fool around with this command just to "see what it does." You use the Rebuild Data command and the Verify Data command (described in the preceding paragraphs) because something bad has happened to your data file, and the QuickBooks technical support engineer decides it's time to pull out the big guns.

Using a Password

You can use a password to restrict access to your QuickBooks data. To do so, choose the File⇨Add/Change Passwords command.

If you're adding a new password, QuickBooks displays the New Password dialog box. To create a new password, you enter the password twice: once into the New Password text box and a second time into the Confirm New Password text box.

If you're changing an existing password, QuickBooks displays the Change Password dialog box. To change the password, you enter the current password into the Enter Old Password text box. Then you enter the new password into both the New Password text box and the Confirm New Password text box.

I apologize for issuing such an obvious warning, but be careful about using passwords, okay? The two big problems that I see are: (1) you've got to remember your password in order to access your QuickBooks Simple Start data, and (2) if to deal with problem 1 you use an easy-to-guess password or you write the password on the monitor with an El Marko, you're not getting much or any benefit from the password.

If you forget a password and cannot for the life of you remember or guess it, you can pay the QuickBooks folks a fee to remove the password from your file. Visit www.quickbooks.com for the current contact information you'll need to track down the QuickBooks number you call for this help.

Updating Company Information and Preferences

When you ran the Setup Interview (which I describe in Chapter 1) you tell QuickBooks Simple Start a bunch of stuff about your company and about the manner you want to account for the company's financial activities. You can change and update almost all of the setup interview information, however, by using the File⇨Company Information command and the File⇨Preferences command.

Changing company information

To change company information for a data file that you've already set up, follow these steps:

1. **Choose File⇨Company Information.**

   QuickBooks Simple Start displays the Company Information dialog box (see Figure 13-6).

2. **Update the company name and address information as necessary.**

   You can change the company name, address, telephone and fax numbers, and the e-mail and Web site information by editing the contents of the Company Name, Address, Country, Phone #, Fax #, E-mail, and Web Site text boxes.

3. **Update the legal information as necessary.**

   You can also change the company's legal name and address by editing the contents of the Legal Name, Legal Address, City/State/Zip, and Legal Country. I'm embarrassed to have to make this point, but just so nobody is confused, changing the information in these boxes doesn't really change, for example, the legal name. Changing the information in these boxes simply updates the QuickBooks Simple Start data file for "legal" changes you've actually already made by following the applicable federal and state laws.

Company Information				☒

Contact Information

Company Name: XYZ Consulting, LLC

Address: 123 Main Street, Redmond, WA 98052

Phone #: 425-555-1234

Fax #: 425-555-1235

E-mail: steve@stephenlnelson.com

Country: US

Web Site:

Legal Information

Legal Name: XYZ Consulting, LLC

Legal Address: 123 Main Street

City/State/ZIP: Redmond WA 98052   Legal Country: US

Report Information

First month in your: Fiscal Year: January   Tax Year: January

Income Tax Form Used: Form 1040 (Sole Proprietor)

Company Identification

Federal Employer Identification Number (FEIN required for Payroll.)

Social Security Number (SSN used on 1099's if no FEIN is entered.)

OK | Cancel | Help

Figure 13-6:
The Company Information dialog box.

4. **Update the accounting information as necessary.**

   You can update QuickBooks Simple Start for a change in your fiscal year and tax accounting year by entering the first month in the fiscal year and in the tax accounting year into the First month in your: Fiscal Year and First month in your: Tax Year boxes. (Almost everybody reading this book will use January as the first month of both their fiscal and tax years.) You can update QuickBooks Simple Start for a change in the tax classification of the business by choosing another entity from the Income Tax Form Used drop-down list box.

   Converting a sole proprietorship or partnership into a regular C corporation is relatively easy. Converting C corporations into S corporations is more complicated (which is too bad because S corporations can be such wonderful tax classifications for small businesses). Converting a corporation into a sole proprietorship or partnership is complicated and often expensive. Changing your tax classifications, therefore, probably requires some outside expert help.

5. **Update your taxpayer identification information as necessary.**

   You can update QuickBooks Simple Start for a new or a corrected taxpayer identification number by editing the contents of the Federal Employer Identification Number text box and the Social Security Number box.

6. **Click OK to save your changes.**

Use preferences to specify how QuickBooks Simple Start handles three accounting tasks: customer payments, estimates, and sales taxes. QuickBooks preferences also control the method of accounting — cash versus accrual — that QuickBooks uses for its reports.

To change QuickBooks Simple Start preferences, follow these steps:

1. **Choose File➪Preferences.**

   QuickBooks Simple Start displays the Preferences dialog box (see Figure 13-7).

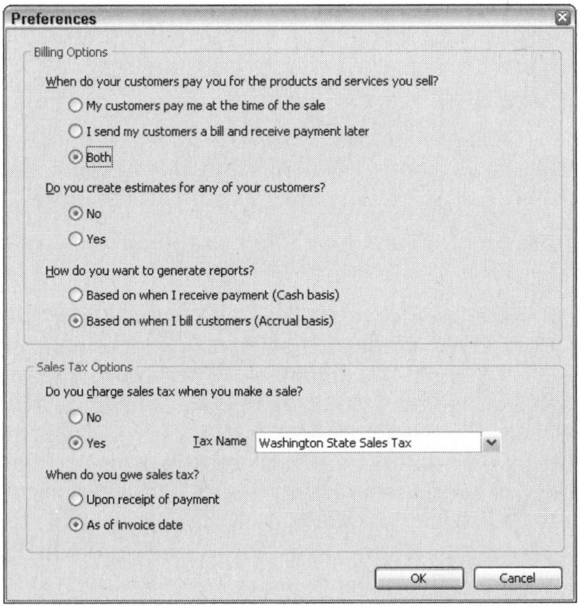

Figure 13-7: The Preferences dialog box.

2. **Indicate when customers pay you for your products or services.**

   You answer the "When do your customers pay you for the products and services you sell?" question so that QuickBooks Simple Start knows how you'll handle customer payments and which customer forms you need. If you indicate that you get paid at the time of the sale, QuickBooks Simple Start knows you only need to produce sales receipts and not invoices — and therefore only lets you record sales receipts. If you indicate that you get paid later, QuickBooks Simple Start knows that you need to produce only invoices and not sales receipts — and therefore only lets you record invoices. If you indicate that you can get paid at any old time, predictably, QuickBooks Simple Start lets you record both sales receipts and invoices.

For information about how invoices work, refer to Chapter 4. For information about how sales receipts work, refer to Chapter 6.

3. **Indicate whether you prepare estimates for customers.**

When you ran through the Setup Interview, you indicated whether you prepare estimates of the amounts you'll later invoice customers. You can change your answer to this question by changing your answer to the "Do you create estimates for any of your customers?" If you do prepare invoices, you can create and print customer estimate forms. You can also easily later create invoices using these estimates.

4. **Choose your accounting method.**

You can prepare your reports either on a cash basis or a pseudo-accrual basis. To tell QuickBooks Simple Start which accounting method you want to use, answer the "How do you want to generate reports?" question. It's really that simple.

In order to do true, by-the-book accrual-based accounting, you probably need to make a bunch of journal entries and very be picky about your bookkeeping. May I suggest you consult your CPA for more information?

5. **Tell QuickBooks Simple Start how you're supposed to handle sales tax.**

Use the Preferences dialog box to tell QuickBooks Simple Start how your business is supposed to handle any sales tax collection or reporting requirements. For example, you answer the "Do you charge sales tax when you make a sale?" question to tell QuickBooks Simple Start whether you even have to charge customers sales tax. If you do charge sales tax, you name the agency you remit the sales tax to using the Tax Name box. Finally, you answer the "When do you owe sales tax?" question to indicate when you, technically speaking, owe the government the sales tax that appears on your sales receipts or invoices. (Sometimes, you owe sales tax when you produce the invoice and sometimes you owe sales tax when you collect from the customer.)

6. **Click OK to save your changes.**

Making Journal Entries

Most of the data you collect as part of "keeping your books" gets entered automatically as part of creating invoices, recording sales receipts, entering checks and credit card charges, and so on. But, unfortunately, some transactions don't get entered automatically or almost automatically. For example, depreciation doesn't get entered automatically.

To enter any missing transactions (like depreciation) you or someone you love needs to record a journal entry. Mechanically, the steps to record journal entries in QuickBooks Simple Start are really very easy. Here's what you do:

1. **Choose Company⇨For Your Accountant⇨Make General Journal Entries.**

   QuickBooks Simple Start displays the Make General Journal Entries window (see Figure 13-8).

   You can page through the general journal entries you've previously created by displaying the Make General Journal Entries window and then clicking the View Previous Journal Entry and View Next Journal Entry command buttons.

2. **Enter the transaction date for the journal entry.**

   This bit of information goes into the Date box. Just as you guessed.

3. **(Optional but a good idea) Enter a transaction number for the journal entry.**

   Whenever I enter journal entries for clients, I always use the prefix "CPA," the year, and then a number. For example, the first general entry I make for 2005 for some client might use an Entry No. of CPA200501. The second general entry might use an Entry No. of CPA200502, and so on.

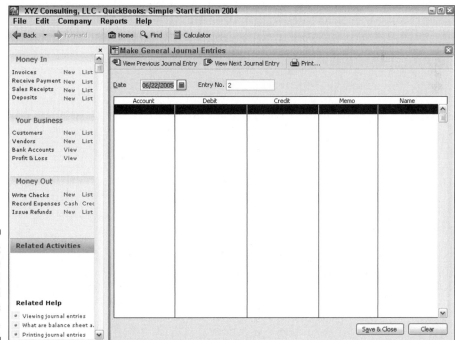

Figure 13-8:
The Make General Journal Entries window.

4. Enter one of the debits or credits for the journal entry.

To enter a debit or credit, first select the appropriate debit or credit account from the Account column. Then enter the debit or credit amount — but be sure to place the amount into the correct column: Debits go in the Debit column, and credits go in the Credit column. You can enter a little memo description in the Memo column, if you want. If you debit or credit an accounts receivable or accounts payable account, you must also name the customer or vendor associated with the accounts receivable or accounts payable transaction.

5. Repeat Step 4 as necessary.

You need to repeat Step 4 to record each debit or credit that's part of the journal entry.

6. Print a copy of the journal entry.

You can print a copy of the journal entry by clicking the Print command button at the top of the Make General Journal Entries window.

7. Click Save & Close when you're done.

Does my discussion here seem almost criminally concise? Here's the problem if you're feeling this way: In order to make general journal entries, you need to understand double-entry bookkeeping. Having solid accounting skills also is helpful. Most business owners don't have this knowledge or these skills. And when that's true, the gnarly work of creating and entering general journal entries is best left to the bookkeeper or CPA.

Part IV
Real-Life Examples

The 5th Wave
By Rich Tennant

"I bought QuickBooks Simple Start to help us monitor and control our office expenses. While I was there, I picked up 7 new games, a couple of screen savers, 4 new mousepads, this nifty pull out keyboard cradle, 3 new speakers..."

In this part . . .

Oftentimes, the tough stuff in accounting isn't the theory. The tough part is figuring out how things work in practice. For this reason, this part's chapters try to supply you with practical information and ideas for handling fixed assets and payroll as well as using QuickBooks Simple Start in a service business and in a retail business.

Chapter 14

Accounting for Fixed Assets

. . . .

In This Chapter

▶ Identifying fixed assets

▶ Recording a fixed assets purchase

▶ Dealing with depreciation

▶ Recording fixed asset sales

▶ Dealing with Section 179 elections

. . . .

*F*ixed assets accounting represents one of the trickier accounting subjects for small businesses. Here's why: When you buy a computer or some piece of equipment, that purchase can't be recorded as an expense. Instead, the asset purchase is recorded as an addition to the firm's assets. The expense associated with using the asset is recognized only later on by recording depreciation. If the asset is disposed of or discarded — such as at the end of the asset's useful life — you have another headache to deal with: recording a gain or loss on the disposal.

In this chapter, I want to guide you through the steps for handling these common situations. But first, I'll identify what fixed assets are and aren't.

Identifying Fixed Assets

You and I need to start this chapter with a definition of what fixed assets are. So I'll do that here. A fixed asset is an item that should be listed on the balance sheet as an asset. Futhermore, a fixed asset's cost gets included in your profit calculations by recording depreciation.

Fixed assets, therefore, include things like computers, machinery, furniture, equipment, and even real estate improvements.

Fixed assets don't, however, include things like pencils and paper you buy because these things don't really belong on the balance sheet as assets. (A couple of pencils and a ream of paper just aren't of high enough value to matter, right?) And fixed assets don't include cash or stock investments or trade accounts receivable. (Even though these items are valuable assets and do belong on the balance sheet's list of assets, these items aren't depreciated.)

Recording a Fixed Asset Purchase

You can record the purchase of a fixed asset when you record the check you wrote to buy the asset or the credit card charge for the asset.

Writing a check for a fixed asset purchase

You use the Write Checks window to record the purchase of a fixed asset you pay for by writing a check. Specifically, you follow these steps:

1. **Click the Write Checks icon and then New.**

   Alternatively, select Write Checks New from the Navigators list. The Write Checks window appears, as shown in Figure 14-1.

2. **Click the Bank Account drop-down list and choose the account from which you want to write this check.**

   This step is very important if you have more than one account. Make sure that you choose the correct account; otherwise, your account balances will be incorrect.

3. **Specify the check date.**

   Click in the Date box and type the check date. You enter the date using the MM/DD/YYYY format. For example, you enter November 26, 2005 as 11/26/2005.

4. **Fill in the Pay to the Order Of line.**

   To specify who the check pays, type the payee name into the Pay to the Order Of box. Or, if you've written a check to this person or party before, you can open the Pay to the Order Of drop-down list box (by clicking the little arrowhead that appears at the right end of the box). When Quick-Books Simple Start displays a list of previous payees, you can select one by clicking its name.

5. Type the amount of the check.

Enter the amount of the fixed asset purchase next to the dollar sign and press Tab. When you press Tab, QuickBooks Simple Start writes out the amount for you on the Dollars line.

6. (Optional) Fill in the Address text box.

You need to fill in this box only if the address isn't there already and you intend to send the check by mail in a window envelope.

7. (Optional) Fill in the Memo line.

You can put a message to the payee on the Memo line. For a fixed asset purchase, the memo line would be a good place to specifically identify the asset you're purchasing.

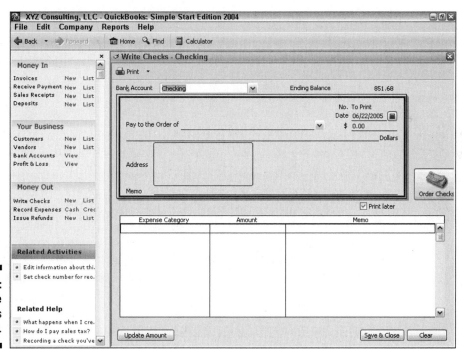

Figure 14-1:
The Write
Checks
window.

8. Move the cursor down to the Expense Category column and enter an appropriate account name for the fixed asset.

This is where the fixed assets stuff gets a little tricky. You need to set up an account for tracking your fixed assets. And I recommend you go further than that. I recommend you set up an account for each major category of fixed assets: computers, equipment, furniture, machinery, and so on. (These are just example fixed asset categories. You might need different categories.)

The first time you enter a "fixed asset category" account name — such as computers — QuickBooks Simple Start asks if you want to set up a new account. When you indicate that you do, the New Account dialog box (see Figure 14-2) displays. All you need to do is specify that the Type is Fixed Asset.

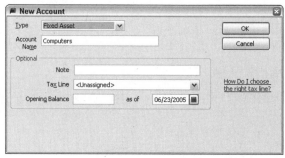

Figure 14-2:
The New
Account
dialog box.

In the future, when you record another fixed asset purchase for a particular category, you won't have to do anything to use the account.

9. Tab over to the Amount column, if necessary, and change the numbers around (see Figure 14-3).

If you purchased more than one fixed asset with a single check and, therefore, are distributing this check across more than one account, make sure that the numbers in the Amount column correctly distribute the check to the appropriate accounts.

10. If you want to, enter words of explanation or encouragement in the Memo column.

Someday, you might have to go back to this check and try to figure out what the fixed asset was. Use the Memo column, as appropriate, to store additional clues.

11. Click Save & Close to finish writing the check and then close the Write Checks window.

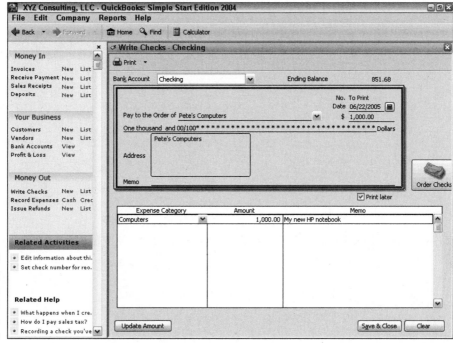

Figure 14-3:
A
completed
check.

As this point, by the way, you've not only recorded the check. You've also added the new fixed asset to your balance sheet.

Charging a credit card for a fixed asset purchase

To record a fixed asset purchase you pay for through a credit card charge, you follow these steps:

1. Select Record Expenses Credit from the Navigators list.

The Credit Card Register window appears, as shown in Figure 14-4.

2. Specify the charge date.

Click in the Date box and type the check date. You enter the date using the MM/DD/YYYY format. For example, you enter November 26, 2005 as 11/26/2005.

3. (Optional) Enter a reference number for the charge.

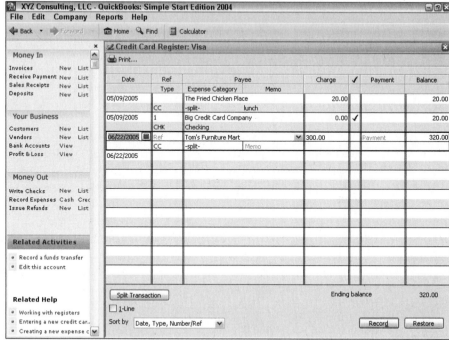

Figure 14-4:
The Credit
Card
Register
window.

4. Fill in the Payee.

To specify who the charge paid, type the vendor or merchant name into the Payee box. Or, if you've written a check to this person before or charged an amount with this person before, you can open the Payee drop-down list box (by clicking the little arrowhead that appears at the right end of the box). When QuickBooks Simple Start displays a list of previous payees, you can select one by clicking its name.

5. Type the amount of the charge.

Use the Tab key or the mouse to select the Charge box. Then, type in the charge amount in the Charge column. You don't want to stick the amount into the Payment column. You use the Payment column when you pay off the credit card balance (or some portion of the credit card balance), as I describe in Chapter 5.

6. (Optional) Fill in the Memo line.

If you want to record additional information about the charge, use the Memo line to record some extra bit of credit card charge or fixed assets information that you want to record but haven't been able to store elsewhere. A little description of the specific thing you purchased might be nice to have three years from now when you look back at this charge. Just an idea.

7. (Optional) Split the charge.

What if the money that you're charging can be distributed across two, three, or four fixed asset accounts? Click the Split Transaction button. QuickBooks Simple Start opens a little, cute, pop-up Split Transaction area that lets you split a charge amount into several different fixed asset categories and amounts (see Figure 14-5). Use the Expense Category column to describe the fixed asset accounts. Use the Amount column to specify the fixed asset amounts.

The individual split transaction details must match (in amount) the total amount you enter into the Charge box in the Credit Card Register window. You can indicate to enter the total of the individual split transaction details into the Charge box. Simply click the Recalc button. Or, if you want to start over, click the Clear button to erase the split transaction details.

8. Click Record to finish recording the credit card charge.

The new fixed asset purchase is added to the QuickBooks Simple Start balance sheet. In fact, take a peek at Figure 14-6. See the $1,300 of fixed assets that balance shows? The $1,300 is a total of the $1,000 computer purchase shown in Figure 14-3 and the $300 furniture purchase shown in Figure 14-5.

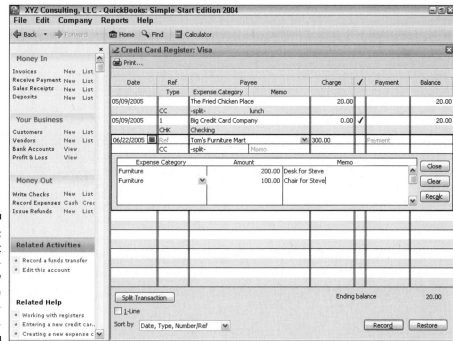

Figure 14-5:
The Credit Card Regis-ter window showing the Split Trans-action area.

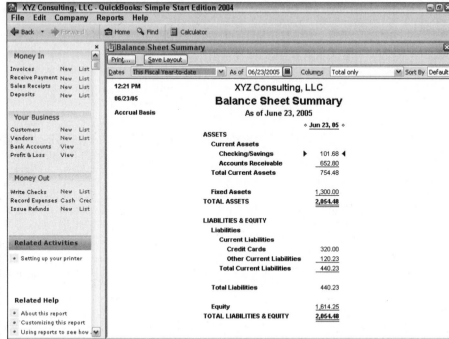

Figure 14-6:
The balance
sheet report
shows your
fixed assets.

Dealing with Depreciation

To count the expense of using (or using up) a fixed asset, you record depreciation. This depreciation increases the expenses shown on the profit and loss statement. And the depreciation adjusts the fixed asset cost shown on the balance sheet.

A simple depreciation example

Let me quickly describe the mechanics of how depreciation works. Suppose you buy a piece of machinery for $1,000 and will be able to use the machinery for five years.

Depreciation simply allocates the $1,000 of cost over the five years of use. One rather straightforward way to make such an allocation would be to charge $200 of depreciation expense each year. Over five years, $1,000 of depreciation would appear on the profit and loss statement (at the rate of $200 a year). And over this same five-year time, the fixed asset cost shown on the balance sheet would start at $1,000, then drop to $800, then to $600, then to $400, and finally to $200.

Depreciation in reality

Despite the conceptual simplicity of depreciation, the actual calculations are not ones you should typically make. You can't simply take the asset cost and divide by the years of use for two big reasons.

First of all, that "cost divided by years of use" approach, which is called *straightline depreciation,* isn't actually used much. Most businesses for most assets use accelerated depreciation, which puts relatively more of the asset's cost into the early years of the asset's life.

Second, income tax accounting rules (which is what most small businesses use) don't let you pick any old "years of use" value. Congress and the Department of Treasury have decided which "years of use" values people should plug into the depreciation calculations. (The charter yacht? Ten years. Your corporate jet? Five years. That ratty old couch in your reception area? Seven years.)

Because the depreciations are tricky and require an understanding of the tax laws you're subject to and maybe an understanding of generally accepted accounting principles, you'll probably get your depreciation numbers from your tax adviser or CPA. (These might be the same person.) In effect, old "Jimmy" will say to you, "Hey, record $300 of depreciation on your computers."

All you need to do, then, is enter the transaction using the given amounts. To enter the depreciation, you make a journal entry.

Making depreciation journal entries

To enter a depreciation journal entry, follow these steps:

1. **Choose Company⇨For Your Accountant⇨Make General Journal Entries.**

   The Make General Journal Entries dialog box appears (see Figure 14-7).

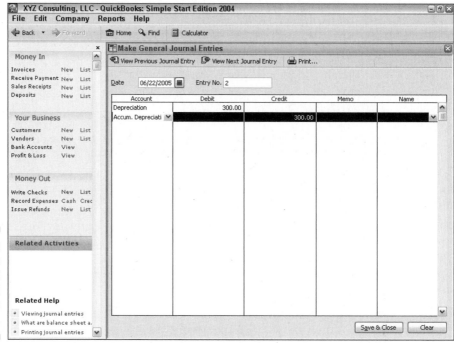

Figure 14-7:
The Make
General
Journal
Entries
dialog box.

2. **Enter the transaction date for the journal entry.**

   You just need to make sure that the transaction date falls in the right year. The right year is the year in which the depreciation expense should be counted.

3. **(Optional) Enter a transaction number for the journal entry.**

4. **Record the depreciation expense.**

   To record the depreciation expense, type **Depreciation** into the first row of the Account column. If this is the first time you've recorded depreciation expense, QuickBooks Simple Start asks if you want to set up a new account. Indicate you do. Then, when prompted by the New Account dialog box, indicate that you want to set up an Expense account with the name "Depreciation." Then enter the depreciation expense amount into the first row of the Debit column.

5. **Record the accumulated depreciation.**

   To adjust the fixed asset cost shown on the balance sheet, type **Accum. Depreciation** into the second row of the Account column. If this is the first time you've recorded accumulated depreciation, QuickBooks Simple Start asks if you want to set up a new account. Indicate you do. Then, when prompted by the New Account dialog box, indicate that you want to set up a Fixed Asset account with the name "Accum. Depreciation." Then enter the accumulated depreciation amount into the second row of the Credit column.

6. **Click Save & Close when you're done.**

   When you finish entering your journal entry — and the darn thing balances — click Save & Close. Figure 14-7, by the way, shows an actual depreciation journal entry that records $300 of depreciation and that adjusts the fixed assets cost shown in the balance sheet by $300.

Recording Fixed Asset Sales

When you sell or dispose of a fixed asset, you need to remove the fixed asset and any of the associated accumulated depreciation from the balance sheet. You also need to compensate for the fact that your depreciation estimates — after all, they were only estimates — were wrong and that you either overdepreciated or underdepreciated the asset.

Recording an asset sale: Example #1

Suppose that you purchased an asset for $1,000, have recorded $300 of depreciation, and are now selling the asset for $500.

The key thing to realize about this example is that although, via the depreciation, you estimated that cost of using the asset to be $300 — that was the depreciation you charged — the actual asset cost was $500. You bought the asset for $1,000 and then later sold it for $500 in cash. In a sense, you underdepreciated the asset by $200.

The amount of underdepreciation gets recorded as a loss on sale using an Other Expense account. Figure 14-8 shows a general entry that records such a transaction. Notice that the first two lines of the journal just reverse the amounts previously debited to the Computers account or credited to the Accum. Depreciation account. The $500 debit to cash shows the cash received from the asset sale. The Other Expenses debit equal to $200 reflects the loss on the sale of the asset.

You could also set up a special expense account to record asset sale losses. If you have questions about how to set up an account, refer to the preceding section, "Making depreciation journal entries."

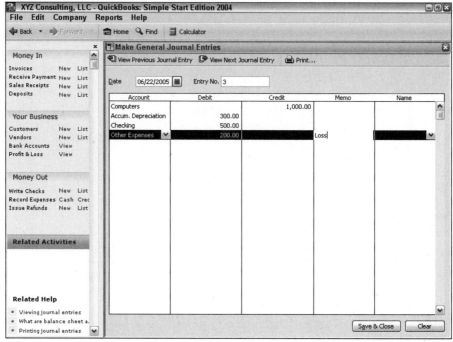

Figure 14-8:
A general journal entry to record an asset sale and $200 loss.

Recording an asset sale: Example #2

Let's change the numbers around a little bit. Suppose that you purchased an asset for $1,000, have recorded $300 of depreciation, and are now selling the asset for $1,500.

The key thing to realize about this example is that while, via the depreciation, you estimated again that cost of using the asset to be $300 — that was the depreciation you charged — there was no cost to using the asset. You bought the asset for $1,000 and then later sold it for $1,500 in cash. The asset didn't depreciate. It appreciated.

The sum of the overdepreciation and appreciation gets recorded as a gain on sale using the Other Income. Figure 14-9 shows a general entry that records such a transaction. Notice that the first two lines of the journal just reverse the amounts previously debited to the Computers account or credited to the Accum. Depreciation account. The $1,500 debit to cash shows the cash received from the asset sale. The Other Income credit equal to $800 reflects the gain on the sale of the asset.

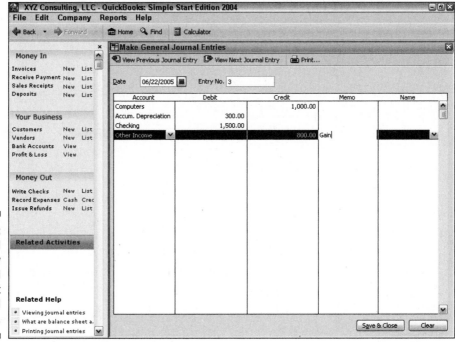

Figure 14-9:
A general
journal entry
to record
an asset
sale and
$800 gain.

You could also set up a special income account to record asset sale gains. If you have questions about how to set up an account, refer to the section, "Making depreciation journal entries."

Recording an asset disposal

One final, perhaps painful, example. Suppose that you purchased an asset for $1,000, have recorded $300 of depreciation, and will throw the thing in the Dumpster tonight when your neighbors aren't looking.

The key thing to realize about this example is that while, via the depreciation, you estimated that cost of using the asset to be $300, the actual asset cost was $1,000. You bought the asset for $1,000 and disposed of the thing in a "transaction" that got you no cash. In a sense, you underdepreciated the asset by $700.

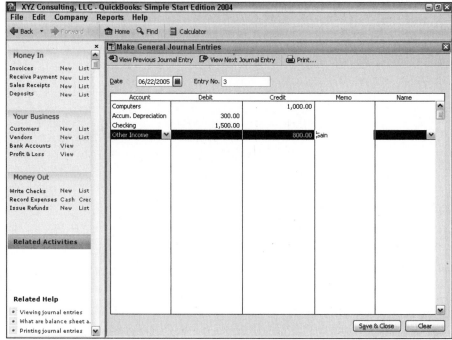

Figure 14-10:
A general
journal entry
to record a
Dumpster
disposal and
$700 loss.

The amount of underdepreciation gets recorded as a loss on disposal using the Other Expense account. Figure 14-10 shows a general entry that records such a transaction. Notice that the first two lines of the journal just reverse the amounts previously debited to the Computers account or credited to the Accum. Depreciation account. The Other Expenses debit equal to $700 reflects the loss on the Dumpster disposal of the asset.

It's a good idea to annually take a peek at your fixed assets records and make sure that you're not showing assets on your balance sheet that no longer exist and that the numbers that appear on the balance sheet make sense. I share this accounting tip for three reasons: First, you probably incur losses when you sell or dispose of old assets, so by not keeping good track of your fixed assets, sales, and disposals, you probably miss deductions. Second, in many jurisdictions, businesses pay personal property taxes (not just real property taxes). By keeping good fixed assets lists and records, you reduce the likelihood that you're paying property taxes on stuff you don't even own. (You might also save on insurance costs for those same "phantom" fixed assets.) Finally, if you never clean up your fixed assets records, they rather quickly become a terrible mess.

Dealing with Section 179 Elections

Tax laws let you immediately write off, or expense, rather than depreciate certain types of assets. This special rule is called a Section 179 election or Section 179 depreciation.

Section 179 depreciation represents a big break for small businesses. You can't, however, use more than a certain amount of Section 179 depreciation in a year: $24,000 in 2002 and $100,000 in 2003, 2004, and 2005. You also need to know some other nitty-gritty details, so confer with your tax adviser if you have questions.

Although you might be tempted to just ignore everything that I've said about depreciation and fixed asset accounts and all the stuff in the preceding paragraphs of this chapter, I suggest you treat Section 179 depreciation just like other depreciation. In other words, I think you use the same step sequences as I give through the earlier sections of this chapter to handle the purchase of a Section 179 asset (see "Recording a Fixed Assets Purchase"), the depreciation of the Section 179 asset (see "Dealing with Depreciation"), and the ultimate sale or disposal of a Section 179 asset (see "Recording Fixed Asset Sales").

What will be different about so-called Section 179 assets is that you'll probably immediately depreciate them. For example, if you buy a $1,000 asset that'll be used for five years, you won't depreciate only $200 of the asset's cost. You'll immediately depreciate the entire $1,000 of asset cost.

I don't feel super-strongly about this "just pretend it's regular depreciation" approach. But I make my recommendation because you need a way to really flag your Section 179 asset purchases. While you will (probably) be able to write off immediately the cost of most fixed assets you purchase (subject to a bunch of complicated rules I'm not covering here), in order to take advantage of this writeoff, you need to carefully report the Section 179 treatment on your tax return. By treating your Section 179 assets as regular assets, they will be very visible. Neither you nor your tax adviser is as likely to forget or omit the Section 179 reporting requirements.

If you say, "Ah the heck with this . . . I'll just write off the purchase of equipment to, hey, I know, the regular old supplies expense account," you might be in trouble. You or your tax adviser might not catch your bookkeeping error and might, as a result, forget or omit to report the information required in order to take the Section 179 writeoff. If that happens and your return is examined, the IRS will probably make you depreciate your fixed assets over the usual economic life. You won't, at that point, be able to go back, plead ignorance, and retroactively make the Section 179 elections. You can only make a Section 179 election on the original timely filed return.

Chapter 15

Processing Payroll

● ●

In This Chapter

▶ Preparing for payroll

▶ Calculating wages and recording a payroll check

▶ Making federal tax deposits

▶ Filing quarterly and annual payroll tax returns

▶ Producing annual wage statements, such as W-2s

▶ Handling state payroll taxes

● ●

A lot of people with small businesses need to deal with payroll. Unfortunately, although all the payroll tax forms and tedious calculations might make you want to have someone else — like a bookkeeper or payroll service — do the work, that's often not an economical solution. Payroll service bureaus (including Intuit's) charge around $1,000 a year — even if you have only one employee. For this reason, I want to provide you with some quick-and-dirty instructions about how to handle simple payroll situations with QuickBooks Simple Start. Oh, sure. It won't be pretty. But I promise you it'll be cheap.

If you're planning to use QuickBooks Simple Start for doing a lot of payroll, do yourself a favor and upgrade to QuickBooks Pro or QuickBooks Premier. The full-featured versions of QuickBooks let you more easily calculate withholding amounts and prepare paychecks.

However, if you've got only a simple payroll need (such as for a single employee who's paid the same amount each month), this chapter explains how you do so.

Getting Ready for Payroll

To prepare payroll checks and summarize the payroll information that you need to prepare quarterly and annual returns, you need to set up some special accounts. You also need to do some paperwork stuff. I describe how to do both things in this section.

Getting QuickBooks Simple Start ready

To do payroll in QuickBooks Simple Start, you need to set up several liability accounts and some payroll expense accounts. Fortunately, doing so is not particularly difficult.

I'm going to describe how you do this task for purposes of United States federal income and payroll taxes. If you employ people in one of the states that has a state income tax — California, say — you might also have to deal with state payroll taxes. But you can track and process these the same way you process the federal taxes. (Some counties and cities even have income taxes, but these should also work the same way.)

I should say that you might also have other taxes to pay if you employ people outside the United States. But, hey, with a couple hundred countries in the world, your best bet is to get specific advice from someone of authority or expertise in the country of employment.

Setting up liability accounts

You need to set up three liability accounts to deal with federal payroll and income taxes:

✔ **Payroll-SS** to track Social Security

✔ **Payroll-MCARE** to track Medicare

✔ **Payroll-FWH** (for *Federal Withholding*) to track federal income taxes owed

To set up a liability account for any of these payroll tax liabilities, follow these steps:

1. **Choose Company⇨Lists⇨Chart of Accounts.**

   QuickBooks displays the Chart of Accounts window. You've probably seen this window about a hundred times before. If you want to see the window right now, though, choose the command and look at your screen.

2. **Right-click the window and choose Add Account.**

   QuickBooks Simple Start displays the New Account window, shown in Figure 15-1.

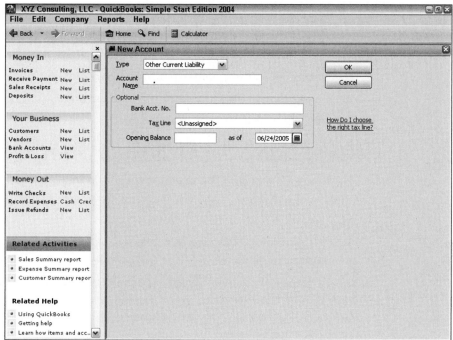

Figure 15-1:
The New
Account
window.

3. Indicate you want to set up an Other Current Liability account.

To do this, select Other Current Liability from the Type drop-down list box. Doing this tells QuickBooks Simple Start that you're going to set up a Liability account.

4. Type the appropriate account name: Payroll-SS, Payroll-MCARE, **or** Payroll-FWH.

Move the cursor to the Account Name text box and type in the right name.

5. Click OK.

6. Repeat Steps 2 through 5 for all the other payroll tax liability accounts you want to add.

Remember that you need at least three payroll tax liability accounts — Payroll-SS, Payroll-MCARE, and Payroll-FWH — for the people you employ in the United States. And if you live in a state with income taxes, you either need to move or set up a fourth account: Payroll-SWH.

The only trick to naming other payroll tax liability accounts is that you need to start each liability account name with the word *Payroll*. No, I didn't just make up this rule arbitrarily. I have a reason for this policy. You can easily create a report that prints information on all the accounts that start with the word *Payroll*.

Setting up a payroll expense account

You also need to set up several payroll expense accounts, which isn't tough. Here's all you have to do:

1. **(If necessary) Choose Company⇨Lists⇨Chart of Accounts.**

   QuickBooks Simple Start displays the Chart of Accounts window.

2. **Right-click the window and choose New.**

   QuickBooks Simple Start displays the New Account window, shown in Figure 15-1.

3. **Enter Payroll-Wages as the expense account name.**

   Move the cursor to the Account Name text box and type **Payroll-Wages**.

4. **Click OK.**

   QuickBooks Simple Start adds the expense account to the chart of accounts and redisplays the Chart of Accounts window.

5. **Repeat Steps 2 through 4 to add expense accounts to track Social Security and Medicare.**

   You also need to set up expense accounts for the company's share of the Social Security taxes and the company's share of the Medicare taxes. You can use Payroll-Comp SS to track the company's share of the Social Security taxes. And you use Payroll-Comp MCARE to track the company's share of the Medicare taxes.

Congratulations, Mr. Bond. You saved the world again. You created the liability and expense accounts that you need to track the amounts you pay employees and the payroll taxes you withhold and owe.

By the way, if you have state or local income taxes, these taxes should be handled the same way as federal income taxes. Just set up equivalent accounts for state and local taxes withheld. If you have state or local payroll taxes that you (the employer) pay, you need to set up liability and expense accounts like those for tracking the employer's portion of Social Security and Medicare. If you have state or local payroll taxes that your employee pays, you need to set up liability and expense accounts like those for tracking the employee's portion of Social Security and Medicare.

Getting the taxes stuff right

You also need to do a couple other things if you want to do payroll the right way in the U.S. of A.

Requesting (or demanding) an employer ID number

First, you need to file the SS-4, or Request for Employer Identification Number form, with the Internal Revenue Service (IRS) so that you can get an employer identification number. You can get this form by calling the IRS and asking for one or by visiting the IRS Web site (www.irs.gov).

In one of its cooler moves, the IRS changed its ways and now lets you apply for and receive an employer identification number over the telephone. You still need to fill out the SS-4 form, however, so that you can answer questions the IRS asks during the short telephone-application process. (You also need to mail or fax the form to the IRS after you have your telephone conversation.)

Or, even cooler, you can apply right online. Here's the URL:

http://sa1.www4.irs.gov/sa_vign/newFormSS4.do

So what about Social Security, Medicare, and withholding taxes?

You need to do two things before you can figure out how to handle all those taxes. First, you need your employees to fill out W-4 forms to let you know what filing status they will use and how many personal exemptions they will claim. Guess where you get blank W-4 forms? That's right . . . from your friendly IRS agent.

You also need to get a *Circular E Employer's Tax Guide* publication. The *Circular E* publication is the pamphlet that tells you how much you should withhold in federal income taxes, Social Security, and Medicare from a person's salary. You can get this form, as well as the additional federal forms that you must fill out to satisfy the government requirements for hiring employees, by calling those friendly people at the Internal Revenue Service. Circular E is also available online at www.irs.gov/publications/p15. To get state tax forms, you need to contact the equivalent tax agency in your state.

Paying someone for a job well done

After you tell QuickBooks Simple Start to get ready to do payroll and you collect the necessary tax information, you're ready to pay someone.

Figuring out the gross wages figure

Determining how much to pay your employees should be pretty easy. Does Raoul make $15 an hour? Did he work 40 hours? Then you owe him $600 because $15 times 40 equals $600. Is Betty's salary $400 a week? Then you owe her $400 for the week.

Calculating that deductions stuff

Your next step — after you know how much you're supposed to pay Raoul and Betty — is to figure out what Uncle Sam says you must withhold.

To determine this amount, you need both Raoul's and Betty's W-4s to find out their filing statuses and personal exemptions. Then just flip to the page in the *Circular E* that describes withholding for persons claiming those filing statuses and weekly pay.

If Raoul is single and claims just one personal exemption, for example, you need to flip to the page that shows withholding amounts for single taxpayers making what Raoul makes each week.

And Betty? Remember that Betty's pay is $400 a week. If Betty's filing status is married filing jointly and she has three personal exemptions, you need to flip to the page that shows withholding amounts for married taxpayers paid weekly.

You determine Social Security and Medicare amounts by multiplying the gross wage figure by a set percentage. Social Security is 6.2 percent of the gross wages up to a specified limit — roughly $90,000 in 2004 and 2005. The Medicare tax is 1.45 percent of the gross wages. Be sure to check your faithful *Circular E* if you think limits come into play for a particular employee. Note, too, that as I'm writing this, Congress is tinkering with the tax laws again. But, of course, Congress is *always* tinkering with the tax laws.

Figuring out someone's net wages

Table 15-1 summarizes the payroll calculations required for our friends Raoul and Betty.

Table 15-1	Payroll for Raoul and Betty		
Item	*Raoul*	*Betty*	*Explanation*
Gross Wages	$600.00	$400.00	Their pay
Withholding	$79.00	$18.00	From *Circular E*
Social Security	$37.20	$24.80	6.2 percent of gross wages
Medicare	$8.70	$5.80	1.45 percent of gross wages
Net Wages	$475.10	$351.40	What's left over

Does Table 15-1 make sense? If it doesn't, take another look at the marked information in Figures 15-2 and 15-3 and read my earlier discussion of how to figure out deductions stuff. All I've really done in the table is reorganize some information, calculate the Social Security and Medicare taxes, and show how Raoul's and Betty's gross pay gets nickeled and dimed by the various taxes they owe.

Working with other taxes and deductions

If you have other taxes and deductions to make and you understand how the federal income taxes, Social Security taxes, and Medicare taxes work, you won't have any problem working with the other taxes — no matter what they are.

State income tax withholding, for example, works like the federal income tax withholding. (Of course, you need to get the state's equivalent to the *Circular E* guide.)

In general, you treat other taxes and the amounts the employee pays similarly.

In fact, the only thing that you need to be careful about is what affects your employees' gross pay for income taxes but not their Social Security taxes — things such as 401(k) deductions and certain fringe benefits. If you have these kinds of things to deal with and you need help, just ask your accountant. (Providing general answers that will work for everyone who reads this paragraph is just too difficult — and actually kind of dangerous, too. Sorry.)

Recording a payroll check

After you make the tax deduction and net wages calculation, you're ready to record the check. Doing so is a little bit tricky, but stick with me; I'll get you through it in no time.

If Betty is milling around your computer, whining, and saying things like, "Gee, Boss, how much longer? I want to get to the bank before it closes," tell her to cool her heels for about three minutes.

Suppose that you're going to record the check by using the register window for your checking account. (As you know, recording the check into the Write Checks window works the same basic way. The difference is that by using the Write Checks window, you can more easily print the payroll check.)

After you display the checking account register window and highlight the first empty row of the register, follow these steps:

1. **Enter the date of the payroll check in the Date field.**

2. **Enter the payroll check number in the Num field.**

3. **Enter the employee name in the Payee field.**

4. **Enter the net wages amount in the Payment field.**

5. **Open the Split Transaction area (see Figure 15-2).**

   You can do so by clicking the Split Transaction button.

6. **In the first row of the Split Transaction area, enter the payroll wages amount in the correct fields.**

   Enter the account **Payroll-Wages**. The amount, of course, should be the gross wages figure (**400.00** in the example).

7. **Enter the employee's federal withholding tax and account in the second row of the Split Transaction area.**

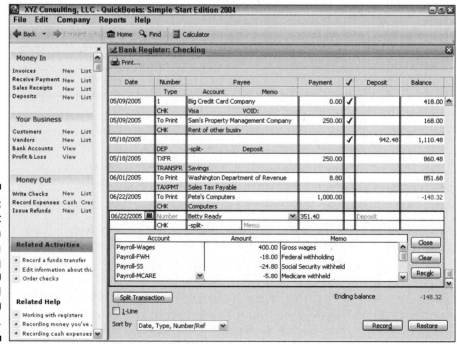

Figure 15-2:
The Split Transaction area recording Betty's $400 wages and her $351.40 paycheck.

Enter the liability account **Payroll-FWH** into the second row of the Split Transaction area. The actual tax withheld amount, which needs to be entered as a negative value, comes from the *Circular E* form (**–18.00** in this example).

8. **Enter the employee's Social Security tax withheld and account in the third row of the Split Transaction area.**

   Enter the liability account **Payroll-SS** into the third row of the Split Transaction area. The amount of the Social Security tax withheld should be 6.2 percent of the employee's gross wages and should be entered as a negative value (**–24.80** in this example). Type this number in the Amount field.

9. **Enter the employee's Medicare tax withheld and account in the fourth row of the Split Transaction area.**

   Enter the liability account **Payroll-MCARE** into the third row of the Split Transaction area. The amount of the Medicare tax withheld should be 1.45 percent of the employee's gross wages (**–5.80** in this example).

   Figure 15-2 shows the Split Transaction area filled out to record Betty's $400 of wages, the taxes poor Betty has to pay on these earnings, and the net wages figure of $351.40. If you have questions about any of these figures, take a peek again at Table 15-1.

10. **If you have other employee-paid payroll taxes, record them in the next empty rows, following the same set of procedures.**

11. **On the next two empty lines of the Split Transaction area, enter your (the employer's) matching share of the Social Security tax.**

    If the employee pays $24.80 of Social Security tax, for example, type **Payroll-Comp SS** in the Account field and **24.80** in the Amount field in the first empty line.

    Then type **Payroll-SS Account** field and **–24.80** in the Amount field in the next line to record the Social Security tax liability.

    Figure 15-3 shows the Social Security and Medicare payroll tax information.

12. **On the next two empty lines of the Split Transaction area, enter your (the employer's) matching share of the Medicare tax.**

    If the employer pays $5.80 of Medicare, for example, use the first empty line to type **Payroll-Comp MCARE** in the Account field or choose the account from the drop-down list box; then type **5.80** in the Amount field.

    Then type **Payroll-MCARE** in the Account section or choose the account from the drop-down list box; then enter **–5.80** in the Amount section in the next line to record the Medicare tax liability.

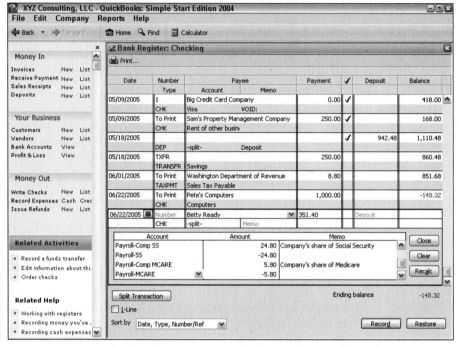

Figure 15-3:
The
employer's
matching
share of
Social
Security and
Medicare
taxes.

The accounts you use to show the payroll taxes withheld and owed are liability accounts. By looking at the balances of these accounts on your Balance Sheet or on the Chart of Accounts window, you can easily see how much you owe the government.

13. **If you have other employer-paid payroll taxes, record these following the employer's matching share of the Social Security and Medicare taxes.**

    You can use this same basic approach to record federal and state unemployment taxes.

14. **Click OK to close the Split Transaction area.**

15. **To record the payroll check and related employer-paid payroll tax information in the register, click Record.**

You did it! You recorded a payroll check and the related payroll taxes. Maybe it wasn't all that much fun, but at least it wasn't very difficult. (Chapter 5 describes how to print checks, just in case you're interested.)

Depositing Taxes

Make no mistake. Uncle Sam wants the money you withhold from an employee's payroll check for federal income taxes, Social Security, and Medicare. Uncle Sam also wants the payroll taxes you owe — the matching Social Security and Medicare taxes, federal unemployment taxes, and so on.

Every so often, then, you need to pay Uncle Sam the amounts you owe.

You can see how much you own in payroll tax withholding amounts by producing a balance sheet and then double-clicking on the Other Current Liabilities value. To produce a balance sheet, choose Reports⇨For Your Accountant⇨ Balance Sheet Summary.

Making this payment is simple. Just write a check payable for the account balances shown in the payroll tax liability accounts. If you have written only the one check to Betty (as shown in Figures 15-4 and 15-5), for example, your payroll liability accounts would show the following balances:

Liability Account	Amount
Payroll-SS	$49.60
Payroll-MCARE	$11.60
Payroll-FWH	$18.00
Total	$79.20

Notice that the Payroll-SS account balance and the Payroll-MCARE account balance include both the employee's and the employer's Social Security and Medicare taxes.

Then you write a check for the $79.20 you owe (see Figure 15-4). The only tricky thing about this transaction is that you transfer the check amount to the payroll liability accounts. In effect, you transfer money from your checking account to the government to pay off the payroll taxes you owe.

The first time you see this sort of transfer, it can be a little confusing. So take a minute to think about it. If you write the check to the government, your checking account doesn't have the money in it anymore, and you don't owe the government the money anymore. Therefore, you need to decrease both the checking account balance and the liability account balance. In QuickBooks, you do so with an account transfer.

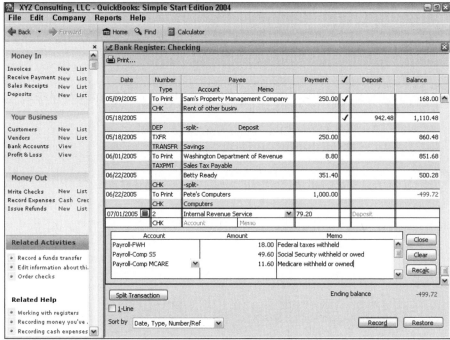

Figure 15-4:
The Split
Transaction
area for
paying
Betty's pay-
roll taxes.

When do you make payroll tax deposits? Good question. Fortunately, it's not one you have to answer. The Internal Revenue Service tells you when you're supposed to deposit your money. In my business, for example, I have to deposit payroll taxes within a couple of days of doing payroll. Some businesses have to deposit more frequently or more quickly. And some businesses get to deposit less quickly or less frequently.

While I am on the subject of federal payroll tax deposits, I should talk about another general rule related to when you need to make the deposit: If your accumulated payroll taxes are less than $1,000, you can just pay the taxes the next time you're supposed to remit payroll taxes: the next payroll date, the next month, or whatever. (This is called the *De Minimis* rule — named after the Congresswoman Dee Minimis, I think.) Don't rely on this *rule,* however, without first checking with either the Internal Revenue Service or your tax adviser.

To make a payroll tax deposit, just run your check with a federal tax deposit coupon to a financial institution qualified as a depository for federal taxes (probably your local bank) or to the Federal Reserve bank serving your geographic area. The IRS should have already sent you a book of coupons as a result of your requesting an employer ID number. And one other thing: Make your check payable to the depository or to the Federal Reserve.

Some businesses are either now, or will shortly be, required to electronically remit payroll tax deposits directly to the U.S. Treasury. The IRS should tell you when that's the case. Talk to your bank if you need to do this.

Filing Quarterly Payroll Tax Returns

At the end of every quarter, you need to file a quarterly 941 payroll tax return that reports the total wages you've paid employees. (By *quarters* here, I'm referring to calendar quarters. You don't do this four times on a Sunday afternoon as you or your couch-potato spouse watch football.)

To get the gross wages totals, print a profit and loss statement and look at the total shown for the Payroll-Wages account. This is the number you'll drop onto the payroll tax return. You can do this by choosing Reports⇨For Your Accountant⇨Profit and Loss Standard. QuickBooks Simple Start displays the profit and loss report, but the dates will probably be wrong, so fix the dates using the From and To boxes, shown in Figure 15-5.

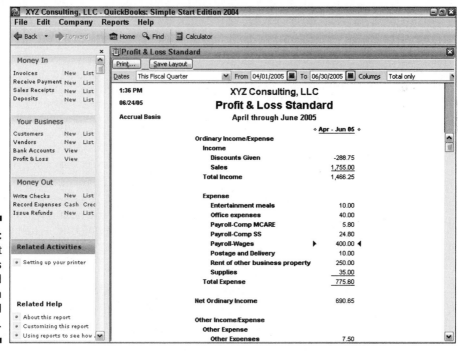

Figure 15-5:
The Profit & Loss Standard report with the payroll information.

The Payroll-Wages amount — $400 in the example — is the gross wages upon which employer payroll taxes are calculated.

The Payroll-Comp MCARE and Payroll-Comp SS amounts show the company-paid payroll taxes. The company's Social Security contributions and Medicare contributions are the amounts you recorded to date for the employer Social Security and Medicare taxes — so you need to double these figures to determine the actual Social Security and Medicare taxes you owe.

Note: If your accountant fills out the 941 for you, you don't even need to read this stuff. Your accountant won't have any problem completing the quarterly payroll tax return by using the QuickBooks Simple Start report and, in fact — I kid you not — will probably even enjoy it.

Computing Annual Returns and Wage Statements

At the end of the year, you need to file some annual returns — like the 940 federal unemployment tax return — and the W-2 and W-3 wages statements. (You'll need to prepare these by hand. Perhaps to protest all the work that small businesses have to go to in order to comply with tax laws, you can prepare these forms by hand using a cheap ballpoint pen. Just an idea.)

As a practical matter, the only thing that's different about filling out these reports is that you need to use a Profit & Loss Standard report that covers the entire year — not just a single quarter. So you need to enter the range of dates in the report window as January 1 and December 31.

The 940 annual return is darn easy if you've been wrestling with the 941 quarterly return. The 940 annual return works the same basic way as those more difficult quarterly tax returns. You print the old payroll report, enter a few numbers, and then write a check for the amount you owe.

Note that you need to prepare any state unemployment annual summaries before preparing the 940, because the 940 requires information from the state returns.

For the W-2 statements and the summary W-3 (which summarizes your W-2s), you just print the old profit and loss report and then, carefully following directions, enter the gross wages, the Social Security and Medicare taxes withheld, and the federal income taxes withheld into the appropriate blanks.

If you have a little trouble, call the IRS. If you have a lot of trouble, splurge and have someone else do it. Any experienced bookkeeper can do the job for you.

Doing the State Payroll Taxes Thing

Yeah. I haven't talked about state payroll taxes — at least not in any great detail. I wish I could provide this sort of detailed, state-specific help to you. Unfortunately, doing so would make this chapter about 150 pages long. It would also cause me to go stark raving mad.

However, you still need to deal with the state payroll taxes. Let me say, though, that you apply to state payroll taxes the same basic mechanics you apply to the federal payroll taxes. For example, a state income tax works the same way the federal income tax works, employer-paid state unemployment taxes work the same way the employer-paid federal taxes work, and employee-paid state taxes work the same way the employee-paid Social Security and Medicare taxes work.

If you're tuned in to how federal payroll taxes work in QuickBooks Simple Start, you really shouldn't have a problem with the state payroll taxes — at least, not in terms of the mechanics.

Chapter 16

Bookkeeping in a Service Business

*Q*uickBooks Simple Start is easy to use. The program's menus use self-descriptive command names. The people who built the program clearly labeled those boxes and buttons you see on windows and dialog boxes. And much of what the program does is pretty simple (printing invoices, recording checks, tallying bank account balances, and so on). However, you can still find yourself in a bit of a pickle if you're new to QuickBooks or accounting and you need to do the bookkeeping. Applying the theory of QuickBooks to a real-life situation — for example, keeping the books for a small service business — can be tricky to figure out.

For this reason, in this chapter, I describe how to use QuickBooks Simple Start in a specific business setting: a small service business. I'll offer some tips on setting up QuickBooks Simple Start, ideas for recording revenue with invoices and sales receipts, and tips on tracking your expenses.

Setting Up for a Service Business

I love service businesses — for a couple of reasons. First, the bookkeeping is pretty easy (at least as compared to businesses that have inventory). Second, and related to the easy bookkeeping, the business profits are usually pretty easy to calculate or estimate. (In a service business, you'll usually know when you're making money and when you're not.)

But even with these advantages, you still need to get QuickBooks Simple Start set up correctly. I offer these four, heartfelt suggestions:

✔ **Use a separate bank account.**

Be sure that you're using a separate bank account for the business's deposits and checks. Oh, I know. The extra bank account might mean you incur extra banking fees. And the extra account might mean that you need to be a bit more formal in your bookkeeping. But having a bank account that's, well, the business's, really will make your bookkeeping easier.

✔ **Consider using several items and income accounts.**

To track your income in detail, use a combination of items and income accounts. This is a really important point, so let me belabor it a bit. Suppose you sell marine engine repair services and that you work on both inboard and outboard engines. You might be tempted to just use a single item (like "Repairs") and a single income account (like "Service"). But that lumping doesn't let you track your sales in much detail. Suppose you instead use items such as: Outboard Parts, Inboard Parts, Outboard Supplies, Inboard Supplies, Outboard Labor, and Inboard Labor. Further suppose that all of the "Outboard" items are grouped together into an Outboard Repairs income account and that all of the "Inboard" items are grouped together into an Inboard Reports income account. By using these more detailed items and income accounts, you'll have a much better idea of where your revenue comes from.

For information on setting up an item and adding income accounts to the chart of accounts, refer to Chapter 3.

✔ **Set up a good Customer List.**

If you enjoy recurring sales to customers, you want to track your sales by customers. This means that you need to add each customer to the Customer List. The two advantages of working with customers you've identified and described using the Customer List are that you can easily see: (1) what you sell to each customer, and (2) what each customer owes you.

For information on setting up a Customer List, refer to Chapter 3.

✔ **But don't go crazy.**

If you have a one-time sale to a customer and collect the cash at the time of the sale — suppose you rent sailboats on the beach in Hawaii — set up a catchall customer called something like "Cash Rentals" and use it to record all your cash sales for the day using a giant, end-of-the-day sales receipt transaction. In other words, if you rented sailboats to 17 customers over the course of the afternoon and in total collected $340 in cash, you can record a single sales receipt transaction for the day in the amount of $340 and to the customer "Cash Rentals."

For information on recording sales receipts, refer to Chapter 6.

Recording Invoices and Sales Receipts

In Chapters 4 and 6, I provide step-by-step descriptions of how to use the Create Invoices window and the Enter Sales Receipts window to record invoices and sales receipts. I'm not going to repeat that information here. I do, however, want to show you what I think a service-business invoice and a service-business sales receipt should look like.

The near-perfect service invoice

Ah, I suppose that the adjective near-perfect is a little inaccurate. But take a look at the invoice shown in Figure 16-1. I want to make several observations about service invoices.

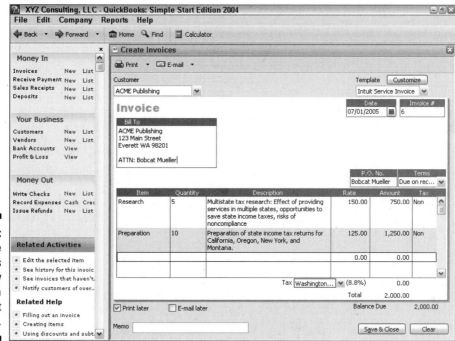

Figure 16-1:
The Create
Invoices
window
showing a
near-perfect
invoice.

Hint #1: Use a Service or Professional Invoice

See the drop-down list box that appears just beneath the Customize button? (Look in the upper-right corner of the window.) You almost certainly want to be either using the Intuit Service Invoice template for your service invoices (which is what I show in Figure 16-1) or the Intuit Professional Invoice template. There's not much difference between the two invoices, so look at both and pick the one that shows the invoice information you want to appear.

Hint #2: Verify that the address information is complete and correct

See the Bill To box? It's the one that provides the billing address information. This sounds so obvious, but make sure that information is complete and correct. Like, dude, obviously, you want to make sure that the company name and address information is correct. But you should also think about whether additional information will speed your invoice's delivery to the person who will pay or will need to approve the payment. For example, if the invoice should go to the accounts payable department, maybe that information should appear on the first line of the address block. Or if the invoice should be sent to the attention of some person, include that information in the address block.

Hint #3: Double-check the invoice date and payment terms

Many businesses — and especially large businesses — will pay an invoice based on a combination of the invoice date and the payment terms. You want to make sure these bits of information are correctly entered. Right?

Hint #4: Use sales-y items and item descriptions

Here's my final nitpicky little point. I think that you should attempt to use richly descriptive and, if possible, sales-y items and item descriptions. I don't think, for example, that I can (as a CPA) send some client a bill for $2,000 and just label the invoice as being "For services rendered." That's not fair to the client. And it's also not very good for my recordkeeping. (What if I later have a question about what I did for the client?) A better approach, I think, is to use items and item descriptions that show the client received good value for the services provided. Look at the item and descriptions I used in Figure 16-1. Aren't those better than a one-line, "For services rendered" item? I think so.

The near-perfect sales receipt

Figure 16-2 shows a pretty darn good example of a sales receipt. Let me throw out some hints and make some observations about such receipts.

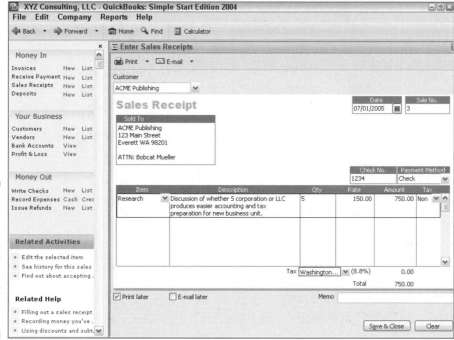

Figure 16-2:
The Enter
Sales
Receipts
window
showing a
near-perfect
sales
receipt.

Hint #1: Get the date right

Just for your own recordkeeping, you want to make sure that this information is right. Otherwise your bank reconciliations will be murderously difficult. And your profit and loss statement and sales reports might also be wrong.

Hint #2: Correctly identify the payment method

You will need to correctly identify the payment method using the Payment Method box. You'll also want to record the check number if the customer or client pays with a check. Without this information, you might later find it really difficult to figure out whether and how some customer paid.

Hint #3: Double-check the quantity and rate inputs

You're typically preparing a sales receipt with some customer looking over your shoulder or breathing down your neck — which is a bummer. But don't go so fast that you goof up the quantity sold or the rate inputs. These two bits of information determine what somebody is paying for your services. Get one of them wrong, and you either charge too little (in which you case you often just lose the revenue) or too much (in which case you probably tick off your customer).

Hint #4: Use sales-y items and item descriptions

As with invoices, if you can, I think you should attempt to use richly descriptive and, if possible, sales-y items and item descriptions. Later on, after the love is gone, your customer or client might look back at the sales receipt and wonder if he or she got a good value. Within reason, a lengthy, richly descriptive list of services keeps the customer happy. Such a list also lets you keep a good record of what you've done.

Recording Business Expenses

With QuickBooks Simple Start, you record your business expenses by writing checks and entering credit card charges. The only tricks are to use a business expense account when you record the check or charge. Figure 16-3 shows the Write Checks window recording $100 of office supplies — clearly a tax-deductible business expense. See how the account shows as "Office Expenses"?

Figure 16-4 shows the Credit Card Register window with the selected transaction recording the charging of $50 of tacos as legitimate business meals. See how the account shows as "Travel Meals"?

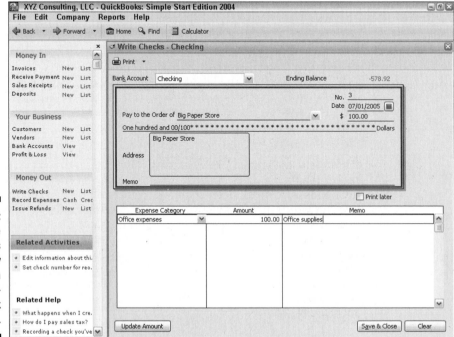

Figure 16-3:
The Write Checks window showing a paid-by-check expense.

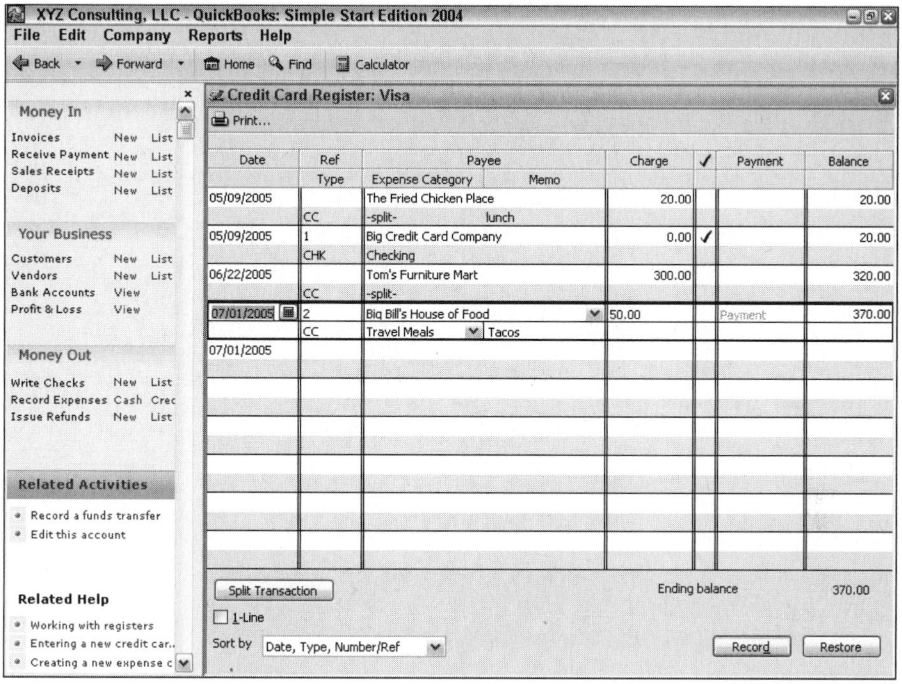

Figure 16-4: The Credit Card Register window showing a business charge for tacos.

Let me make just two comments about the expense accounts you use for recording your business expenses:

- ✔ Try to stick with the standard set of QuickBooks expense accounts. The standard set of accounts ties rather nicely to the tax return deduction categories that you'll need to later report. So working with the standard set of expense accounts makes it easy to later prepare your tax return. The other thing is — and here I'm just being honest — people tend to make a mess when they add a bunch of expense accounts.

- ✔ If you write a check or make a credit card charge that pays a personal rather than a business expense, use the owner's draws, partner's draws, dividends, or distributions account. (Figure 16-5 shows an owner's draw.) In other words, if you do ignore my earlier admonition to use a separate business bank account just for your business expenses (see "Setting Up for a Service Business"), don't compound that mistake by mixing personal and business expense accounts. The "everything-is-mixed-up" approach pretty quickly means that you don't know whether your business is making or losing money. And the approach means you or your poor accountant will find it nearly impossible to economically prepare an accurate tax return.

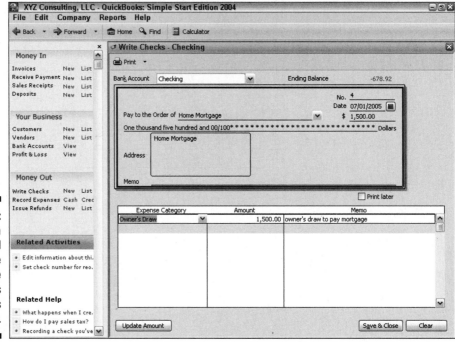

Figure 16-5:
Recording a personal expense paid by the business as an owner's draw.

Did you know that if you're a U.S. business, you're required by law to maintain an accounting system that clearly reflects income . . . so it's not just a good idea to keep accurate financial records — it's also the law.

If you pay personal expenses out of a corporate or LLC bank account, you might be weakening the liability protection offered by the corporation or LLC. If this is a big deal to you, you might want to confer with your attorney for more information.

Chapter 17

Retailing with QuickBooks Simple Start

*T*his chapter describes how to use QuickBooks Simple Start for a small retailing business. I must, however, caution you at the very start: The bookkeeping techniques I describe here aren't for large retailing businesses. Your retailing business should probably be doing less than $500,000 in annual sales and maybe less than $200,000 in annual sales in order to safely use the, er, quick-and-dirty methods discussed here.

The big accounting challenge with retail accounting is your inventory. Ideally, you want to keep a perpetual inventory system that means you keep close track of every inventory dollar and take note of each item as it moves into your store, sits on the shelf, and then moves out of the store and into some shopper's car. Such a system lets you know exactly what's selling — and what's not. And that information means that you'll sell more and carry less inventory. Unfortunately, perpetual inventory accounting for a retail business requires a point-of-sale system. And point-of-sale systems are expensive. And they also require more accounting knowledge. So very small retailers often use a periodic inventory accounting system — and that's what I describe in this chapter. One final, important comment: Intuit makes a great point-of-sale system called QuickBooks Point of Sale (full cost: roughly $1,500 including a cheap PC) that you can use when you're ready.

Setting Up for a Retail Business

I offer these four suggestions for setting up QuickBooks Simple Start for small retailing businesses:

✔ **Use a separate bank account.**

Be sure that you're using a separate bank account for the business's deposits and checks. The extra bank account might mean you incur extra banking fees and that you need to be a bit more formal in your bookkeeping. But having a business bank account really will make your bookkeeping easier. (See the later chapter section, "Recording Non-Inventory Business Expenses.")

✔ **Set up at least one inventory account and one cost of goods sold account.**

You need an inventory account to record the value of the inventory you hold at month-end and year-end. (The inventory account will use the Other Current Asset account type.) You also need a cost of goods sold account to tally the costs of the items you sell your customers. (The cost of goods sold account will use the Cost of Goods Sold account type.) If you want to track your inventory and cost of goods sold in more detail, in fact, you can use more than one inventory and cost of goods sold account. (For each inventory account, you use a corresponding cost of goods sold account.) But note that you don't want to go hog wild by setting up a bunch of inventory and cost of goods sold accounts. If you think you need lots of detailed information about your inventory and cost of goods sold, the correct course is to set up a point-of-sale system using something like the QuickBooks Point of Sale software. By using a point-of-sale system, you get inventory and cost of goods sold information by the item.

For information on adding inventory and cost of goods sold accounts to the chart of accounts, refer to Chapter 3.

✔ **Set up a good Customer List**.

If you enjoy recurring sales to customers, you might want to track your sales by customers. (This would especially be the case if you allow your customers to buy on account and then later bill them.) To track sales by customers, add each recurring customer to the Customers List. In this way, you can easily see: (1) what you sell to each customer, and (2) what each customer owes you.

For information on setting up a Customer List, refer to Chapter 3.

✔ **Set up some catchall Customer Lists.**

For your one-time or occasional customers for whom you collect the cash or charge the person's credit card at the time of the sale, set up catch-all "customers" for each payment method. For the cash or check sales, for example, you can use a "customer" labeled something like "Cash or Check." For the VISA and MasterCard charges, you can use a "customer" labeled something like "VISA and MC." You can also set up an American Express customer labeled "Amex" and a Discover card customer labeled "Discover." You'll use these groupings to record your daily sales using end-of-the-day sales receipt transactions. (I talk more about how to do this in the later chapter section, "Recording Invoices and Sales Receipts.")

For information on recording sales receipts, refer to Chapter 6.

Recording Invoices and Sales Receipts

Refer to Chapters 4 and 6 for step-by-step descriptions of how to use the Create Invoices window and the Enter Sales Receipts window to record invoices and sales receipts. In this section, I show you what I think a retail-business invoice and sales receipt should look like.

A reasonable retail invoice

Take a look at the invoice shown in Figure 17-1. It shows an imaginary sale of office supplies to some accountant, which is about as boring as it gets. But I want to use it to provide several hints about how to make reasonable retail invoices.

Hint #1: Use a Product Invoice

You almost certainly want to be using the Intuit Product Invoice "template" for your service invoices (which is what I show in Figure 17-1). This invoice template provides a bunch of boxes for describing a product sale, the mechanics of the sale, and any payment terms. To set the invoice template to Intuit Product Invoice, open the drop-down list box that appears just beneath the Customize button (this appears in the upper-right corner of the window) and choose Intuit Product Invoice.

Hint #2: Verify the address information is complete and correct

This sounds so obvious, but make sure that information is complete and correct. Obviously, you want to make sure that both the billing and the shipping information are correct. Note, too, that you might also want to think about adding information that will speed your invoice's delivery to the person who will pay or will need to approve the payment. For example, if the invoice should go to the accounts payable department, maybe that information should be added to the Bill To address block. Or if the shipment should be delivered directly to Joe-Bob in the warehouse, maybe that information should be included in the Ship To address block.

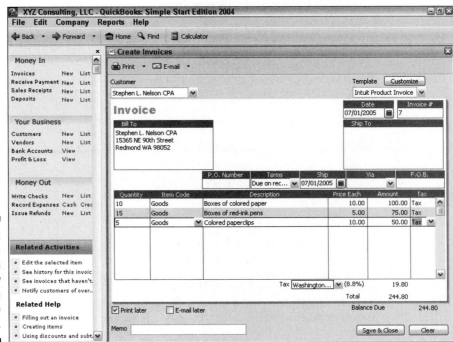

Figure 17-1:
The Create Invoices window showing a reasonable invoice.

Hint #3: Double-check the invoice date and payment terms

Many businesses — and especially large businesses — will pay an invoice based on a combination of the invoice date and the payment terms. You want to make sure these bits of information are correctly entered. Right?

Hint #4: Resist the urge to use multiple items

Now I grant you, this hint seems counterintuitive. But see the item used for each line of the invoice shown in Figure 17-1? Why, goodness sakes, every invoice line item shows as "Goods." Can that be right? Yeah, it is. You can't track inventory levels by item in QuickBooks Simple Start. (And, for retailers, you can't actually track inventory levels by item very well with the fully-featured version of QuickBooks.) So, what you do is use a single item for everything. Just like I used "Goods" as the item for each product billed with the invoice shown in Figure 17-1.

A reasonable sales receipt

Figure 17-2 shows a reasonable retail sales receipt. Let me throw out some hints and make some observations about such receipts.

Hint #1: Get the date right

Just for your own recordkeeping, you want to make sure that this information is right. Otherwise your bank reconciliations will be even more difficult.

Hint #2: Use a separate sales receipt for each deposit

Because of the heavy transaction volumes that even small retailers see, you typically want to record a sales receipt for each deposit into the bank account — rather than for each sale. In other words, you'll use your cash register or handwritten receipts to provide sales receipts for customers. And then, at the end of the day, when you count the money in the till and prepare your bank deposit, you record a single sales receipt transaction for each deposit into your bank account. Your cash and check sales, for example, will be bunched together and recorded as sale to the customer labeled something like "Cash and Check." (This is what I show in Figure 17-2.)

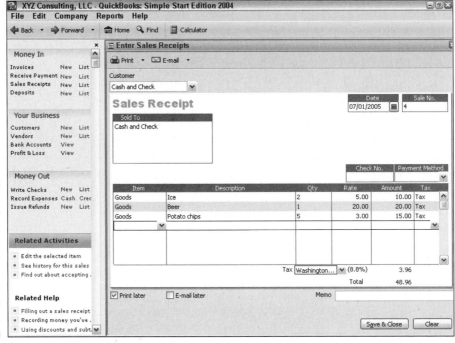

Figure 17-2:
The Enter
Sales
Receipts
window
showing a
reasonable
retail sales
receipt.

If you accept VISA and MasterCard charges, you'll also bunch these together and record them in a separate sales receipt transaction for the customer "VISA and MC." And if you accept American Express or Discover credit cards, you'll treat the daily sales for these payment sources in the same way.

Let me now justify my suggestion that you use this slap-dash bookkeeping trick for your daily sales: I think you should use the quick-and-dirty sales accounting method I've described here for three reasons:

✔ The method is fast, so you're more likely to religiously do your bookkeeping for sales each day.

✔ The method is easy so you're less likely to screw things up. And that seems like a good idea.

✔ The method produces accurate measures of total sales and accurate bank account balances, and in many cases, that's as good as it gets for the small retailer.

In the interest of fairness, however, let me say that my method suffers from two serious weaknesses:

✓ You don't know what your sales are at an item-level or customer-level, so you won't know which products or customers are hot and which aren't. (If it's really important to you to know sales by items and customers, you must invest in a real point-of-sale system like QuickBooks Point of Sale.)

✓ Unless you're the one running the cash register, you don't have any built-in controls to minimize discrepancies between the cash register's records and QuickBooks records. And you don't have any built-in controls to reduce the chances that the person running the cash register is dipping into the till for a little, off-the-books bonus.

Hint #3: Work to minimize sales-related errors and theft

In the preceding paragraph, I noted that my slap-dash accounting system suffers from some control weaknesses. For this reason, I want to suggest that you should work to minimize this weakness, if possible, with some manual or jury-rigged control procedures. For example, you can yourself run the cash register to eliminate employee theft. Or you can put up one of those little signs that says, "If you don't get a receipt, it's free." (That forces the sales clerk to create paper receipts so there's a hard copy record of all sales, including the cash sales that are easiest to pocket.) You can also create a little manual reconciliation procedure to compare the numbers you're recording in QuickBooks with the numbers shown on the sales tape produced by the cash register or the total of the handwritten paper receipts.

Recording Inventory and Cost of Goods Sold

You need to record three types of transactions in order to accurately account for your inventory and cost of goods sold: inventory purchases, inventory sales, and physical inventory adjustments. All three transactions are described in the paragraphs that follow.

Inventory purchases

To record an inventory purchase, you would write a check and then use an inventory account rather than an expense account to show what the check pays. Figure 17-3 shows an example of just this. The Write Checks window shows a $50,000 check written to Acme Wholesaling. The Expense Category shows as inventory.

As I mention in the earlier section, "Setting Up for a Retail Business," the inventory account should use the Other Current Asset account type.

If you purchase inventory with a credit card charge, you use the same basic account. You record the credit card charge in pretty much the usual manner — you just have to make sure you set the Expense Category to Inventory.

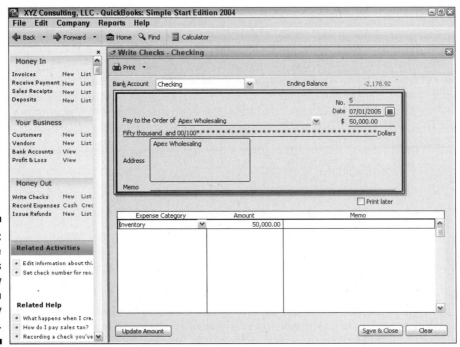

Figure 17-3: The Write Checks window showing an inventory purchase.

Inventory sales

To record the sale of inventory, you move dollars from the inventory account to the cost of goods sold account using a general journal entry transaction. This transaction simultaneously reduces your inventory account balances and counts the inventory's cost as an expense.

Now here's the rub. How in the world can you know the dollar value you're supposed to move from inventory to cost of goods sold? You can't know precisely, can you? You might not know or remember what you sold. And even if you did, you probably don't know for sure exactly that the sold items cost. So what do you do?

Well, here's the answer. You guess at the cost of inventory sold using your gross margin percentage. For example, just to keep the math easy, say you always automatically mark up items by 300 percent. If you purchase some item for $25, you mark the item up by 300 percent, or $75, and then sell it for $100. If you always mark things up by 300 percent, your gross margin percentage equals 75 percent. And you can calculate the cost of inventory items sold using this formula:

Sales * (1 – gross margin percentage)

If sales for the day equal $500 and the gross margin percentage equals 75 percent, for example, the cost of inventory items, or goods, sold can be calculated using this formula:

$500 * (1 – .75)

which equals $125.

Figure 17-4 shows a general journal entry that moves dollars from the inventory account to the Cost of Goods Sold account. You would enter a general journal entry like this every time you record sales. For example, if you record sales on a daily basis, you would also want to record your cost of goods sold on a daily basis.

Chapter 13 describes how to use the Make General Journal Entries window to record journal entries. If you're familiar with how journal entries work, however, don't even bother to flip to Chapter 13. Just choose the Company⇨ For Your Accountant⇨Make General Journal Entry command and enter the needed debits and credits.

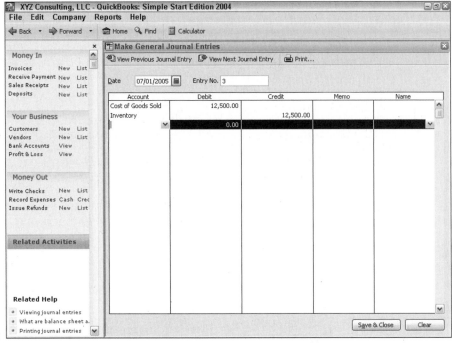

Figure 17-4:
A general
journal
entry for
recording
cost of
goods sold.

As I mention in the earlier section, "Setting Up for a Retail Business," the cost of goods sold account should use the Cost of Goods Sold account type.

Physical inventory adjustments

Your inventory and cost of goods sold numbers won't be exactly correct, even if you try really hard, because of two, corrupting influences:

- ✔ Your gross margin percentage won't be exactly correct because you'll have some markdowns and hopefully better-than-average markups on some products.

- ✔ Some of your inventory will be stolen and some will be discarded.

For these two reasons, you'll need to periodically count all the items in your inventory, figure out what you originally paid for them, and then adjust your QuickBooks records to match what your physical inventory counts and costing shows.

This makes sense, right? Suppose that QuickBooks says you have $30,000 of inventory. But you've just done a painfully thorough physical count of the items you hold in inventory. Also suppose that you've also methodically researched the costs of every single item. Your research shows you hold only $25,000 of stuff. What you need to do in this case, therefore, is reduce your inventory balance by $5,000. And you do that by moving dollars from inventory to cost of goods sold. Figure 17-5 shows the Make General Journal Entries window recording just such a transaction.

Because we're on the subject of physical inventory counts, let me throw out a couple of related comments:

✔ **You really need to do at least an annual physical inventory.**

Usually businesses do the physical inventory at year-end so that you have a good inventory balance number and a good cost of goods sold number at the year-end. (Retailers often use fiscal years that have funny ending dates for just this reason: They don't want to be burdened with doing a physical inventory during, for example, Christmas.)

✔ **You should calculate a new actual gross margin percentage for the year after you do your physical inventory.**

This is might be obvious to you, but after the first year of business — the year when you have to use a gross margin percentage based on your markup in your inventory sale transactions — you should instead use the previous year's actual gross margin percentage. For example, suppose that in your first year, based on your markup, you used a 75 percent gross margin percentage, as shown below:

	Dollars	*Percent*
Sales	$300,000	100%
Cost of Goods	$75,000	25%
Gross Margin	$225,000	75%

But suppose that, after taking into account some shoplifting and then some markdowns, the actual percentage turned out to be 66.66 percent, as shown below:

	Dollars	*Percent*
Sales	$300,000	100%
Cost of Goods	$75,000	25%
Physical adj.	$25,000	8.33%
Gross Margin	$200,000	66.66%

In the next year's inventory sale transactions, you should use the 66.66 percent gross margin percentage. In this manner, you effectively recognize a bit of shoplifting and markdown each time you record the cost of goods sold — rather than all at once at the end of the year.

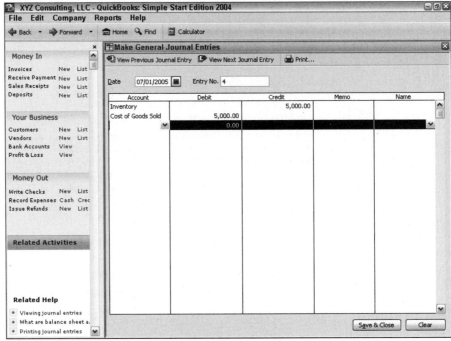

Figure 17-5:
A general journal entry for recording a physical-to-book inventory adjustment.

Recording Non-Inventory Business Expenses

As I describe in some detail in Chapter 5, you record your business expenses by writing checks and entering credit card charges. The only tricks are to use a business expense account when you record the check or charge. Figure 17-6 shows the Write Checks window recording $2,000 to pay rent.

Figure 17-7 shows the Credit Card Register window with the selected transaction recording the charging of $50 of tacos as business meals. (The business meals expense category is Travel Meals.)

I've said this a handful of places elsewhere in the book, but just because I have a compulsive personality, let me make two suggestions about your business expense accounts:

✔ Stick with the standard set of QuickBooks expense accounts. The standard set of accounts ties rather nicely to the tax return deduction categories that you'll need to later report. So working with the standard set of expense accounts makes it easy to later prepare your tax return. The other thing is — and here I'm just being honest — people tend to make a mess when they add a bunch of expense accounts.

✔ If you write a check or make a credit card charge that pays a personal rather than a business expense, use the owner's draws, partner's draws, dividends, or distributions account. In other words, if you do ignore my admonition to use a separate business bank account just for your business expenses (see "Setting Up for a Retail Business"), don't compound that mistake by mixing personal and business expense accounts. The "everything-is-mixed-up" approach pretty quickly means that you don't know whether your business is making or losing money. And the approach means you or your poor accountant will find it nearly impossible to economically prepare an accurate tax return.

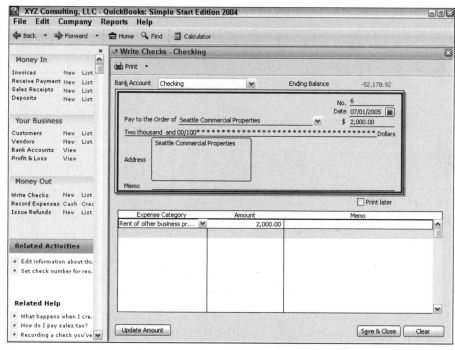

Figure 17-6:
The Write Checks window showing a paid-by-check expense.

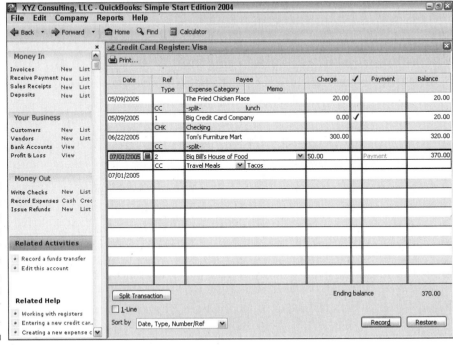

Date	Ref Type	Payee / Expense Category	Memo	Charge	✓	Payment	Balance
05/09/2005		The Fried Chicken Place		20.00			20.00
	CC	-split-	lunch				
05/09/2005	1	Big Credit Card Company		0.00	✓		20.00
	CHK	Checking					
06/22/2005		Tom's Furniture Mart		300.00			320.00
	CC	-split-					
07/01/2005	2	Big Bill's House of Food		50.00		Payment	370.00
	CC	Travel Meals	Tacos				
07/01/2005							

Ending balance   370.00

Figure 17-7:
The Credit
Card
Register
window
showing a
business
charge for
tacos.

When you pay personal expenses out of a corporate or LLC bank account, you weaken the liability protection offered by the corporation or LLC. If this is a big deal to you, you might want to confer with your attorney for more information.

Other Bookkeeping Stuff

You need to regularly complete a handful of other bookkeeping tasks. Here they are:

✔ **Bank reconciliations.**

When you get your monthly bank statements, be sure to reconcile your bank account. The reason I say this is that by reconciling your bank account, you'll catch bookkeeping errors and omissions. Those catches will not only mean that you have better bank account balances information. Those catches will mean that your profit and loss statements are more accurate.

Reconciliations for retail businesses are really tedious because the credit card companies bunch batches of credit card deposits. For example, you might have recorded $100 in American Express charges for Monday, $200 for Tuesday, and $50 for Wednesday. But you won't see these three transactions on your bank statement. You'll see one transaction for $350. You can go nearly mad dealing with this phenomenon. So one thing you might want to do is just wait to enter credit card transactions until you see the actual deposit made by the credit card company. This approach is especially easy if you can get to an online copy of your bank statement so you can enter credit card deposits every few days.

✔ **Customer collections.**

If you allow some customers to pay on account, on a regular basis — perhaps monthly — you'll want to produce the Invoices That Haven't Been Paid report (choose Reports➪Invoices That Haven't Been Paid) and see who you need to call about their past-due accounts. This is awkward. But a simple fact of business life is that some people are deadbeats. And you sometimes need to rattle their cages a bit in order to get paid for the work you do.

✔ **Regular data file backups.**

You ought to back up your QuickBooks data file at least once a month (see Chapter 13).

Part V
The Part of Tens

The 5th Wave   By Rich Tennant

"It's a football/math program. We're tackling
multiplication, going long for division, and
punting fractions."

In this part . . .

As a writing tool, laundry lists aren't something high school English teachers encourage. But you know what? The old laundry list format is pretty handy for certain types of information.

With this in mind (and, of course, with deepest apologies to my high school English teacher, Mrs. O'Rourke), this part simply provides you with ten-item (or almost ten-item) lists of information about QuickBooks, bookkeeping, taxes, and business finance.

Chapter 18

Ten Tips for Business Owners

In This Chapter

▶ Supplying your own signature

▶ Signing checks correctly

▶ Looking over canceled checks before your bookkeeper does

▶ Selecting a QuickBooks bookkeeper

▶ Using the right resources for your business

▶ Keeping things simple

*I*f you run a business and you use QuickBooks, you need to know the information in this chapter. You can get this information by sitting down with your certified public accountant over a cup of coffee at $170 an hour. Or you can read this chapter.

Sign All Your Own Checks

I have nothing against your bookkeeper. In a small business, however, people — especially full-charge bookkeepers — can bamboozle you too darn easily. By signing all the checks yourself, you keep your fingers on the pulse of your cash outflow.

Yeah, I know this practice can be a hassle. I know that you can't easily spend three months in Hawaii. I know that you have to wade through paperwork every time you sign a stack of checks.

Tag-Team Check-Signing in Partnerships

By the way, if you're in a partnership, I think that you should have at least a couple of the partners cosign checks.

Don't Sign a Check the Wrong Way

If you sign many checks, you might be tempted to use a John Hancock–like signature. Although scrawling your name illegibly makes great sense when you're autographing baseballs, don't do it when you're signing checks. A clear signature, especially one with a sense of personal style, is distinctive. A wavy line with a cross and a couple of dots is really easy to forge.

Which leads me to my next tip. . . .

Review Canceled Checks before Your Bookkeeper Does

Be sure that you review your canceled checks before anybody else sees the monthly bank statement.

This chapter isn't about browbeating bookkeepers. But a business owner can determine whether someone is forging signatures on checks only by being the first to open the bank statement and by reviewing each of the canceled check signatures.

If you don't examine the checks, unscrupulous employees — especially bookkeepers who can update the bank account records — can forge your signature with impunity. And they won't get caught if they never overdraw the account.

I won't continue this rant, but let me mention one last thing: Every time I teach CPAs about how to better help their clients with QuickBooks, I hear again and again about business owners who haven't been careful about keeping an eye on the bookkeeper — and have suffered from embezzlement and forgery as a result.

If you don't follow these procedures, you will probably eat the losses, not the bank.

Choose a Bookkeeper Who Is Familiar with Computers

Don't worry. You don't need to request an FBI background check.

In fact, if you use QuickBooks, you don't need to hire people who are familiar with small-business accounting systems. Just find people who know how to keep a checkbook and work with a computer. They shouldn't have a problem understanding QuickBooks.

Of course, you don't want someone who just fell off the turnip truck. But even if you do hire someone who rode into town on one, you're not going to have much trouble getting that person up to speed with QuickBooks.

Find a Smart-but-Economical CPA

You might guess that, because I'm a CPA, I think this. But you should find a smart but economical CPA to help you with two critically important areas: your accounting and your federal and state income taxes.

The accounting stuff is probably obvious, right? You might need help getting your accounting system to produce reports that let you see how your business is doing. Without an accounting system that shows which months, which products, which services, and which customers are profitable, you're flying blind.

A CPA — more than any other professional — is the right person to get your accounting system producing this sort of information. Of course, you won't need that much help. You've got this book. But if there are any questions I've left unanswered. . . .

The taxes thing is more subtle. After all, what about doing your tax returns yourself with something like TurboTax? Or what about using one of the inexpensive national tax preparation services? Or that lady who lives down the street?

The problem with any of these other cheap tax approaches, in my opinion, is that you're unlikely to spot those wonderful, big tax-saving opportunities that come along with regularity in a business. Such as, is it time to incorporate? Should you elect "S" status? Is it time to set up a Section 105(b) plan? (Does the lady down the street even know what a Section 105(b) plan is?) Stuff like that.

Neither TurboTax (which is a great product) nor someone who's been through an 11-week course about tax preparation so she can get a $10-an-hour job (even if she's a smart, honest worker) can supply these sorts of insights. A good CPA often can. And that should mean a business can save thousands of dollars in tax a year. Thousands.

How do you find a good but economical CPA? Ask around. You've got friends. Some of them have businesses. One of these friends with a business (probably more than one!) has located a good economical CPA.

While You're at It, Find a Good Attorney, Too

You know what? While you're asking your friends about tax advisers, ask them for the name of a good attorney, too.

All you need to do is avoid one big mistake over a decade — a bad real estate lease, an ugly employee termination, or a terrible investment — and you'll have paid for your attorney's annual fees several times over.

Choose an Appropriate Accounting System

When you use QuickBooks Simple Start, you use a cash-basis accounting rather than an accrual-basis accounting.

Cash-basis accounting is fine when a business's cash inflow mirrors its sales and its cash outflow mirrors its expenses. This situation isn't the case, however, in many businesses. A contractor of single-family homes, for example, might have cash coming in (by borrowing from banks) but might not make any money. A pawnshop owner who loans money at 22 percent might make scads of money, even if cash pours out of the business daily.

As a general rule, when you're buying and selling inventory, accrual-basis accounting works better than cash-basis accounting.

As another general rule, if you can, you want to use cash-basis accounting if at all possible because it's easier and you tend to save taxes when you do so.

You want to think about which accounting method you use. Specifically, you want to consider the usual, general rules. And you want to think about whether cash-basis or accrual-basis accounting works best in your business. (The best accounting method is the one that lets you easily figure out when and where you're making money.)

Just so you know, QuickBooks Simple Start sort of allows you to do accrual-basis accounting because it'll let you count revenues when you invoice a customer. But QuickBooks Simple Start doesn't let you do a completely accrual-based accounting of your revenues and expenses. Don't be fooled by some of the references you see to "accrual-basis accounting" in the QuickBooks Simple Start program. To do true accrual-based accounting, you need to upgrade to one of the full-featured versions of QuickBooks.

If QuickBooks Simple Start Doesn't Work for Your Business, Upgrade

QuickBooks Simple Start is a great small-business accounting program.

However, if QuickBooks Simple Start doesn't seem to fit your needs — if, for example, you need a program that works better for a manufacturer or that includes some special industry-specific feature — you might want one of the more complicated (but also more powerful) small-business accounting packages.

The first thing you should consider is upgrading to one of the more fully featured versions of QuickBooks like QuickBooks Pro or QuickBooks Premium.

If a QuickBooks Upgrade Doesn't Work, Look Around a Bit More

Another possibility is another popular (and more powerful) full-featured Windows accounting program: Peachtree Accounting for Windows from Peachtree (www.peachtree.com).

If programs like QuickBooks Pro, QuickBooks Premium, or Peachtree Accounting don't work, you might want to talk to your accountant about industry-specific packages. (For example, if you're a commercial printer, some vendor might have developed a special accounting package just for commercial printers.)

I'm amazed that PC accounting software remains so affordable. You can buy a great accounting package — one that you can use to manage a $5 million or a $25 million business — for a few hundred bucks. Accounting software is truly one of the great bargains in life.

Chapter 19

Tips for Handling (Almost) Ten Tricky Situations

As your business grows and becomes more complex, your accounting does, too. I can't describe and discuss all the complexities you'll encounter, but I can give you some tips on handling (just about) ten tricky situations.

In QuickBooks, you make journal entries by using the General Journal Entry window, which you get to by choosing Company⇨For Your Accountant⇨ Make Journal Entries.

Tracking Asset Depreciation

To track the depreciation of an asset that you've already purchased (and added to the chart of accounts), you need two new accounts: an asset type of account called something like Accumulated Depreciation and an expense account called something like Depreciation Expense.

If you have a large number of assets, keeping track of the accumulated depreciation associated with specific assets is a good idea. You can do this either outside of QuickBooks (like in an Excel spreadsheet or with your tax return) or inside QuickBooks (by using individual accounts for each asset's original cost and accumulated depreciation).

After you set up these two accounts, you can record the asset depreciation with a journal entry such as the following one that records $500 of depreciation expense:

	Debit	*Credit*
Depreciation expense	$500	
Accumulated depreciation		$500

The federal tax laws provide a special form of depreciation called Section 179 depreciation. Section 179 depreciation enables you to depreciate the entire cost of some assets, which is a big break for small businesses. You can't, however, use more than a certain amount of Section 179 depreciation in a year: $24,000 in 2002 and $100,000 in 2003, 2004 and 2005. You also need to know some other nitty-gritty details, so confer with your tax adviser if you have questions.

Selling an Asset

When you sell an asset, you need to back out (get rid of) the asset's account balance, record the payment of the cash (or whatever) that somebody pays you for the asset, and record any difference between what you sell the asset for and its value as a gain or loss.

If you purchase a piece of land for $5,000 but later resell it for $4,000, for example, you use the following journal entry to record the sale of this asset:

	Debit	*Credit*
Cash	$4,000	
Loss	$1,000	
Asset		$5,000

You might need to set up another income account for the gain or another expense account for the loss. Refer to Chapter 1 for information on setting up new accounts.

Selling a Depreciable Asset

Selling a depreciable asset works almost identically to selling an asset that you haven't been depreciating. When you sell the asset, you need to back out (or get rid of) the asset's account balance. You also need to back out the asset's accumulated depreciation (which is the only thing that's different from selling an asset that you haven't been depreciating). You need to record the payment of the cash (or whatever) that somebody pays you for the asset. Finally, you count as a gain or a loss any difference between what you sell the asset for and what its net-of-accumulated-depreciation value is.

This process sounds terribly complicated, but an example will help. Suppose that you purchased a $5,000 piece of machinery and have accumulated $500 of depreciation thus far. Consequently, the asset account shows a $5,000 debit balance, and the asset's accumulated depreciation account shows a $500 credit balance. Suppose also that you sell the machinery for $4,750 in cash.

To record the sale of this depreciable asset, you would use the following journal entry:

	Debit	*Credit*
Cash	$4,750	
Accumulated depreciation	$500	
Asset		$5,000
Gain		$250

If you have a bunch of assets, you probably want to set up individual accounts for each asset's original cost and its accumulated depreciation. The individual accounts make it much easier to make the journal entry shown in the preceding paragraph.

Owner's Equity in a Sole Proprietorship

Actually, tracking owner's equity in a sole proprietorship is easy. You can use the single account that QuickBooks sets up for you, called Opening Bal Equity, to track what you've invested in the business. (You might want to rename this account something like Contributed Capital.)

To track the money you withdraw from the business, you can set up and use a new owner's equity account called something like Owner's Draws. Table 19-1 gives an example of owner's equity accounts in a sole proprietorship.

Table 19-1	An Example of Owner's Equity Accounts in a Sole Proprietorship
Account	*Amount*
Contributed capital	$5,000
Retained earnings	$8,000
Owner's draws	($2,000)
Owner's equity (total)	$11,000

Owner's Equity in a Partnership

To track the equity for each partner in a partnership, you need to create three accounts for each partner: one for the partner's contributed capital, one for the partner's draws, and one for the partner's share of the distributed income.

Amounts that a partner withdraws, of course, get tracked with the partner's draws account.

Suppose that a partner's share of the partnership's profits gets allocated to the partner's profit share account. (Your partnership agreement, by the way, should say how the partnership income is distributed among the partners.) Table 19-2 gives an example of owner's equity accounts in a partnership.

Table 19-2	An Example of Owner's Equity Accounts in a Partnership	
Account	*Partner A's Amount*	*Partner B's Amount*
Contributed capital	$5,000	$7,000
Profit share	$6,000	$6,000
Draws	($3,000)	($4,000)
Equity (total)	$8,000	$9,000

Owner's Equity in a Corporation

Yikes! Accounting for the owner's equity in a corporation can get mighty tricky mighty fast. In fact, I don't mind telling you that college accounting textbooks often use several chapters to describe all the ins and outs of corporation owner's equity accounting.

As long as you keep things simple, however, you can probably use three or four accounts for your owner's equity:

- **A capital stock par value account** for which you get the par value amount by multiplying the par value per share by the number of shares issued.

- **A paid-in capital in excess of par value account** for the amount investors paid for shares of stock in excess of par value. You get this amount by multiplying the price paid per share less the par value per share by the number of shares issued.

- **A retained earnings account** to track the business profits left invested in the business.

- **A dividends paid account** to track the amounts distributed to shareholders.

Table 19-3 shows an example of owner's equity accounts in a corporation.

Table 19-3	An Example of Owner's Equity in a Corporation
Account	*Amount*
Par value	$500
Paid-in capital in excess of par value	$4,500
Retained earnings	$8,000
Dividends paid	($3,000)
Shareholder's equity	$10,000

Multiple-State Accounting

Small businesses often get confused about multistate accounting, so I'll give you a bird's-eye view. The basic rule is that if you're conducting business in a state, you owe that state income taxes on a slice of your business profits.

To determine the "slice of profits" that's apportioned to a state, you use a three-factor formula that averages the sales percentage in a state, the payroll percentage in a state, and the property percentage in a state. While this sounds complicated, it actually isn't. For example, suppose that you run a small business that generates 50 percent of its sales in California, pays 10percent of its payroll in California, but has no property in California. To determine the slice of business profits that get apportioned to California, you make the following calculation:

California slice of profits equals (50%+10%+0%)/3 or 20 percent.

And, using these example numbers, 20 percent of your business profit gets reported to and, presumably, taxed by California.

Now that you know how multistate tax calculations work, it's pretty easy to come up with ways to get the information you need from QuickBooks.

- ✔ To get the sales by state, you need to use separate income accounts for each state in which you sell. If you can look at your profit and loss statement and see that you generated $50,000 in California, $30,000 in Washington, and $20,000 in Oregon, you know that California represented 50 percent of your sales, Washington 30 percent, and Oregon 20 percent.

- ✔ To get payroll by state, you need to use separate wages expense accounts. For example, if you look at your profit and loss statement and see that you paid $20,000 in California wages and $20,000 in Washington wages, you know that 50 percent of your wages were California wages and 50 percent of your wages were Washington wages.

- ✔ To get property by state, you need to use separate asset accounts for things you own from out of state. For example, if the balance sheet shows you're holding $100,000 of assets, but that $20,000 of these assets are located in Oregon, you know that 20 percent of your property is Oregon property. A couple of final comments about multistate accounting: First, ask your CPA for help with the calculations and the rules. What I've said in the preceding paragraphs is correct for many states, but there are all sorts of little exceptions and gotchas you'll have to deal with when you actually start doing multistate accounting. Second, be aware that much interstate commerce is exempt from multistate taxation. (For example, if you just sell stuff from your Washington store into California and that's all you do, California probably can't tax you.)

Getting a Loan

Getting a loan is the hard part. After you get the money, recording it in QuickBooks is easy. All you do is record a journal entry that increases cash and that recognizes the new loan liability. For example, if you get a $5,000 loan, you record the following journal entry:

	Debit	Credit
Cash	$5,000	
Loan payable		$5,000

You'll already have a cash account set up, but you might need to set up a new liability account to track the loan.

Repaying a Loan

To record loan payments, you need to split each payment between two accounts: the interest expense account and the loan payable account.

For example, suppose that you're making $75-a-month payments on a $5,000 loan. Also, suppose that the lender charges 1 percent interest each month. The following journal entry records the first month's loan payment:

	Debit	Credit	Explanation
Interest expense	$50		Calculated as 1 percent of $5,000
Loan payable	$25		The amount left over and applied to principal
Cash		$75	The total payment amount

The next month, of course, the loan balance is slightly less (because you made a $25 dent in the loan principal, as shown in the preceding loan payment journal entry). The following journal entry records the second month's loan payment:

	Debit	Credit	Explanation
Interest expense	$49.75		Calculated as 1 percent of $4,975, the new loan balance
Loan payable	$25.25		The amount left over and applied to principal
Cash		$75.00	The total payment amount

Get the lender to provide you with an amortization schedule that shows the breakdown of each payment into interest expense and loan principal reduction.

You can record loan payments by using the Write Checks window. Just use the Category column to specify the interest expense account and the loan liability account.

Chapter 20

(Almost) Ten Little Ideas for Saving Big on Business Taxes

. . . .

In This Chapter

▶ Using pension plan devices

▶ Taking business vacations

▶ Choosing to expense, not depreciate

▶ Incorporating your business

▶ Thinking about using the Sub S election

▶ Opting for the best of both worlds

▶ Putting your kids to work

▶ Moving your business

. . . .

*O*kay. I'm a little nervous about this. In fact, I had this crazy idea that maybe I should somehow camouflage this chapter. Perhaps name it something like "Don't Read This" or "Really Boring Stuff You Probably Don't Want to Know Anyway." My nervousness, I should point out, doesn't stem from the material. I dare say that what you can find here in this little chapter might provide you more value than almost anything else in this book. And because this chapter talks about how you can probably save at least hundreds — and very probably thousands — of dollars on taxes, well, by definition, the material is interesting.

No, here's the problem: What I talk about here is easily misunderstood. And if you misunderstand something I say here and then get just slightly mixed up in the way that you implement some strategy or follow some snidbit of advice, well, all bets are off. I can pretty well guarantee you a real mess.

So here's what I need you to do if you really want to save money on taxes:

1. **Read through the tax-saving ideas that I present in this chapter.**

   Make sure that you understand (as best you can) the gist of each gambit.

2. **Sit down with your tax adviser and ask for help implementing the two or three ideas that make the most sense in your situation.**

By following these two steps, two other important things happen. One, you do the background research (just by reading this chapter) into which tax-saving tricks work in your situation. And, two, you get the expert advice typically necessary to make sure that you don't mess up and, thereby, find yourself in a heap of trouble.

And now let the tips begin.

Trick 1: Benefit from the Appropriate Pension Device

Let me start with the biggie. Pension plans. Here's the deal. If you're self-employed, you can set up a pension fund that pretty much lets you stash as much money as you want into things like Individual Retirement Accounts, SEP/IRAs, SIMPLE IRAs, 401(K)s, and some of their more exotic brothers and sisters — plans that go by the names of Paired Plan Keoghs and Defined Benefit Plans.

Although this angle doesn't sound very exciting, if your business is profitable, these plans give you a way to put money into tax-deductible, tax-deferred investment choices. In doing so, not only do you build wealth outside of your business — which is important for reducing risk — but you also save a heap of taxes.

I should clarify the risk-reduction angle here. In most states, money that you store in pension plans is not available to creditors. This protection means that if you go bankrupt, you might be able to save the money in your pension. And if someone sues you, again, you might be able to save the money in your pension. If you have questions about this possibility, ask your attorney.

The tax savings are easy to underestimate. Suppose that you have $10,000 of profit and you're considering saving this money. Further, suppose that your marginal income tax rate — the top combined state and federal rate you pay on your last dollar of income — is 33 percent. In this case, if you save the $10,000 into a pension plan, you'll actually get a $3,300 tax savings, which is pretty impressive. With this method, much of the money you save actually comes from the tax savings.

You can calculate how big a tax savings you'll enjoy by multiplying your pension plan contribution by the marginal income tax rate. Remember, though, that you can further boost your tax savings and your pension plan contributions by saving your tax savings. In other words, you can also use the initial tax savings — $3,300 in this example — to augment the amount of the pension contribution. By saving your savings, you generate further savings.

Okay, all this business about pension fund contributions probably doesn't sound all that exciting. But before you say to yourself, "Man, this guy is boring," let me tell you two things you might not know:

✔ **My guess is that your marginal tax rate is higher than you think:** If you have a successful business in a state with income tax, you might easily be paying a 33 percent tax rate on your last dollars of income. And if you have a really successful business, you might be paying close to 50 percent. People often miss this fact — and get confused because average tax rates are lower. But we live in a country with very progressive tax rates. And small businesses often get hit harder by this progressivity than they realize. But anyway, that's the first thing you need to take away from this discussion of pension plan angles.

✔ **You can probably save way more money in pension plan accounts than you realize:** What you're probably thinking is, "Oh, yeah, I know you put a couple of grand into an IRA and a bit more into a 401(K)." But you don't realize that other, almost-secret pension plans, are available. And some of these other, almost-secret pension plans let you stash away oodles and oodles of money. For example, 401(K) plans (when you combine both the employee and the employer share) now let you save up to $40,000 a year. With the help of a pension consultant, you can even set up pension plans that let you save $50,000 or $100,000 a year by using something called a Defined Benefit Plan.

I'm not going to spend any more time on this pension plan stuff. I have other tax tips to talk about. But do recognize that if you want to build wealth outside of your business, you can do so by using pension plan devices that provide you with just scads of tax savings.

While the tax breaks associated with pension fund options like those described in the preceding paragraphs seem like no-brainers, don't go to the work of setting up a pension plan for yourself or for employees if you can save just as much through traditional IRA accounts. For example, an individual can save up to $3,000 of earned income, and a married couple can save up to $6,000 of earned income in an IRA if the taxpayer or taxpayers aren't covered by some other qualified pension plan. If these IRA contribution limits are all you want to save, you don't need a formal pension plan. And you're only wasting your money by paying some plan administrator $2,000 or $3,000 a year to maintain such a plan.

Trick 2: Don't Take Any More Personal Vacations

Okay, I really, really want you to talk to your tax adviser about this gambit. In fact, I'm not going to tell you about this trick unless you promise me that you'll consult a tax adviser first. Okay?

That caveat given, let me point out something that a tax adviser told me a while back. He said to me, "Steve, you're basically an idiot to be taking personal vacations."

Now this guy wasn't telling me I should stop taking my family to Hawaii. He knows firsthand how gloomy and gray Seattle looks in February. His point, really, was that I could probably get many of the same benefits from business travel.

Rather than Hawaii, for example, he suggested a really good conference in sunny Phoenix. In this way, my plane ticket, the car rental, and the hotel all become business travel deductions. Of course, I can't write off my family's airplane tickets. But, in truth, many of the family's typical travel expenses — the hotel and car rental, to name just two — do become deductible if I follow his suggestion.

The only real trick to this gambit is that the travel needs to be real business travel. You can't simply call a family vacation a business trip. You need to be doing real business.

By the way, I haven't actually taken this "don't take any family vacations" advice. I have a little problem unwinding on vacation anyway. And trying to take a working vacation just doesn't work for someone with my particular set of personality disorders. But you might be different. If what you really want from a vacation is some sun (or snow), a change of scenery, and a chance to see another part of the country or world, well, you might be able to get all these things on a tax-deductible business trip.

You promised me earlier that you would check with a tax adviser before attempting this gambit on your own. You need to meet very specific criteria to deduct travel expenses as business expenditures.

Trick 3: Don't Depreciate — Expense

I mention the Section 179 election in a handful of places elsewhere in this book. But because this is a powerful tax-saving gambit, let me again say that, in general, you can immediately expense up to the first $100,000 of depreciable stuff you buy in a year. (Usually, you have to depreciate depreciable stuff, thereby spreading out the deduction over the estimated economic life of the thing you bought.) In this way, you boost your deductions without actually having to suffer a cash outflow. Note that if you buy more than $400,000 of stuff in a year, the election amount gets phased out.

Trick 4: Incorporate

In some circumstances, you can incorporate a business and save substantial income taxes. This step is tricky, though, because when you incorporate, the new corporation typically becomes a new taxpayer, which means that it's also subject to income taxes (except in the special case where you make the Sub S election, which I talk about in the very next trick).

The neat thing about corporations — at least for shareholder employees — is that they let you provide lots of tax-free fringe benefits to all your employees, including you.

But let me explain exactly how the corporation thing works. First, suppose you have a sole proprietorship that makes $100,000 a year. In this situation, you can't provide any tax-deductible fringe benefits to yourself, and you must pay taxes on the entire $100,000 of income. (By the way, a partnership can't for the most part provide tax-deductible fringe benefits to partners either.)

Okay. Now suppose you incorporate the exact same business, pay yourself a salary of $60,000, and provide a generous fringe benefits package worth around $20,000. In this case, the money you spend on the fringe benefits isn't taxable. And you can provide an incredibly rich fringe benefits package, including complete health insurance and even a generous medical expenses reimbursement plan. The medical expenses reimbursement plan, by the way, might include money for things like kids' orthodontia, new air conditioning that your allergist recommends for your house, and the backyard swimming pool your physician prescribes for your arthritis.

Now before you run off to your attorney's office and incorporate, let me share with you the two complicating factors in this "incorporate and provide yourself with massive fringe benefits" trick:

✔ **You must provide the same set of fringe benefits to all your employees.** Obviously that's not a big deal if the only employees are you and your spouse or maybe you and the other shareholder. But what if your kids work for the business, too? Or maybe you employ a bunch of other people? Do they all deserve, for example, a physician-prescribed backyard swimming pool? You see the problem.

✔ **You also face what people usually call the double-taxation problem.** Here's how this works. You can only pay yourself a fair salary. So, in the case where your business makes $100,000 and, out of this amount, you pay $60,000 in salary and another $20,000 in fringe benefits, you have another $20,000 in leftover profits. These profits — these corporate profits — are taxed at the corporate tax rates. Corporate tax rates run 15 percent on the first $50,000 of income and then rather quickly rise to rates that roughly run 35 percent to 40 percent. Now that doesn't sound so bad, I guess, but any money the corporation distributes to shareholders is taxed again as a dividend. So here's what happens to that last $20,000 of profit you can't pay out as a salary and can't pay out in fringe benefits:

  • First, it's subject to a 15 percent corporate tax, which reduces the $20,000 to $17,000 because the corporate tax amounts to $3,000.

  • Then, when you pay out the remaining $17,000 as a dividend, you are subjected to another income tax — this time, the individual income tax, which will probably run roughly another 30 percent, or $5,100.

So you are taxed twice on the same money. And as a result, your $20,000 rather quickly dwindles to around $12,000 because of the roughly $3,000 corporate income tax and the roughly $5,000 personal income tax. Bummer.

Now before you shake your head, let me share a little secret. And this is another thing you need to discuss with your tax adviser. The double-taxation thing maybe isn't as bad as it seems if you're saving a good deal of money on the fringe benefits thing. For example, returning again to the case in which you're thinking about incorporating a business that makes $100,000 a year, the $20,000 of deductible fringe benefits might save you around $6,000 in taxes. The double-taxation penalty might cost you an extra $3,000 in corporate income taxes. So in that case, you're still $3,000 ahead.

I want to say one other thing about the double-taxation thing. Although the IRS looks very closely at the salaries that corporations pay to shareholder employees, I think that, in practice, you have a bit of wiggle room. Check with your tax adviser; but maybe in good years, you can pay yourself a $10,000 bonus, which adds to your salary and reduces your taxable corporate profits. Or maybe in good years, you invest extra money in the business. Perhaps the good years, for example, are when you buy the new equipment you regularly need. These sorts of tricks might further reduce the damage done by double taxation.

One other way to avoid the double-taxation problem is to elect Sub S status. If you do so, however, you don't get to deduct fringe benefits for shareholder employees.

In terms of actual mechanics, and for the reasons given in the first pages of Chapter 1, your attorney probably won't have you set up an actual corporation. Instead, he or she will set up an LLC and then ask the IRS to treat the LLC as a corporation for tax purposes.

Trick 5: Consider the Sub S Election

Okay, here's another tricky technique. And again, this is not something that you want to do without the help of a tax adviser! Those two warnings in place, let me say that you can sometimes save quite a bit of money by incorporating a business and then electing S corporation status. A corporation that elects S status doesn't get taxed at the corporate level on its profits. The profits just get allocated to the shareholders, and they then pay the personal income taxes on the corporate profits. What you save by using this option isn't income taxes but something that's often equally annoying: self-employment taxes.

Self-employment taxes are what self-employed persons pay in lieu of Social Security and Medicare taxes. In effect, they are equivalent to Social Security and Medicare taxes.

To explain how this election works, I need to set up an example. Suppose that you run a sole proprietorship and you make $60,000 a year in profits. In this case, you must pay self-employment taxes (equivalent to Social Security and Medicare taxes) of 15.3 percent, or roughly $9,000. That's a bummer, right?

Well, if you incorporate and then tell the IRS that you want to be treated as a special type of corporation called an S corporation, you can split your $60,000 into two categories: wages and dividends. The weird part is that only your wages are subject to the self-employment taxes. You see where I'm going, right? Say, for example, that you're now incorporated, and that you take $30,000 of your $60,000 of profit and treat that money as wages. And then you take the other $30,000 of profit and treat that money as dividends. In this case, you pay self-employment taxes of around $4,500. Why? Because the 15.3 percent self-employment taxes you pay are levied only on the wages you make — not on the dividends.

The only trick in this deal is that you have to pay yourself a reasonable salary. If you're a plumber and plumbers make $50,000 a year where you live, for example, you can't pay yourself $30,000.

Trick 6: Enjoy the Best of Both Worlds

If you read Trick 4, you know that regular corporations, called C corporations, provide a neat tax-saving opportunity in the form of deductible fringe benefits. And that's pretty sweet. But if you read Trick 5, you know that Sub S corporations provide a different tax-savings opportunity — the self-employment taxes gambit (plus they let you avoid the double-taxation trap).

If you have to choose between one classification and the other, you need to sit down and work out the numbers, of course. But consider that this might not be an "either-or" option. Maybe you really have two businesses. In this case, you might want to treat the smaller business as a C corporation and the larger, more-profitable business as an S corporation. In this way, you might actually get to enjoy the best of both worlds.

Just so you don't waste any time on this, you can't be artificial in creating the second business. The IRS has the ability to come in, look at the reality of your situation, and recategorize whatever you've done so it matches reality. For example, I have a CPA practice. But I can't decide to put individual tax returns and planning into a C corporation and then business tax returns and planning into an S corporation. That's clearly my being bogus. But if I also had, say, a travel agency, I could set up separate corporations for the travel agency business and for the public accounting practice. And one could be an S corporation, and one could be a C corporation.

Trick 7: Create Some Legitimate Job for Your Kids

Here's a clever trick I saw the partners of a CPA firm recently do. They put together a brochure that described all the services their firm offers to individuals. The brochure, of course, included pictures of the sorts of families they serve. And the models in the pictures were the partners' kids, who were, of course, fairly paid.

The neat thing about this trick is that the first bit of money a kid earns isn't taxable because of the standard deduction. So the partners effectively turned several thousand dollars of taxable "partner" income into nontaxable "partners' kids" income.

Note: My understanding is that the partners took the money that each kid was paid and stashed it away into that kid's college savings fund.

Trick 8: Relocate Your Business

Different states and cities have different income tax rates, so you want to be careful about where you locate your business. Now clearly, you don't want to pick a location purely for tax reasons. That truly would be a case of letting the tail wag the dog. But you ought to look at the tax burden of each of the locales from which you can operate your business. I save about $4,000 a year, for example, by operating my business from the suburbs rather than from downtown Seattle.

If you do consider the tax consequences of relocating your business, be sure to consider not just income taxes but also other taxes, such as payroll taxes like unemployment and workmen's compensation and even indirect taxes, such as minimum wage requirements. Recently, I was happy (Not!) to see that Washington state, where I live, forces employers to pay the nation's highest hourly minimum wage and the nation's second highest unemployment tax rate.

Part VI
Appendixes

The 5th Wave   By Rich Tennant

"Can't I just give you riches or something?"

In this part . . .

Appendixes are like basements. Why? You use them to store stuff that you want to keep but don't know where else to put. In the appendix that follows, I discuss how to zero in on profit.

Appendix

If Numbers Are Your Friends

You don't need to know much about accounting or about double-entry bookkeeping to use QuickBooks Simple Start, which, as you know, is most of its appeal. But if you're serious about this accounting business or serious about your business, consider finding out a bit more; setting up QuickBooks and understanding all the QuickBooks reports will be easier, and you'll be more sophisticated in your accounting, too.

 Just because the accounting in this appendix is a little more complicated doesn't mean that you can't understand it. To make this whole discussion more concrete, I use one big example. Hope it helps you! If nothing else, it'll inspire you to get into the rowboat rental business.

Keying In on Profit

Start with the big picture. The key purpose of an accounting system is to enable you to answer the burning question, "Am I making any money?"

Accounting is that simple. Really. At least conceptually. So, throughout the rest of this appendix, I just talk about how to calculate a business's profits in a reasonably accurate but still practical manner.

Let me introduce you to the new you

You just moved to Montana for the laid-back living and fresh air. You live in a cute log cabin on Flathead Lake. To support yourself, you plan to purchase several rowboats and rent them to visiting fly fishermen. Of course, you'll probably need to do quite a bit of fly-fishing, too. But just consider that the price you pay for being your own boss.

Different names, same logic

I don't see any point in hiding this nasty little accounting secret from you: Accountants call this cost-allocation process by different names, depending on what sort of cost is being spread out.

Most of the time, the cost allocation is called *depreciation*. You depreciate buildings, machinery, furniture, and many other items as well. But

allocating the cost of a natural resource — such as crude oil that you pump, coal that you dig up, or minerals that you extract — is called *depletion*. And allocating the cost of things that aren't tangible — copyrights and patents, for example — is *amortization*.

The first day in business

It's your first day in business. About 5 a.m., ol' Peter Gruntpaw shows up to deliver your three rowboats. He made them for you in his barn, but even so, they aren't cheap. He charges $1,500 apiece, so you write him a check for $4,500.

Peter's timing, as usual, is impeccable. About 5:15 a.m., your first customers arrive. Mr. and Mrs. Hamster (pronounced ohm-stair) are visiting from Phoenix. They want to catch the big fish. You're a bit unsure of your pricing, but you suggest $25 an hour for the boat. They agree and pay $200 in cash for eight hours.

A few minutes later, another couple arrives. The Gerbils (pronounced go-bells) are very agitated. They were supposed to meet the Hamsters and fish together, but the Hamsters are rowing farther and farther away from the dock. To speed the Gerbils' departure, you let them leave without paying. But you're not worried. As the Gerbils leave the dock, Ms. Gerbil shouts, "We'll pay you the $200 when we get back!"

Although you don't rent the third boat, you do enjoy a sleepy summer morning.

About 2 p.m., the Hamsters and Gerbils come rowing back into view. Obviously, though, a problem has occurred. You find out what it is when the first boat arrives. "Gerbil fell into the lake," laughs Mr. Hamster. "Lost his wallet, too." Everybody else seems to think that the lost wallet is funny. You secretly wonder how you're going to get paid. No wallet, no money.

You ask Mr. Gerbil if he would like to come out to the lake tomorrow to pay you. He says he'll just write you a check when he gets home to Phoenix. Reluctantly, you agree.

Look at your cash flow first

I've just described a fairly simple situation. But even so, answering the question, "Did I make any money?" isn't going to be easy. You start by looking at your cash flow: You wrote a check for $4,500, and you collected $200 in cash. Table A-1 shows your cash flow.

Table A-1	The First Day's Cash Flow	
	Cash In and Out	*Amount*
Add the cash in:	Rent money from Hamsters (pronounced ohm-stairs)	$200
	Rent money from Gerbils (pronounced *go-bells*)	$0
Subtract the cash out:	Money to purchase rowboats	($4,500)
Equals your cash flow:		($4,300)

To summarize, you had $200 come in but $4,500 go out. So your cash flow was –$4,300. (That's why the $4,300 is in parentheses.) From a cash-flow perspective, the first day doesn't look all that good, right? But does the cash-flow calculation show you whether you're making money? Can you look at it and gauge whether your little business is on the right track?

The answer to both questions is no. Your cash flow is important. You can't, for example, write a $4,500 check unless you have at least $4,500 in your checking account. But your cash flow doesn't tell you whether you're making money. In fact, you might see a couple of problems with looking just at the cash flow of the rowboat rental business.

Depreciation is an accounting gimmick

Here's the first problem: If you take good care of the rowboats, you can use them every summer for the next few years. In fact, suppose that the rowboat rental season, which runs from early spring to late autumn, is 150 days long and that your well-made rowboats will last 10 years.

- **You can probably rent the rowboats for 1,500 days.**

  (150 days a year times 10 years equals 1,500 days)

- **Each rowboat costs $1,500.**

  The depreciation expense for each rowboat is only $1 per day over 1,500 days. That's a whopping $3 for all three boats.

Do you see what I'm saying? If you have something that costs a great deal of money but lasts for a long time, spreading out the cost makes sense. This spreading out is usually called *depreciation.* The little $1 chunks that are allocated to a day are called the *depreciation expense.*

Accountants use the terms *cost* and *expense* to mean distinctly different things. A cost is the price you pay for something. If you pay Peter Gruntpaw $1,500 for a rowboat, the rowboat's cost is $1,500. An expense, on the other hand, is what you use in a profit calculation. The little $1 chunks of the rowboat's $1,500 cost (that are allocated to individual days) are expenses.

If this depreciation stuff seems wacky, remember that what you're really trying to do is figure out whether you made any money your first day of business. And all I'm really saying is that you shouldn't include the whole cost of the rowboats as an expense in the first day's profit calculation. Some of the cost should be included as an expense in calculating the profit in future days. That's fair, right?

Accrual-basis accounting is cool

You don't want to forget about the $200 that the Gerbils owe you either. Although Mr. Gerbil (remember that the name's pronounced go-bell) might not send you the check for several days, or even for several weeks, he will pay you. You've earned the money.

The principles of accounting say that you should include sales in your profit calculations when you earn the money and not when you actually collect it. The logic behind this "include sales when they're earned" rule is that it produces a better estimate of the business you're doing.

Suppose that the day after the Gerbils and Hamsters rent the rowboats, you have no customers, but Mr. Gerbil comes out and pays you $200. If you use the "include sales when they're earned" rule — or what's called *accrual-basis accounting* — your daily sales look like this:

	Day 1	*Day 2*
Sales	$400	$0

If you instead use what's called *cash-basis accounting* (in which you count sales when you collect the cash), your daily sales look like this:

	Day 1	*Day 2*
Sales	$200	$200

The traditional accrual-based accounting method shows that you have a good day when you rent two boats and a terrible day when you don't rent any boats. In comparison, when you use cash-basis accounting your sales record looks as if you rented a boat each day, even though you didn't. Now you know why accrual-basis accounting is a better way to measure profit.

Accrual-basis accounting also works for expenses. You should count an expense when you make it, not when you pay it. For example, you call the local radio station and ask the people there to announce your new boat rental business a couple of times for a fee of $25. Although you don't have to pay the radio station the day you make the arrangements for your announcement, you should still count the $25 as an expense for that day.

Now you know how to measure profits

With what you now know, you're ready to measure the first day's profits. Table A-2 is a profit and loss statement for your first day in business.

Table A-2	A Profit and Loss Statement for the First Day	
Description	*Amount*	*Explanation*
Sales	$400	Rental money from the Hamsters and Gerbils
Expenses		
Depreciation	$3	3 rowboats × $1/day depreciation
Advertising	$25	Radio advertising
Total expenses	$28	Depreciation expense plus the advertising
Profit	$372	Sales minus the total expenses

Although the first day's cash flow was terrible, your little business is quite profitable. In fact, if you really do make about $370 a day, you'll recoup your entire $4,500 investment in less than three weeks. That's pretty darn good.

Some financial brain food

Now that you know how to measure profits, I can fill you in on some important conceptual stuff:

- ✔ **You measure profits for a specific period of time.**

  In the rowboat business example, you measured the profits for a day. Some people actually do measure profits (or they try to measure profits) on a daily basis. But most times, people use bigger chunks of time. Monthly chunks of time are common, for example. And so are three-month chunks of time. Everybody measures profits annually — if only because the government makes you do so for income tax accounting.

- ✔ **When people start talking about how often and for what chunks of time profits are measured, they use a couple of terms.**

  The year you calculate profits for is called the *fiscal year*. The smaller chunks of time for which you measure profits over the year are called *accounting periods* or *interim accounting periods*.

  You don't need to memorize the two new terms. But now that you've read them, you'll probably remember them.

- ✔ **The length of your accounting periods involves an awkward trade-off.**

  Daily profit and loss calculations show you how well you did at the end of every day, but you have to collect the data and do the work every day. And preparing a profit and loss statement is a great deal of work.

  I made the example purposefully easy by including only a few transactions, but in real life, you have many more transactions to worry about and fiddle with.

- ✔ **If you use a quarterly interim accounting period, you don't have to collect the raw data and do the arithmetic very often, but you know how you're doing only every once in a while.**

  In my mind, checking your profits only four times a year isn't enough. A lot can happen in three months.

In the Old Days, Things Were Different

If you're new to the arithmetic and logic of profit calculation — which is mostly what modern accounting is all about — you won't be surprised to hear that not all that long ago, most people couldn't and didn't do much profit calculating.

What they did instead was monitor a business's financial condition. They used — well, actually, they still use — a *balance sheet* to monitor the financial condition. A balance sheet just lists a business's assets and its liabilities at a particular point in time.

Suppose that at the start of your first day in the rowboat rental business — before you pay Peter Gruntpaw — you have $5,000 in your checking account. To make the situation interesting, $4,000 of this money is a loan from your mother-in-law, and $1,000 is cash that you've invested in your business.

Here's a key to help you understand the balance sheets and cash flow in this section:

✔ A business's *assets* consist of the things the business owns.

✔ *Liabilities* consist of the amounts the business owes.

✔ *Equity* is the difference between the business's assets and its liabilities. Interestingly, equity also shows the money the owners or shareholders or partners have left in the business.

✔ If you correctly calculate each of the numbers that go on the balance sheet, the total assets value always equals the total liabilities and total owner's equity value.

Your balance sheet at the beginning of the day looks like the one in Table A-3.

Table A-3	The Balance Sheet at the Beginning of the Day	
Description	**Amount**	**Explanation**
Assets	$5,000	The checking account balance.
Total assets	$5,000	Your only asset is cash, so it's your total, too.
Liabilities and owner's equity	$4,000	The loan from your mother-in-law.
Total liabilities and owner's equity	$4,000	Your only liability is that crazy loan.
	$1,000	The $1,000 you put in.
Total liabilities and owner's equity	$5,000	The total liabilities plus the owner's equity.

If you construct a balance sheet at the end of the first day, the financial picture is only slightly more complicated. Some of these explanations are too complicated to give in a sentence, so the paragraphs that follow describe how I got each number.

Even if you don't pay all that much attention, I recommend that you quickly read through the explanations. Mostly, I want you to understand that if you try to monitor a business's financial condition by using a balance sheet, as I've done here, the picture gets messy. Later in this appendix, I talk about how QuickBooks Simple Start makes all this stuff easier.

Table A-4 shows the balance sheet at the end of the first day.

Table A-4	The Balance Sheet at the End of the Day	
	Description	*Amount*
Assets		
	Cash	$700
	Receivable	$200
	Rowboats	$4,497
Total assets		$5,397
Liabilities and owner's equity		
	Payable	$25
	Loan payable	$4,000
Total liabilities		$4,025
	Owner's equity	$1,000
	Retained earnings	$372
Total liabilities and owner's equity		$5,397

Cash, the first line item shown in Table A-4, is the most complicated line item to prove. If you were really in the rowboat rental business, of course, you could just look at your checkbook. But if you were writing an appendix about being in the rowboat rental business — as I am — you'd need to be able to calculate the cash balance. Table A-5 shows the calculation of the cash balance for your rowboat rental business.

Table A-5	The First Day's Cash Flow		
Description	*Payment*	*Deposit*	*Balance*
Initial investment		$1,000	$1,000
Loan from mother-in-law		$4,000	$5,000
Rowboat purchase	$4,500		$500
Cash from Hamsters		$200	$700

The $200 receivable, the second line item shown in Table A-4, is the money the Gerbils owe you.

The third line shown in Table A-4, the Rowboats balance sheet value, is $4,497. This is weird, I'll grant you. But here's how you figure it: You take the original cost of the asset and deduct all the depreciation expense that you've charged to date. The original cost of the three rowboats was $4,500. You've charged only $3 of depreciation for the first day, so the balance sheet value, or net book value, is $4,497.

The only liabilities are the $25 you owe the radio station for those new business announcements (shown on the seventh line in Table A-4) and that $4,000 you borrowed from your mother-in-law (shown on the eighth line in Table A-4). I won't even ask why you opened that can of worms.

Finally, the owner's equity section of the balance sheet shows the $1,000 you originally contributed (see line 10 in Table A-4) and also the $372 of money you earned (see line 11 in Table A-4).

It's not a coincidence that the total assets value equals the total liabilities and total owner's equity value. If you correctly calculate each of the numbers that go on the balance sheet, the two totals are always equal.

A balance sheet lists asset, liability, and owner's equity balances as of a specific date. It gives you a financial snapshot at a point in time. Usually, you prepare a balance sheet whenever you prepare a profit and loss statement. The balance sheet shows account balances for the last day of the fiscal year and interim accounting period. (I think that it's kind of neat that after only a few pages of this appendix you're reading and understanding such terms as *fiscal year* and *interim accounting period*.)

What Does an Italian Monk Have to Do with Anything?

So far, I've provided narrative descriptions of all the financial events that affect the balance sheet and the income statement. I described how you started the business with $5,000 of cash (a $4,000 loan from your mother-in-law and $1,000 of cash that you yourself invested). At an even earlier point in this appendix, I noted how you rented a boat to the Hamsters for $200, and they paid you in cash.

Although the narrative descriptions of financial events — such as starting the business or renting to the Hamsters — make for just-bearable reading, they are unwieldy for accountants to use in practice. Partly, this awkwardness is because accountants are usually (or maybe always?) terrible writers. But an even bigger problem is that using the lots-and-lots-of-words approach makes describing all the little bits and pieces of information that you need difficult and downright tedious.

Fortunately, about 500 years ago, an Italian monk named Lucia Pacioli thought the same thing. No, I'm not making this up. What Pacioli really said was, "Hey, guys. Hello? Is anybody in there? You have to get more efficient in the way that you describe your financial transactions. You have to create a financial shorthand system that works when you have a large number of transactions to record."

Pacioli then proceeded to describe a financial shorthand system that made it easy to collect all the little bits and pieces of information needed to prepare income statements and balance sheets. The shorthand system he described? *Double-entry bookkeeping.*

This system enabled people to name the income statement or balance sheet line items or accounts that are affected and then give the dollar amount of the effect. The profit and loss statement and the balance sheet line items are called *accounts*. You need to remember this term.

A list of profit and loss statement and balance sheet line items is called a *chart of accounts*. You might already know this term from using QuickBooks.

Pacioli also did one wacky thing. He used a couple of new terms — *debit* and *credit* — to describe the increases and decreases in accounts.

- ✔ Increases in asset accounts and in expense accounts are debits. Decreases in liability, owner's equity, and income accounts are also debits.

- ✔ Decreases in asset and expense accounts are credits. Increases in liability, owner's equity, and income accounts are also credits.

Keeping these terms straight is a bit confusing, so refer to Table A-6 for help.

I'm sorry to have to tell you this, but if you want to use double-entry bookkeeping, you need to memorize the information in Table A-6. If it's any consolation, this information is the only chunk of data in the entire book that I ask you to memorize. Or, failing that, mark this page with a dog-ear so that you can flip here quickly, or just refer to the Cheat Sheet.

Table A-6   The Only Stuff in This Book That I Ask You to Memorize

Account Type	Debits	Credits
Assets	Increase asset accounts	Decrease asset accounts
Liabilities	Decrease liability accounts	Increase liability accounts
Owner's equity	Decrease owner's equity accounts	Increase owner's equity accounts
Income	Decrease income accounts	Increase income accounts
Expenses	Increase expense accounts	Decrease expense accounts

And now for the blow-by-blow

The best way to help you understand this double-entry bookkeeping stuff is to show you how to use it to record all the financial events that I've discussed thus far in this appendix. Start with the money that you've invested in the business and the money that you foolishly borrowed from your mother-in-law. You invested $1,000 in cash, and you borrowed $4,000 in cash. Here are the double-entry bookkeeping transactions — called *journal entries* — that describe these financial events.

Journal Entry 1	**To Record Your $1,000 Investment**	
	Debit	Credit
Cash	$1,000	
Owner's equity		$1,000

Journal Entry 2	**To Record the $4,000 Loan from Your Mother-in-Law**	
	Debit	Credit
Cash	$4,000	
Loan payable to mother-in-law		$4,000

If you add up all the debits and credits in a journal entry, you get something called a *trial balance*. A trial balance isn't all that special, but you use it to prepare profit and loss statements and balance sheets easily. If you add up the debits and credits shown in journal entries 1 and 2, you get the trial balance shown in Table A-7.

Table A-7	Your First Trial Balance	
	Debit	**Credit**
Cash	$5,000	
Loan payable to mother-in-law		$4,000
Owner's equity		$1,000

This trial balance provides the raw data needed to construct the rowboat business balance sheet at the start of the first day. If you don't believe me, take a peek at Table A-3. Oh sure, the information shown in Table A-7 isn't as polished. Table A-7 doesn't provide labels, for example, that tell you that cash is an asset. And Table A-7 doesn't provide subtotals showing the total assets (equal to $5,000) and the total liabilities and owner's equity (also equal to $5,000). But it does provide the raw data.

Take a look at the journal entries you would make to record the rest of the first day's financial events:

Journal Entry 3	To Record the Purchase of the Three $1,500 Rowboats	
	Debit	**Credit**
Rowboats	$4,500	
Cash		$4,500

Journal Entry 4	To Record the Rental to the Hamsters	
	Debit	**Credit**
Cash	$200	
Sales		$200

Journal Entry 5	To Record the Rental to the Gerbils	
	Debit	**Credit**
Receivable	$200	
Sales		$200

Journal Entry 6	To Record the $25 Radio Advertisement	
	Debit	**Credit**
Advertising expense	$25	
Payable		$25

Journal Entry 7	To Record the $3 of Rowboat Depreciation	
	Debit	**Credit**
Depreciation expense	$3	
Accumulated depreciation		$3

To build a trial balance for the end of the first day, you add all the first day journal entries to the trial balance shown previously in Table A-7. The result is the trial balance shown in Table A-8.

Table A-8	The Trial Balance at the End of the First Day	
	Debit	**Credit**
Balance sheet accounts		
Cash	$700	
Receivable	$200	
Rowboats — cost	$4,500	
Accumulated depreciation		$3
Payable		$25
Loan payable		$4,000
Owner's equity		$1,000

(continued)

Table A-8 (continued)

	Debit	Credit
Profit and loss statement accounts		
Sales		$400
Depreciation expense	$3	
Advertising expense	$25	

The trial balance shown in Table A-8 provides the raw data used to prepare the balance sheet and profit and loss statement for the first day.

If you look at the accounts labeled "Balance sheet accounts" in Table A-8 and compare these to the balance sheet shown in Table A-4, you see that this trial balance provides all the raw numbers needed for the balance sheet. The only numbers in Table A-4 that aren't directly from Table A-8 are the subtotals you get by adding up other numbers.

If you look at the accounts labeled as "Profit and loss statement accounts" in Table A-8 and compare them to the profit and loss statement shown in Table A-2, you see that this trial balance also provides all the raw numbers needed for the profit and loss statement. Again, the only numbers in Table A-2 that aren't directly from Table A-8 are the subtotals you get by adding up other numbers.

Blow-by-blow, part II

If you understand what I've discussed so far, you grasp how accounting and double-entry bookkeeping work. I want to show you about a half dozen more example transactions, however, to plug a few minor holes in your knowledge.

When you collect money you've previously billed, you record the transaction by debiting cash and crediting receivables (or accounts receivable). In the rowboat business, you make this basic entry when Mr. Gerbil later pays you the $200 he owes you for the first day's rental.

Journal Entry 8   To Record a Payment by a Customer

	Debit	Credit
Cash	$200	
Receivable		$200

Don't record a sale when you collect the cash. The sale has already been recorded in journal entry 5. When you pay the radio station for the advertising, you record the transaction by debiting accounts payable and crediting cash.

Journal Entry 9	To Record Your Payment of $25 to the Radio Station	
	Debit	**Credit**
Payable	$25	
Cash		$25

The one other thing I want to cover — ever so briefly — is *inventory accounting.* Accounting for items you buy and resell or the items you make and resell is a bit trickier. And I don't have room to go into a great deal of detail.

When you buy items to resell, you debit an asset account, often named Inventory. If you purchase 300 of the $10 thingamajigs you hope to resell for $25 each, you record the following journal entry:

Journal Entry 10	To Record the Cash Purchase of Thingamajigs	
	Debit	**Credit**
Inventory	$3,000	
Cash		$3,000

When you sell a thingamajig, you need to do two tasks: record the sale and record the cost of the sale. If you need to record the sale of 100 thingamajigs for $25 each, for example, you record the following journal entry:

Journal Entry 11	To Record the Sale of 100 Thingamajigs for $25 Apiece	
	Debit	**Credit**
Receivable	$2,500	
Sales		$2,500

You also need to record the cost of the thingamajigs that you've sold as an expense and record the reduction in the value of your thingamajig inventory. That means that if you reduce your inventory count from 300 items to 200 items, you need to adjust your inventory's dollar value. You record the following journal entry:

Journal Entry 12	To Record the Cost of the 100 Thingamajigs Sold	
	Debit	*Credit*
Cost of goods sold	$1,000	
Inventory		$1,000

The cost of goods sold account, by the way, is just another expense. It appears on your profit and loss statement.

How does QuickBooks Simple Start help?

If you (or someone else) keep the books for your business manually, you actually have to make these journal entries. But if you use QuickBooks Simple Start (or any other version of QuickBooks) to keep the books, all this debiting and crediting business usually goes on behind the scenes. When you invoice a customer, QuickBooks debits accounts receivable and credits sales. When you write a check to pay some bill, QuickBooks debits the expense and credits cash.

In the few cases in which a financial transaction isn't recorded automatically when you fill in some on-screen form, you need to use the General Journal Entry window. To display the General Journal Entry window, choose Company⇨For Your Accountant⇨Make General Journal Entries. You use the General Journal Entry window to create journal entries.

QuickBooks automatically builds a trial balance, using journal entries it constructs automatically and any journal entries that you enter by using the General Journal Entry window. QuickBooks prepares balance sheets, profit and loss statements, and several other reports as well, using the trial balance. (Curiously, QuickBooks Simple Start doesn't produce a trial balance report, although the full-fledged versions of QuickBooks do. You can see the trial balance numbers, however, by printing a general ledger report. To print the general ledger report, choose Reports⇨Accountant Reports⇨General Ledger

Two Dark Shadows in the World of Accounting

The real purpose of accounting systems, such as QuickBooks, is simple: Accounting systems are supposed to make succeeding in your business easier for you. You might think, therefore, that the world of accounting is a friendly place. Unfortunately, this scenario isn't quite true. I'm sorry to report that two dark shadows hang over the world of accounting: *financial accounting standards* and *income tax laws.*

The first dark shadow

"Financial accounting standards," you say. "What the heck are those?"

Here's the quick-and-dirty explanation: *Financial accounting standards* are accounting rules created by certified public accountants. These rules are supposed to make reading financial statements and understanding what's going on easier for people. (I happen to believe that just the opposite is often true, in case you're interested.) But because of what financial accounting standards purport to do, some people — such as bank loan officers — want to see profit and loss statements and balance sheets that follow the rules. The exact catchphrase is one that you might have heard before: "Prepared in accordance with generally accepted accounting principles."

Unfortunately, the rules are very complicated. The rules are inconsistently interpreted. And actually applying the rules would soon run most small businesses into the ground. (And as you were running your business into the ground — you'll be happy to know — your certified public accountant would make a great deal of money helping you figure out what you were supposed to be doing.) So what should you do about this first dark shadow?

✔ **Well, first of all, know that the rules exist.** Know that people like your banker honestly think that you should follow a super-complicated set of accounting rules. Even when the banker doesn't understand the rules.

✔ **Also, don't get sucked into the financial accounting standards tar pit.** Tell people — your banker included — that you do your accounting in the way that you think enables you to best manage your business. Tell people a small business like yours can't afford to have an in-house staff of full-time CPAs. And finally, tell people that you don't necessarily prepare your financial statements "in accordance with generally accepted accounting principles."

Do attempt to fully and fairly disclose your financial affairs to people who need to know about them. Lying to a creditor or an investor about your financial affairs or getting sneaky with one of these people is a good way to end up in jail.

The second dark shadow

And now here's the second dark shadow: income tax accounting laws. You know that Congress enacts tax legislation to raise revenue. And you know that it does so in a political environment strewn with all sorts of partisan voodoo economics and social overtones. So you won't be surprised to find out that the accounting rules that come out of the nation's capital and your state capital also don't make much sense for running a business.

You need to apply the rules when you prepare your tax return, of course. But you don't have to use them the rest of the year. A far better approach is to do your accounting in a way that enables you to best run your business. That way, you don't use accounting tricks and gambits that make sense for income tax accounting but foul up your accounting system. At the end of the year, when you're preparing your tax return, have your tax preparer adjust your numbers so that they conform to income tax accounting laws.

The Danger of Shell Games

This appendix is longer than I initially intended. I'm sorry about that. I want to share one more thought with you, however. And I think that it's an important thought, so please stay with me just a little longer.

You could use the accounting knowledge that this appendix imparts to do the bookkeeping for a very large business. As crazy as it sounds, if you had 3,000 rowboats for rent — perhaps you have rental outlets at dozens of lakes scattered all over the Rockies — you might actually be able to keep the books for a $200,000,000-a-year business. You would have to enter many more transactions, and the numbers would all be bigger, but you wouldn't necessarily be doing anything more complicated than the transactions in this appendix.

Unfortunately, the temptation is great — especially on the part of financial advisers — to let the money stuff get more complicated as a business grows. People start talking about sophisticated leasing arrangements that make sense because of the tax laws. Some customer or vendor suggests some complicated profit-sharing or cost-reimbursement agreement. Then your attorney or accountant talks you into setting up a couple new subsidiaries for legal reasons. (You thought you understood that there was also some tax reason, but that might have just been your imagination.)

All these schemes make accounting for your business terribly complicated. If you choose to ignore this complexity and go on your merry way, very soon you won't know whether you're making money. (I've seen plenty of people go this route — and it isn't pretty.) On the other hand, if you truly want to do accurate accounting in a complex environment, you need to spend a great deal of cash for really smart accountants. (This tactic, of course, supposes that you can find, hire, and afford these really smart accountants.)

If you're unsure about how to tell whether something is just too complicated, here's a general rule you can use: If you can't easily create the journal entries that quantify the financial essence of some event, you're in trouble.

So, what should you do? I suggest that you don't complicate your business's finances — not even if you think that the newfangled, tax-incentivized, sale-leaseback profit plan is a sure winner. Keep things simple, my friend. To win the game, you have to keep score.

Index

• **F** •

Notes

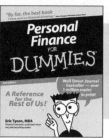

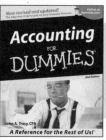
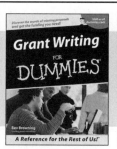

FOR DUMMIES®

A world of resources to help you grow

HOME, GARDEN & HOBBIES

0-7645-5295-3

0-7645-5130-2

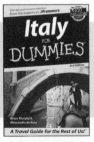

(Guitar)

0-7645-5106-X

Also available:

Auto Repair For Dummies
(0-7645-5089-6)

Chess For Dummies
(0-7645-5003-9)

Home Maintenance For
Dummies
(0-7645-5215-5)

Organizing For Dummies
(0-7645-5300-3)

Piano For Dummies
(0-7645-5105-1)

Poker For Dummies
(0-7645-5232-5)

Quilting For Dummies
(0-7645-5118-3)

Rock Guitar For Dummies
(0-7645-5356-9)

Roses For Dummies
(0-7645-5202-3)

Sewing For Dummies
(0-7645-5137-X)

FOOD & WINE

0-7645-5250-3

0-7645-5390-9

0-7645-5114-0

Also available:

Bartending For Dummies
(0-7645-5051-9)

Chinese Cooking For
Dummies
(0-7645-5247-3)

Christmas Cooking For
Dummies
(0-7645-5407-7)

Diabetes Cookbook For
Dummies
(0-7645-5230-9)

Grilling For Dummies
(0-7645-5076-4)

Low-Fat Cooking For
Dummies
(0-7645-5035-7)

Slow Cookers For Dummies
(0-7645-5240-6)

TRAVEL

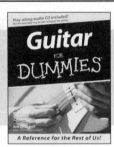

0-7645-5453-0

0-7645-5438-7

0-7645-5448-4

Also available:

America's National Parks For
Dummies
(0-7645-6204-5)

Caribbean For Dummies
(0-7645-5445-X)

Cruise Vacations For
Dummies 2003
(0-7645-5459-X)

Europe For Dummies
(0-7645-5456-5)

Ireland For Dummies
(0-7645-6199-5)

France For Dummies
(0-7645-6292-4)

London For Dummies
(0-7645-5416-6)

Mexico's Beach Resorts For
Dummies
(0-7645-6262-2)

Paris For Dummies
(0-7645-5494-8)

RV Vacations For Dummies
(0-7645-5443-3)

Walt Disney World & Orlando
For Dummies
(0-7645-5444-1)

Available wherever books are sold. Go to www.dummies.com or call 1-877-762-2974 to order direct.

FOR DUMMIES®

Plain-English solutions for everyday challenges

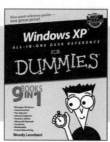

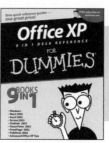

FOR DUMMIES®

Helping you expand your horizons and realize your potential

INTERNET

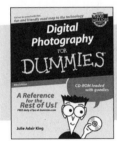

0-7645-0894-6

0-7645-1659-0

0-7645-1642-6

Also available:

America Online 7.0 For Dummies
(0-7645-1624-8)

Genealogy Online For Dummies
(0-7645-0807-5)

The Internet All-in-One Desk Reference For Dummies
(0-7645-1659-0)

Internet Explorer 6 For Dummies
(0-7645-1344-3)

The Internet For Dummies Quick Reference
(0-7645-1645-0)

Internet Privacy For Dummie
(0-7645-0846-6)

Researching Online For Dummies
(0-7645-0546-7)

Starting an Online Business For Dummies
(0-7645-1655-8)

DIGITAL MEDIA

0-7645-1664-7

0-7645-1675-2

0-7645-0806-7

Also available:

CD and DVD Recording For Dummies
(0-7645-1627-2)

Digital Photography All-in-One Desk Reference For Dummies
(0-7645-1800-3)

Digital Photography For Dummies Quick Reference
(0-7645-0750-8)

Home Recording for Musicians For Dummies
(0-7645-1634-5)

MP3 For Dummies
(0-7645-0858-X)

Paint Shop Pro "X" For Dummies
(0-7645-2440-2)

Photo Retouching & Restoration For Dummies
(0-7645-1662-0)

Scanners For Dummies
(0-7645-0783-4)

GRAPHICS

0-7645-0817-2

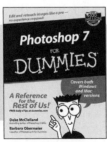

0-7645-1651-5

0-7645-0895-4

Also available:

Adobe Acrobat 5 PDF For Dummies
(0-7645-1652-3)

Fireworks 4 For Dummies
(0-7645-0804-0)

Illustrator 10 For Dummies
(0-7645-3636-2)

QuarkXPress 5 For Dummies
(0-7645-0643-9)

Visio 2000 For Dummies
(0-7645-0635-8)

FOR DUMMIES®

The advice and explanations you need to succeed

  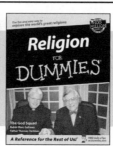
 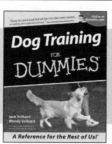 
  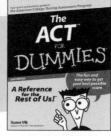

PCs For Dummies®, 10th Edition

Cheat Sheet

My PC!

Fill in the following essential information about your computer.

Make and model: _____

Serial number: _____

Network name (if any): _____

Microprocessor: _____

RAM (MB): _____

Hard drive capacity (GB): _____

Keys to press on startup to enter PC Setup program:

_____

Drive A is ❏ 3 1/2-inch floppy ❏ Missing

Drive C is ❏ My PC's first hard drive

Other drives

Drive ___ is a hard drive.

Drive ___ is a hard drive.

Drive ___ is a CD-ROM drive.

Drive ___ is a DVD drive.

Drive ___ is a CD-R/RW drive.

Drive ___ is a DVD-R type of drive.

Drive ___ is a Zip drive.

Drive ___ is _____.

Drive ___ is _____.

What Plugs into What?

Circle the proper connection for your PC goodies.

Keyboard: Keyboard port USB

Mouse: Mouse port USB

Printer: Printer port USB

USB hub? Yes No

Other USB devices

NIC Scanner Modem

Sound gizmo Digital camera Webcam

External USB drives: _____

_____

_____

FireWire? Yes No

FireWire devices: _____

_____

_____

Important Phone Numbers

My dealer: _____

Sales rep (name/ext.): _____

Dealer tech support: _____

Operating system support: _____

ISP: _____

ISP tech support: _____

Computer guru: _____

For Dummies: Bestselling Book Series for Beginners

PCs For Dummies, 10th Edition

Cheat Sheet

Helpful PC Hints

The help key in Windows and in most other programs is F1.

Always save your stuff. Save when you first create something, save as you go along, save when you stand up to take a break, and save before you close your programs.

Delete only the files or folders that you created yourself.

It's okay to delete a shortcut file; doing so doesn't delete the original.

When you mess up, immediately press Ctrl+Z, the Undo keyboard command. That should right whatever transgression you just committed.

Always unplug the computer console before you open it.

It's okay to connect USB devices to the computer while the computer or the device is on.

Get used to working with the mouse by playing some computer games, especially card games.

The best gift you can buy your PC is more memory.

Remember to unmount any digital memory card before you yank it out of the memory card reader. Ditto for a CD: Properly eject the CD by using Windows rather than pressing the Eject button on the CD drive. Ditto again for DVDs.

The key to understanding software is to know what a file is.

When e-mailing a graphical image, be sure to save or convert the image into the JPG file format.

Internet Info

Internet login name: _____

Internet password: (Write down elsewhere)

My e-mail address: _____

My e-mail password: (Write down elsewhere)

My ISP's domain name: _____

My e-mail address on Yahoo!: _____

My Yahoo! e-mail password: (Write down elsewhere)

Hotmail e-mail address: _____

Hotmail password: (Write down elsewhere)

Other e-mail address: _____

For Dummies: Bestselling Book Series for Beginners